START AND RUN
A PROFITABLE CONSULTING BUSINESS

START AND RUN
A PROFITABLE CONSULTING BUSINESS
A step-by-step business plan

Douglas A. Gray, B.A., LL.B.

Self-Counsel Press
(a division of)
International Self-Counsel Press Ltd.
Canada   U.S.A.

Printed in Canada

First edition: March, 1985; Reprinted: October, 1985
Second edition: August, 1986; Reprinted: August, 1987; August, 1988; November, 1989

Canadian Cataloguing in Publication Data

Gray, Douglas A.
    Start and run a profitable consulting business

    (Self-counsel series)
    Bibliography : p.
    ISBN 0-88908-648-6

    1. Consultants.   2. New business enterprises.
I. Title.   II. Series.
HD69.C6G73 1986   658.4'6'023   C86-091403-8

Self-Counsel Press
(a division of)
International Self-Counsel Press Ltd.
Head and Editorial Office
1481 Charlotte Road
North Vancouver, British Columbia V7J 1H1

U.S. Address
1704 N. State Street
Bellingham, Washington 98225

CONTENTS

LIST OF SAMPLES

LIST OF TABLES

To Eleanor and Diana, the two women in my life.

INTRODUCTION

This book is designed primarily for the beginning or potential consultant, but consultants who have been in practice for a considerable time should also find it helpful. The purpose of the book is to provide essential information and practical step-by-step guidelines to assist you in starting and developing a successful and profitable consulting business. All the information necessary to set up and maintain your own business is included in this book.

The book is organized to reflect a typical consulting business, from getting the original idea to generating income sufficient for your needs and expectations. You will assess your consulting potential and determine your marketable skills in chapter 2. In chapters 3 through 13 you will learn all the basic steps you have to consider before starting your business. Chapters 14 and 15 deal with the marketing techniques essential to success. Without effective ongoing marketing, you simply will not succeed. The final chapters 16, 17, and 18 inform you how to negotiate a consulting assignment from the first interview to the proposal to obtaining a contract. Chapter 19 discusses ways of expanding your practice.

The tables, samples, and appendices have been provided to make the text as meaningful as possible. There are many good reference books that can assist you further; these are listed in the Bibliography and have been divided into various section headings for easy reference by subject area. A detailed source list of further information is contained in Appendix 1. Consulting is basically a knowledge industry, and access to ways of improving your knowledge should assist you in marketing your skill more effectively.

Each chapter in this book stands independently but is linked to the others. If you know little about consulting or being in business, you should read the chapters sequentially to appreciate the need for dealing with basic business considerations. Consulting is first of all a business, which can succeed or fail like any other business. Understanding and managing the business side of consulting is as essential as performing the consulting service.

Every year the demand for consultants increases as our society becomes more complex. Business, education, health care, government, military, labor unions, social services, churches, and volunteer organizations employ consultants on a regular basis. Consulting in North America has become a multi-billion dollar industry.

Consultants are people who are determined to succeed, who thrive on challenge, and who believe in themselves.

Consultants are entrepreneurs in the knowledge field. Consultants are individuals who believe that they are competent and capable of rendering a worthwhile service to others.

Consulting offers a continual challenge and can present opportunities for freedom, growth, and satisfaction far beyond those of employment or other forms of business. This book increases your chances of capitalizing on the opportunities and assisting your business success.

Note: This book aims to highlight common consulting practices accurately. However, the information is general in nature, and no legal, tax, or financial advice is given. If legal or other expert assistance is required, you should obtain the services of competent professionals.

Laws are constantly changing and neither the author nor the publisher can accept any responsibility for changes to the law or practice that occur after the printing of this publication.

1

UNDERSTANDING THE CONSULTING BUSINESS

a. WHAT IS A CONSULTANT?

A consultant is someone who has an expertise in a specific area or areas and offers unbiased opinions and advice for a fee. The opinion or advice is rendered exclusively in the interests of the client and can cover review, analysis, recommendations, and implementation. A consultant generally works in conjunction with the resource personnel of the client, but uses employees, sub-consultants, or others as required for the specific project and in accord with the agreement.

A consultant is not an employee but an independent contractor, usually self-employed, contracted to perform a short-term or long-term task and paid on an hourly, daily or project basis or other fee arrangement.

There are numerous consulting opportunities in the private and public sector. Table #1 provides a brief summary of some of the major consulting areas. The consulting profession has grown extensively over the past 15 years and is now one of the major service industries in North America. The outlook for continued growth of consulting in the 1980s is very positive. Demand exceeds the projected supply.

TABLE #1
MAJOR CONSULTING SUBJECT AREAS

Acoustics	Construction services
Actuarial services	— Management
Advertising	— Heating/ventilating/air-conditioning
Architecture	— Inspection and estimates
Association management	Curriculum development
Audiovisual services	Data processing
Automation	— Computer hardware
— Office	— Computer software/programming
— Industrial	— Systems analysis
Building management	Direct marketing
Business administration	Economic research, analysis, forecasting
Business forms and systems	Editorial services
Cable television	Educational services
Career guidance	—Curriculum development
Communication	— School/camp selection
— Electronic	Electronics
— Interpersonal	Employee benefit planning
Community relations	— Pension planning
Conference and convention planning and management	— Profitsharing
	Energy management and conservation

TABLE #1 — Continued

Engineering
— Aeronautical
— Chemical
— Civil
— Electrical
— Electronics
— Environmental
— Industrial
— Marine
— Mechanical
— Mining
— Nuclear
— Petroleum
Estate planning
Executive development and recruitment
Exhibit planning and design
Financial management
— Banking
— Budgeting
— Investment counseling
Food facilities design
Food retailing
Food services
Foreign licensing
Forestry
Franchising
Freight transportation and shipping
Fundraising
Furnishings
Government relations
— Municipal
— State/provincial
— Federal
Graphics
Health services administration
Heating
Hospital administration
Hotel and motel management
House publications
Human factors engineering
Human relations
Human resources development
— Employee selection and training
— Employee surveys
— Industrial psychology
— Personnel productivity
Immigration and naturalization
Industrial/manufacturing services
— Industrial classification
— Industrial development
— Industrial testing
— Production management
Information storage and retrieval
Insurance

Interior design
— Color
— Furnishings
— Lighting
International business and trade
Inventory control
Labor relations
Land use planning
Landscaping
Leasing
— Equipment
— Transportation
Library design and services
Licensing
Lighting
Lithography
Mail order
Marketing programs and services
Marketing research and analysis
Marriage and family relations
Material handling
Materials science
Mergers and acquisitions
Microforms
Museum and exhibit planning and design
National security and defense
Naturalization
New product design
New product introduction
Nutrition
Office design
Office management
Operations research
Opinion polls
Organization analysis and development
Packaging
Personal image
Personnel
Planning (long range, strategic)
Political campaigning
Pollution control
— Air
— Noise
— Water
Product design
Professional practice management
Public relations
Publishing
Purchasing
Real estate
Records management
Recreation planning
Reliability and quality control
Religion

TABLE #1 — Continued

Relocation services	Social services
Research and development	Sports
Safety services	Standardization
— Accident investigation	Statistical services
— Expert witness	Stockholder relations
— Fire protection	Systems analysis
— Product liability	Taxes
— Program design and installation	Technology transfer
Sales	Telecommunications
— Forecasting	Television and radio
— Management	Traffic and parking
— Personnel recruiting	Transportation
— Policy and planning	Urban renewal
— Retail/wholesale	Utilities management
Salvage and reclamation	Venture capital
Sanitation	Wage and salary administration
Security (investigation and loss prevention)	Warehousing
Shipping	Women's issues and concerns
Small business development	

The consulting industry prospers in most economic conditions. The amount of income that a consultant can earn is, of course, related to many factors, including the field of knowledge and level of expertise in that field. The degree of profit is also directly related to how effectively time is managed and how efficiently the business is administered. New consultants spend a large portion of time managing the task, researching their field of expertise, improving on techniques, and marketing their expertise. Most of these tasks are essential but unbillable hours.

b. WHO GOES INTO CONSULTING?

Basically, consultants are people with a marketable skill, a perceptive mind, a need for independence and challenge, an ability to communicate with others and persuade them to follow advice, a desire to help others in an effective way, and a wish to be an agent of positive change. In general, the people who go into consulting include:

- People frustrated with their current careers, who see the solutions for problems but are unable to effectively influence decision-makers

- People who want a stimulating, dynamic, growing career that satisfies the need for personal development

- People dissatisfied with the lack of challenge, opportunity or creativity in their existing jobs

- People graduating from school with training but little experience who wish to work for a large consulting firm

- People who are between jobs and seeking new opportunities and careers

3

- People who see that they may be laid off and wish to establish themselves in a business to earn a livelihood; these people may start on a part-time basis while still employed

- Retired people who have expertise and wisdom to offer

- People who wish to supplement their present income by using their managerial expertise or technical or academic skills

- People with work experience and industry knowledge or other skills who want to combine a family life with work at home

- People who understand government operations and the contract process, or who have built up contacts in government, politics or industry over the years

c. WHY DO ORGANIZATIONS USE CONSULTANTS?

There are many reasons why the private and public sector need consultants for problem solving. Some of these reasons are discussed below.

1. Temporary assistance

Clients frequently wish to supplement skills in their organization by hiring trained, proven, motivated consultants on a short-term or long-term basis. Consultants may be hired on a project, seasonal or new funding basis.

By hiring consultants, clients do not have to contend with the training, instruction, and long-term commitment for salaries and fringe benefits entailed in hiring a skilled employee. Recruitment costs alone for a skilled employee can be considerable and cannot be justified for short-lived or cyclical need. Consultants are independent contractors and therefore no tax deductions or fringe benefits are involved.

2. Objective review

Consultants are retained as impartial advisors without any vested interest in the outcome of the recommendations. Internal staff may not be able to see the problems or may not be sufficiently objective. A consultant can perform a competent and thorough analysis of the issues. It is easier psychologically for personnel to adapt to external advice rather than the internal advice of someone who may be acting out of self-interest.

3. Third-party request for problem identification and resolution

Banks are naturally concerned about any signs of a problem that might put their investment at risk. A bank may need to know whether the problems are related to administrative, personnel, financial, market or product difficulties and how the problems can be solved. Only an outside consultant's opinion would be credible.

4

4. Surviving a crisis

A business owner suffering from serious business problems may seek an outside consultant to investigate causes and recommend solutions.

5. Initiating change

A consultant can act as a catalyst in stimulating ideas in a highly structured organization that otherwise might be resistent to change due to its size, bureaucracy and institutionalized nature.

6. Obtaining funding

Many non-profit organizations or small and medium size businesses need assistance in obtaining grants or loans for their continued survival. They may lack the expertise, ability or time to research the availability of funding and prepare a persuasive application. Consultants with an expertise in this area act as advisors or agents.

7. Selecting personnel

A client might hire a consultant for recruitment of key executives. The consultant is looked upon as being independent and unbiased with the expertise and time to selectively screen and recommend prospective candidates.

8. In-house education

Consultants are hired to provide in-house training to keep staff informed of new management and supervisory techniques or technical knowledge and to improve employee morale.

9. Dealing with internal personnel difficulties

Outside consultants are retained to review and make recommendations on internal structure, for example, consolidation of departments or services or elimination of redundant employees or executives. The consultant's report provides the rationale for making the decisions. The consultant then leaves and is not affected by the decision.

Consultants can also be used to resolve conflicts between various levels of management. The consultant plays an arbitrating or mediating role that permits frustrations to be expressed so that energy can be directed toward constructive resolution.

10. Delay tactics

Consultants can be hired to perform research studies which take the pressure off a company that is being exposed to public or government scrutiny. This also permits the organization to use the excuse of a consultant's study to justify a delay in decision-making. The consultant is frequently asked to take the brunt of any media attention by being the contact person, which reduces media attention toward the organization concerned.

11. Executive assistance

An executive who is aware of his or her personal limitations may request that a consultant review a problem situation, provide advice on how to deal with it, and possibly follow up with implementation.

12. Government regulatory compliance

Government regulations at all levels are constantly changing, and companies are frequently not prepared or trained to comply. Consultants may be retained to provide expertise to assist a company in complying economically, efficiently, and with the least amount of trauma to the organization.

13. Socio-economic and political changes

Socio-economic and political matters are always in a state of flux. These changes present opportunities for consultants. For example, pollution problems create a need for environmental protection experts, and fuel shortages create a need for energy conservation experts.

14. Government excess funds

Consultants benefit considerably from the expenditure of large amounts of government money. The government may be funding the private sector with the hope of stimulating the economy; there may be political reasons before an election; there may be a balance in a department's budget that is quickly spent before the end of the budget year, so as not to reduce the allotment requested by that department the following fiscal year. Governments also frequently hire consultants to assess needs and provide solutions, and to conduct in-house training.

d. REGULATIONS AFFECTING CONSULTANTS

Some professional organizations are empowered by legislation to exercise rights of practice, membership, and discipline. However, there is no government control or regulation of consultants as such. The term consultant is similar to the term accountant: anyone can use the word to describe his or her activity without credentials, experience, competence or accountability.

There are many consulting organizations for specific areas of consulting, but membership is voluntary. These organizations or associations have little power or authority to investigate complaints.

Management consultants can apply to become a member of the Institute of Management Consultants. This group provides guidelines for professional practice.

The benefits of membership in a consulting association include:

(a) Certification status if the consultant meets minimum acceptable standards of skill and knowledge

(b) Opportunities for self-development in seminars and workshops

(c) Interaction and networking with other consulting professionals

(d) Representation of the membership's areas of interest to government and other professional bodies

(e) A code of ethics and code of conduct

(f) Keeping current on issues in the area of consulting by means of a newsletter or other publication.

2

SELF-ASSESSMENT

a. INTRODUCTION

Many consultants open a business without ever doing a thorough, honest appraisal of their strengths and weaknesses. If you haven't identified your skills, attributes and talents, how can you determine your specialty areas and the target market? How are you able to package and sell your services and take advantage of opportunities? Without this awareness it is difficult to project the self-confidence necessary to operate your business and respond to questions a potential client might ask you.

Most consultants never go through the steps outlined in this chapter, and that gives you a distinct competitive advantage. To know yourself — your strengths and weaknesses — is to have power and a prescription for success.

[handwritten margin note: X Experience as corporate visual organisation presentations models 3D.]

b. ASSESSING YOURSELF AND YOUR MARKETABLE SKILLS

The following exercise is important to help you determine the direction you should take in your new consulting business. For the maximum benefit, take all the time you need to complete each stage. Be honest and candid with yourself. The material you are preparing is for your information and benefit only.

SELF-ASSESSMENT

1. Summarize your own autobiography. Review and detail all facets of your past, including work positions, projects you have done, education, credentials you have obtained, free time activities including hobbies and sports, family and personal relationships. Include all the work experiences performed during summers, weekends or holidays. Start with the most current time period and work backwards.

2. List all the areas of your special interest, achievement, knowledge, and personal satisfaction.

3. List all your skills, that is, things that you can do. Skills are developed or acquired abilities such as instructing, administering, researching, and problem-solving.

4. List all your talents. Talents are a natural endowment, often a unique "gift" or special, often creative, attribute. Frequently a talent is a combination of skills. Think of any evaluations that may have been made about you or comments made by your friends in which your talents were observed, for example.

5. List all your attributes. Attributes are inherent characteristics such as an analytical or inquiring mind, intuition or sensitivity. Various studies have found the following attributes essential to successful consultants:

- Good physical and mental health

- Professional etiquette and courtesy
- Stability of behavior
- Self-confidence
- Personal effectiveness and drive; that is, responsibility, vigor, initiative, resourcefulness and persistence
- Integrity, that is, the quality that engenders trust
- Independence; the successful consultant must be self-reliant and not conform to the opinions of others. The consultant must be able to form judgments in the areas of his or her competence and experience
- Intellectual competence
- Good judgment; the faculty of sound appraisal with complete objectivity
- Strong analytical or problem-solving ability; the ability to analyze, assemble, sort, balance, and evaluate the basic factors of problem situations of different degrees of complexity
- Creative imagination; the ability to see the situation with a fresh perspective
- Ability to communicate and persuade, with above-average facility, in oral, written and graphic formats
- Psychological maturity; the successful consultant is always ready to experience people, things and events as they really are with their unique individual characteristics; to view them in perspective and to take the action needed in a calm and objective manner without being diverted from a sound, logical and ethical course by outside pressure
- Skill in interpersonal relationships, including an ability to gain the trust and respect of client personnel, enlist client participation in the solution of problems, apply the principles and techniques of change, and transfer knowledge to client personnel; a receptiveness to new information or points of view expressed by others; and an orientation toward the people aspect of problems.
- Technical knowledge, which means an all-encompassing knowledge of the business and also recognizing lack of skill where it exists and seeking to acquire that skill or employing people with that skill

6. List all the skills and attributes you lack that you believe are necessary for a consulting business.

7. List the skills and attributes you lack related to being a consultant that you believe you can improve; write down how that will happen and how long it will take. Prioritize.

8. Of the skills and attributes that you believe you cannot improve, state how that will affect your consulting business choices, if at all.

9. Speak to friends, relatives or family members who know you well and whose judgment, candor, and goodwill you respect. Ask them to think about your strengths and weaknesses as they see them, and prepare a list. Also ask them to outline the skills, talents, and attributes they believe you possess and those you lack.

10. Update and modify the personal inventories you previously prepared.

11. Review your list of skills, talents, and attributes and provide specific examples where each trait was used that could have a marketing application in providing consulting services.

12. Prioritize the 10 activities that gave you the most pleasure and personal satisfaction. Outline how well you did these activities. Don't over-estimate or under-estimate your abilities.

13. List the top 10 skills or talents, starting with the most important, that you feel are basic to your consulting practice.

14. Imagine the type of consulting projects you would like to do and write them down in detail and why you would like to do them. Then review your notes and identify the skills, talents and attributes required to successfully complete these projects.

15. Imagine your personal life in the future. What direction are you currently headed in with your family and career, socially, financially, spiritually, and personally? What effect would a consulting business have on your existing lifestyle? Would the long hours and pressure of the first 6 to 12 months create strains in the family? Are you interested in marketing your abilities locally, regionally, nationally or internationally? What effect will these decisions have on you and the people in your life?

16. Think of all the consulting opportunities that might be available to you. Consultants sell themselves as people who have solutions to problems or needs, so look for problems/need situations. Focus only on existing or potential problem/need situations that relate to your area of interest and consulting expertise.

17. Increase your awareness of additional consulting opportunities by using the following resources.

(a) The Bibliography in this book

(b) Consulting newsletters will stimulate your ideas on managing your practice, marketing your skills, determining consulting opportunities and keeping current on events related to the consulting industry. A list of consulting newsletters is in the Bibliography.

(c) Magazines and newspapers; you should attempt to read everything you can relating to your specialty and general awareness of current events. Subscribe to trade journals related to your area of interest. Get on all the free mailing lists that are of interest or relevant to your specialty area. Read your local daily newspaper and, in Canada, *The Globe and Mail* and *The Financial Post;* in the United States, *The New York Times, The Washington Post* and *The Wall Street Journal.* There are other newspapers, of course, that you might prefer to read, but these provide a general indication of trends and interpretation of important events, all of which could have a bearing on opportunities for your business. There are numerous excellent business magazines which can stimulate further ideas and sources of contacts and information. Browse through your local international news outlet for an indication of the publications available. Another alternative is your public library.

(d) Consulting and professional associations; contact with the associations will provide you with an opportunity to obtain information related specifically to your specialty from newsletters, publications, meetings or other consultant contacts. A list of the major consulting associations is in Appendix 2.

If there is a local association of consultants, either of a general or specialized nature relevant to your needs, try to attend a number of meetings and ask a lot of questions.

The reference book, *Consultants and Consulting Organizations Directory,* available in public libraries, lists consultants in various specialties throughout the United States and Canada.

The SBA (U.S.) sponsors SCORE, which is an organization providing consulting for beginning businesses without charge. The FBDB (Canada) sponsors CASE, which is a program where consultants at a very nominal rate provide expertise and research skills to beginning small businesses. You may wish to take advantage of their expertise to assist you in the business side of consulting.

(e) Government agencies and publications; depending on the area of your interest, you may want to get on the mailing list of government organizations or departments that have regular publications distributed free or at a nominal charge to the public. The government, of course, is a major purchaser of consulting services, and very large sums of money are expended every year directly and indirectly for that purpose. Sources of procurement and contracts information are outlined in Appendix 1.

(f) Public and university libraries; there is a vast amount of information that is current and accessible to you for research or general ideas in your local public or university libraries. Most of the major libraries have the various directories listed in the Bibliography and Appendix 1.

(g) Continuing education courses and seminars; universities have continuing education courses pertaining to business and related services. The SBA (U.S.) and the FBDB (Canada) have small business seminars and workshops on an ongoing basis, as well as numerous publications pertaining to successful small business management.

(h) Competitors; attempt to identify the competitors in your specific field. Determine what their style and method of operation is, how long they have been in business, how they market themselves, what they charge, and who their clientele is, if possible. Try to ascertain why they are successful, if they are, and how you can best distinguish yourself and find your own niche in the market. You want to have your own unique style if comparisons are made between you and your other competitors by a prospective client.

18. Define the consulting service areas that you would like to provide (refer to Table #1 showing the major fields of consulting activity).

19. Identify who you believe could be possible clients and why.

20. Project how you would like to operate your consulting business. List the important stages and time frames of your business over the next year, three years, and five years.

21. List how you intend to market your services; that is, create a demand for your service and make potential clients realize that you exist. This question will be answered in another chapter, but it is helpful to go through the reflective exercise yourself.

You should now have a comprehensive, detailed and exhaustive guideline for your successful consulting business. Review it, update it and modify it on a regular basis. You should feel confident that you have developed a realistic framework for the next important stages of your business development.

3

SETTING UP YOUR BUSINESS

You have now assessed your skills, attributes, and abilities and have determined your area of interest and expertise. Various administrative matters have to be understood, considered and dealt with before embarking on your road to success.

This chapter and the next 10 chapters deal with the administrative fundamentals. The challenging and fun part — that is, successfully marketing your consulting — is explained later.

Before setting up your office and opening your doors to the public, many matters have to be considered. Your fee structures, marketing plan, and business plan, which includes your cash flow projections, will all determine how much revenue you must generate to pay your overhead. It is wise to be conservative on anticipated revenue and the lead time it will take to reach a breakeven point. Your legal, tax, accounting, and financial advisors will influence your initial decisions. These important aspects are covered in other chapters.

This chapter discusses how to establish the basics of an office while controlling your expenses. With thorough review and comparison of the costs of the key overhead areas, you should require minimal capital investment and keep your overhead and risk at a safe level.

a. START-UP COSTS AND MONTHLY EXPENSES

There are many factors that determine what your costs and expenses are going to be, such as whether you are going to use your own home or rent an office, whether you are going to buy, finance or lease new or used furniture and equipment, and whether you intend to hire staff or do the typing yourself. Your individual finances and needs and how shrewd you are in business and negotiating will clearly affect your overhead.

1. Start-up costs

Start-up costs vary widely depending upon your choices and circumstances. Table #2 lists average start-up expenses. Sample #1 is a start-up expense checklist as a guide for estimating initial costs of your business. It is important to keep a record of your estimated and actual costs during the start-up and first year of operation for overhead expenses as well as for your cash flow projections. The date to pay column should assist you in scheduling your cash flow or other funds to meet the initial expenses. You should be able to fill in the estimated costs schedule after you have thoroughly done your research. Further details on aspects of start-up costs are covered later.

TABLE #2
AVERAGE START-UP EXPENSES

Item	Price Range*		
Business licenses and permits	$ 20	to	$ 100
Business announcement or brochures	250	to	500
Supplies and stationery	100	to	250
Equipment (unless rented, then add rental charge)	500	to	3,000
Rental deposit on office (first and last months)	0	to	800
Utility and phone deposits	0	to	250
Insurance	100	to	300
Legal and accounting	500	to	1,500
Professional or business membership expenses	100	to	300
Answering service deposit (first and last months)	100	to	150
Miscellaneous	200	to	500
TOTAL START-UP COSTS	$1,870	to	$7,650

*Low range assumes the use of home office with outside secretarial service. High range assumes renting an office with one half-time secretary.

2. Monthly overhead expenses

Naturally, monthly expenses will vary widely depending upon the type of consulting service you are planning to operate. Sample #2 should assist you in planning and budgeting for your possible overhead expenses.

3. Personal expenses

Personal monthly overhead expenses obviously influence your cash flow needs and the amount of resources available to invest in your business. When you prepare your business plan, (see chapter 6), you will take into account your personal needs. It will be helpful, though, to consider your personal cash flow needs while planning your business expense outlay. See Sample #3 as a guide for detailing your personal expenses.

b. SELECTING A NAME

Selecting your name is an important decision both from an image and a legal perspective. It is essential to be aware of the implications of selecting your name to make it correct from the outset.

SAMPLE #1
START-UP EXPENSE CHECKLIST

Expense	Date to pay	Estimated cost	Actual cost
Business licenses and permits	_____	$ _____	$ _____
Business announcement or other initial business development including brochures	_____	_____	_____
Supplies and stationery	_____	_____	_____
Equipment/furniture	_____	_____	_____
Rental deposit on office (if outside home: first, second and last months)	_____	_____	_____
Telephone installation and deposits	_____	_____	_____
Utility deposits (if outside home)	_____	_____	_____
Insurance (health, life, liability, theft, etc.; unless paid monthly or quarterly)	_____	_____	_____
Legal and accounting	_____	_____	_____
Professional or business membership or expenses	_____	_____	_____
Answering service deposit (first and last months)	_____	_____	_____
Other	_____	_____	_____
Cushion for unexpected costs (contingency)	_____	_____	_____

1. General considerations

Many consultants do business under their own names, for example, "David R. Jones, Educational Consultant." The business card and letterhead stationery would also show the address and telephone number (with area code) and a brief description of the service. The description could read, for example, "Research studies and project management."

Many consultants prefer to use their own name because they are offering a personal service and promoting and selling themselves. The drawback of using your name is that it implies a one-person operation; this could cause a client to doubt your capacity to complete a project if you are ill or injured. For this reason, and by personal choice, some consultants prefer to use the phrase, "David R. Jones and Associates, Educational Consultants." This implies a business with more than one person and a resource base of skilled consultants.

Many consultants contract with sub-consultants as required, depending upon the job project. This cuts down on overhead, provides depth and flexibility,

SAMPLE #2
MONTHLY EXPENSE CHECKLIST

Expense	Date to pay	Estimated cost	Actual cost
Office rent (if outside home)	_____	$ _____	$ _____
Printing and supplies (not paid for by clients)	_____	_____	_____
Equipment (monthly payment and/or what you need to set aside for future cash purchases)	_____	_____	_____
Preparation of tax return and other accounting expenses (prorated, or if specific time owed then state)	_____	_____	_____
Legal services (projected and prorated)	_____	_____	_____
Typing and secretarial services	_____	_____	_____
Telephone	_____	_____	_____
Utilities (if outside home)	_____	_____	_____
Insurance costs (prorated over 12 months)	_____	_____	_____
Retirement contribution if applicable estimated costs prorated)	_____	_____	_____
Savings (for yourself and your business)	_____	_____	_____
Loan payment	_____	_____	_____
Taxes (including social security or pension plan prorated over 12 months)	_____	_____	_____
License renewal prorated	_____	_____	_____
Advertising	_____	_____	_____
Answering service	_____	_____	_____
Subscriptions	_____	_____	_____
Books and reference material	_____	_____	_____
Marketing	_____	_____	_____
Entertainment and promotion	_____	_____	_____
Automobile	_____	_____	_____
Travel (in town or out)	_____	_____	_____
Conventions, professional meetings, trade shows	_____	_____	_____
Professional development	_____	_____	_____
Salary (what you need to meet personal expenses)	_____	_____	_____
Miscellaneous	_____	_____	_____

15

SAMPLE #3
PERSONAL MONTHLY EXPENSE CHECKLIST

Budget for the month of _____

ITEM	BUDGET	ACTUAL	DEVIATION
Food	$ _____	$ _____	$ _____
Housing:			
Monthly payment	_____	_____	_____
Taxes (if owned)	_____	_____	_____
Insurance	_____	_____	_____
Clothing	_____	_____	_____
Auto:			
Payment	_____	_____	_____
Gasoline	_____	_____	_____
Repairs	_____	_____	_____
Insurance	_____	_____	_____
Utilities:			
Electricity	_____	_____	_____
Heat (if not electric)	_____	_____	_____
Telephone	_____	_____	_____
Other (water, gas)	_____	_____	_____
Personal spending (gifts)	_____	_____	_____
Credit cards (not covered elsewhere)	_____	_____	_____
Installment and other loans	_____	_____	_____
Life insurance	_____	_____	_____
Taxes	_____	_____	_____
Recreation	_____	_____	_____
Travel	_____	_____	_____
Investment, including saving	_____	_____	_____
Donations	_____	_____	_____
Medical and dental	_____	_____	_____
Education (family)	_____	_____	_____
Miscellaneous	_____	_____	_____
TOTALS	$ _____	$ _____	$ _____

and expands consulting contract opportunities. Other name variations include "Jones Educational Associates" or "Educational Consulting Associates."

It is important to describe the nature of the services you are offering, and not limit the future development of your consulting service. For example, if you are a hospital consultant, you may not want to state on your letterhead or business card "specializing in personnel development" if you could receive other spin-off consulting work outside the limits of description of personnel development. Don't use the word "freelance," as it may not project the professional image you want to create.

Some consultants prefer not to use their own name in the firm's name for a number of reasons. One reason is that the consultant does not want an employer to be aware that a consulting business is being operated part-time. Another reason is that if goodwill is developed under a company's name rather than an individual's, a higher price might be obtained if the consulting practice is sold.

If you decide to incorporate your business, you must have the name approved by the responsible government department and the name must end in Ltd. or Limited, Inc. or Incorporated, or Corp. or Corporation. Advantages and disadvantages of forming a corporation are discussed in chapter 4.

2. Fictitious name

If you are operating your proprietorship or partnership business under a name other than your own, you are required in most jurisdictions to register your fictitious name. Filing for fictitious names does not apply to corporations.

The procedures vary from area to area. The costs generally range from $10 to $75. Ask your lawyer about the requirements for your area. The procedure generally is to fill out forms disclosing the people behind the name and, in some cases, placing an ad in the local newspaper or legal gazette outlining the information in the filing documents.

c. SELECTING AN OFFICE

Most beginning consultants operate out of their homes. As the practice grows, the decision might be made to move into an office space.

Normally consultants go to the client's office, but occasionally clients wish to meet the consultant at the consultant's place of business.

1. Home office

There are several advantages to operating our of your home. You save money on gas and rent. The stress of commuting to work is reduced. You are able to deduct from income tax the portion of your home you are using for business purposes. (The tax deductions you can use when you have a home office are covered in chapter 9.)

Being close to the family is an important consideration for some consultants.

There are also disadvantages of having a home office. You may be distracted by your family members during the work day. Your presence may be distracting to your family members. The mix of home and office dynamics could negatively affect your private life. You could turn into a workaholic due to the proximity of your office. Your home might be distant from your clients' offices, which would make it difficult for your clients to visit you. If clients come to your home on occasion, you would want your home to present a positive impression so as not to detract from your professional image. Your home address on your stationery and business card could present a questionable image to prospective clients who may wonder about your business competence. Clients may view you as a freelancer, and be more likely to question your fees.

Due to the limitations of working out of your home, you may wish to consider a professional identity package provided by various office service businesses. This includes a mail drop address and telephone answering service, as well as other features you may desire.

The mail drop means having an address that is recognizable as a business and, depending upon the location, as a prestigious address. The staff at this location are able to receive or send out courier packages for you and receive envelopes or messages from clients who may stop by "your" office, etc.

These services can generally be found under "secretarial services" or "stenographers — public" in the yellow pages of the telephone directory. A post office box number has a negative effect in terms of your credibility and business reliability, and should be avoided if possible.

Having a personalized telephone answering service connected to your telephone at home allows you the freedom of knowing your telephone calls are being handled in a professional manner whether you are at home or out making calls. By keeping the answering service informed of your schedule for the day, your callers will receive the appropriate response and know when the call might be returned.

Generally, it's not a good idea to use an answering machine; they don't present a professional image, callers get the impression that you are a one-person operation (which, of course, you are), and you may be perceived as a freelancer, which has a negative connotation to some.

2. Office outside of home

You may wish to get an office outside your home when circumstances and finances justify it. Having your own office address increases credibility and stature when dealing with clients or prospective clients. Studies have shown that consultants are able to collect higher fees for performing the same work when operating out of an office.

When considering an office location, factors such as expense, image of business address, your proximity to clients, and referral possibilities should be examined.

Try to look at your long range goals over two years and imagine what your office needs might be. It is costly to pay for new office stationery and other start-up costs and several moves may create an image of instability.

(a) Office sharing arrangement

You may wish to look for an office with complementary professional or business tenants and prospective business clients. You have your own office and generally supply your own personal office furniture, but the rent expenses of the overall office and the receptionist's salary are shared on a proportional basis by the tenants. The secretarial expenses are negotiated depending upon use.

If you do seek out a pooling arrangement, try to have a minimal notice period to leave the premises. You may wish to leave due to expansion, inability to pay the rent or personality conflicts. It is fairly common to have a three-month notice provision. Make sure that the terms of your rental relationship are in writing and signed by the necessary parties before you begin your relationship.

As a general caution, avoid sharing space with a client. You could have a falling out or the client could attempt to use your time for free or look on you as staff.

(b) Sharing same private office

Two or more people may use the same office space. The parties agree on the costs of furnishing the office, unless it was already furnished, and an agreement would be worked in terms of the hours and days of use. Costs of this arrangement are negotiated on a per use basis.

(c) Office rental package

There are firms in the business of renting packaged office space. There can be anywhere from 5 to 50 tenants or more. Each tenant has a private office, and there is a common reception area.

The office package arrangement is a good source of potential contacts for networking or prospective clients, depending upon the mix of the tenants.

Frequently telephone answering and office furniture is included in the package price as well as a nominal number of hours of secretarial time per month. The rental arrangement may be a minimum two or three-month notice to vacate, or a six-month or one-year lease arrangement. Prices and terms of various office package arrangements may be negotiable if there is competition in that market-place in your community.

There are several other advantages of an office package arrangement. Frequently other services are available which save you considerable money on staff and equipment. These include:

(a)   Street mailing address — not a post office box number

(b) Postage metered mail for prompt delivery and a professional appearance

(c) Typing — a variety of typestyles available on modern equipment for letters, reports, invoices, statements, etc.

(d) Dictaphone transcription

(e) Secretarial services, including letter composition and editing using correct business language and form

(f) Photocopying — a bond copier with various features including collating could be available to produce quality copies on your letterhead, transparencies or address labels

(g) Word processing services with the advantages of speed, efficiency, and storage and retrieval capacity.

(d) Occasional office

You can rent a board room or an office for as short a time as an hour, or half day or a day. The cost is negotiable. The occasional office space can be found through office rental package services described earlier. Some firms require that you have a telephone answering or professional identity package arrangement with them before you are able to rent occasional space.

(e) Leased space

Leasing space does have its disadvantages, and it is most important that you consult your accountant and a competent lawyer familiar with commercial leases before signing anything. You should shop around for space to make sure you have the best arrangement for your needs and to assist you in negotiating.

Leases are generally for a period of one to five years. There are basically three types of lease payment formulas. The terminology may vary, but the concepts are the same. The first type, called a "net" lease means that the base rent is the total rent. In other words, the flat negotiated rate is the only monthly payment you have to make.

The second type of rent, "double net," is similar to the first except you have to pay a pro rata share of any tax increases over the base tax period outlined in your lease. If the taxes increase substantially, you could have extra overhead you had not anticipated.

The third type, "triple net" rent, can be very expensive. The base rent is just the beginning. All other landlord costs, such as taxes, insurance, maintenance, repair, improvements, management and administration fees are passed on proportionately to the tenants. This could increase your monthly rent by 50% to 100%. The other problem with this type of rent structure is the uncertainty of not knowing for budgeting purposes your rental overhead expenses.

A variation of this third formula involves paying the landlord a percentage of your gross revenue. Naturally, for a professional consultant, this is an unacceptable arrangement.

Some of the clauses to be wary of when you are considering a lease include restrictions on your ability to sublet or assign your lease, liabilities and duties of the landlord and tenant, the use you intend for the premises, limitations on alterations or improvements to the premises, acceleration clauses in case of default, and a requirement for your personal guarantee if you are doing business as a corporation.

If you are still interested in signing a lease, attempt to negotiate as many attractive features as possible. All leases are negotiable and there are no standard clauses. Your lawyer can properly advise you and possibly negotiate the lease on your behalf.

Some tips on negotiating your lease include:

(a) Rather than negotiating a three-year lease, for example, try to negotiate a one-year lease with two additional one-year options. This way you minimize the risk in case you cannot afford the lease or in case you need to expand or the premises are otherwise unsuitable for your needs.

(b) Consider offering the last two or three months rent as a deposit. If you default the lease and leave before the end of the term, the deposit monies go to the landlord, and you are free of any further liability.

(c) Put in the lease that alterations or improvements you intend to make will be at the landlord's expense.

(d) Attempt to get the first few months free of rent as an incentive for you to lease the premises.

(e) Try to get out of paying the last month's security deposit rent, if possible. If it is not possible, try to negotiate with the landlord to pay you interest at a fixed rate on the security deposit money.

Another factor in leasing space is the additional expense for furniture and equipment for your office and reception area, plus the additional costs of a secretary or receptionist. All these additional costs have to be carefuly factored out to ensure there is sufficient cash flow to justify the commitment.

3. Equipping an office

Equipping an office is not too expensive if you buy secondhand furniture. You can obtain good used business furniture from bankruptcy sales, auction sales, or through the classified section in the newspaper. The type and quality of furniture that you select naturally will relate to your type of consulting clientele and the image that you want to project.

There are certain basic things you need for your office, including desk, chairs, tables, lamps, bookcases, file cabinet, typewriter, calculator, telephone answering device (optional), tape recorder (as a dictaphone, to record meetings, to record consulting or marketing ideas), card file and/or address file, clock, postage meter and briefcase.

4. Office supplies

The basic supplies you need include business cards, letterhead stationery and printed envelopes, brochures, records for bookkeeping, invoices, filing folders, and various types of calendars.

(a) Business stationery, cards, envelopes

Your business stationery is very important as it represents you, your image, and your business. It should present a professional and conservative image. It should state your name, your business name, the type of consulting (if applicable), address, postal/zip code and telephone number with area code.

All your stationery should correspond with the format and image of your business card. Choose a good quality paper stock. Purchase blank pages of your letter stock so that your second page will match the color of the first. Neutral shades for colors, such as beige, ivory or white, create a professional impression. You have a choice between litho (flat) or thermo (raised) ink. The thermo's raised, glossy appearance creates a richer effect. The cost of raised letter is not much more than flat, but extra time is required for printing. As the printing business is very competitive, be sure to compare rates.

Some consultants prefer to have a logo on their business card. Have a graphic artist prepare the logo or see *Design Your Own Logo,* another title in the Self-Counsel series.

(b) Brochures

Depending upon the type of consulting practice that you have and the nature of clientele you wish to attract, brochures may be part of your marketing plan. Naturally, brochures are less expensive by quantity. You may choose to request the services of a promotional writer to assist you in preparing the text for a brochure that will effectively outline the services you provide for your specific clientele or market. Such services can be found under the "sales promotion services" section of the yellow pages. For printing, check for competitive rates and allow yourself considerable lead time to obtain the best rate. One color ink on colored stock is less expensive than two inks and can be just as effective.

(c) Record-keeping documents, invoices, and file folders

These items are necessary for the orderly maintenance of projects, systems, and good business management. The types of record-keeping documents are outlined in chapter 8.

(d) Calendars

For recording appointments, telephone calls, and deadlines you should have a desk calendar, a wall calendar, and a daily diary that you carry with you. The time that you spend on client files must be recorded in detail for proper billing and for your protection in the event of a dispute.

5. Personnel

(a) Secretarial staff

Most beginning consultants do not have the workload or cash flow to justify hiring a secretary. Some consultants prefer to type the documents and correspondence themselves, but even if you are a good typist, you will make more money consulting or finding new clients than you will typing. Some consultants have a family member do the typing, but this can create strains on the family relationship.

It is far more cost efficient and practical to "rent" a secretary. In many cases, the typing costs related to a client file can be billed directly to the client, in addition to your fees. You then have verification from the typing service if there is any question on your account.

Find a professional typing service that offers temporary or one-time service. Ask how much lead time is required, what the turn-around time is, and what other services they offer. Interview several professional typing services and ask to see sample copies of their reports, newsletters, and correspondence so that you can judge the professional quality of the work.

It is essential that word processing services be available. As a consultant, you will be producing large quantities of material that require neat, clean, and correctly styled typing. A word processor can produce this quality, and store your contracts, proposals, form letters, reports, and mailing lists for retrieval.

A professional secretarial service can also look after all your correspondence and document needs including preparing invoices and reminder letters for your receivables. You can ask the secretarial service if one staff member will work on your file so that person will become familiar with your style. A dictaphone tape for transcription is a considerable benefit in terms of consistency and saving time when one person gets accustomed to your method of dictating.

(b) Retaining other consultants

Employing another consultant as an independent contractor, in other words, a sub-consultant, is a common technique to reduce overhead and increase your resource base and efficiency. There are times when you might need specialized skills or additional help to be able to satisfy a potential client contract. Try to develop a sub-contracting network of consultants you can call on when needed Many consultants take on projects they could not complete themselves and sub-contract portions to another consultant.

It is important to maintain your position with your client as the main source of information and communication. Your client need not know that you have sub-contracted out a part of the job.

d. SELECTING A TELEPHONE SYSTEM

Your telephone, in many ways, is your lifeline to a successful consulting practice. Many consultants start out using their home telephone number and a telephone answering device, but there are problems with this. Inexpensive alternatives exist. The important consideration is the impression your telephone system gives your clients or prospective clients and how effectively you receive incoming messages.

1. A separate phone at home

Many consultants operating out of their home prefer to have a separate line for their consulting practice apart from their personal line. This saves the frustration of having children answer your phone or family members tying up the phone with their personal calls.

2. Business line terminating at answering service

You may wish to have an office number that does not go to your home, but terminates at your answering service. Your answering service could then phone you at home (if those were your instructions) and advise you of a phone message.

Alternatively, you could telephone the answering service from time to time to pick up messages. You could then return calls on your personal line. The advantage of this system is that you save on the monthly line charges for a business telephone installed in your home, but have a telephone answering capacity.

When selecting an answering service, it is very important to consider the personal aspect of the service. An answering service that has only 40 to 60 lines will generally be more attentive, know your business better, and personalize the responses so that the caller is unaware it is an answering service. Compare various answering services and ask for references from their clients.

The quality of your answering service is vital to the reputation and goodwill of your business. In many cases the person answering the phone will be the first representative of your firm to the caller. A drawback of the larger answering service companies with trunk lines and hundreds of customers is that the switchboard operators are frequently very busy and therefore unable to personalize your phone messages. Another factor is the turnover that can occur in personnel. With the larger answering services, it is very difficult to hide the fact that it is an answering service.

3. Business line terminating at home and answering service

Your business line can pass through an answering service's switchboard. All calls may be intercepted by the answering service, if those are your instructions, or with a switch on your phone unit, you can decide to answer the phone yourself for certain periods of the day. The answering service staff can be told the appropriate procedures for incoming phone calls. There are additional monthly line charges for this system.

4. Overline

An overline feature allows an incoming phone call to come through on a second line while you are on the first line. This is an appropriate feature if you intend to use your business phone regularly, as your phone would otherwise ring busy for an incoming phone call if you just had one line. Too many busy signals give a negative impression, and may result in the loss of a prospective client. The other technique, as mentioned earlier, is to give out your business telephone number for incoming calls and use your personal phone for outgoing calls.

5. Measured business line

A measured business line can reduce your monthly phone charges for service in half. The reduced base rate has a limit of 50 outgoing phone calls per month. No limit is placed on the number of incoming calls. If you make more than 50 outgoing calls in a month, you are charged an additional fee per phone call (approximately 11¢, but it varies).

If you make many outgoing phone calls, this system is not economical. Some people use the measured line system for incoming calls and their personal phone for outgoing calls.

6. Shared line

A number of people may agree to share a common telephone number. Usually it is a feature offered through a telephone answering service for one of their unused lines. Telephone expenses are reduced considerably. The phone is answered "4444," "Suite 100" or some such non-descriptive phrase, or it can be answered "consulting office" if there are two or more consultants receiving calls on the same line.

7. Remote call forwarding

Remote call forwarding allows telephone calls to one number to be automatically redirected to another number without the caller being aware. For example, if you are going to be at a location other than your home office and want to receive all calls there temporarily, you can dial a predetermined code and the number you want calls redirected to. Anyone phoning your number may hear the phone ringing, but it is not ringing at your home or office, but at the number you designated the calls be redirected to. You therefore do not miss incoming or expected phone calls.

8. Telephone answering devices

The purpose of a telephone answering device (TAD) is to help you avoid losing critical calls if you are away from your office. It also acts as an efficient office screening agent. The TAD answers the phone, gives a message, and accepts a message from the caller on your behalf. After you have dictated your message into the machine, call your own number to listen with a critical ear to the impression of your message.

There are six basic kinds of answering machines. Due to the intense competition in this market area, comparative pricing is recommended if you are in the market for a TAD.

(a) *Announce only* answers the telephone with one or more pre-recorded announcements up to several minutes long

(b) *Announce/record* gives a pre-recorded message and allows the caller to leave a message.

(c) *Call screening* can help you avoid unwanted calls. By turning the volume higher, you can listen to caller's messages without their knowledge. If you wish, you can pick up the telephone, interrupt the regular answering cycle, and talk to the caller

(d) *Record* can record a conversation. This is useful if you need proof that you have communicated important information to another party. In many jurisdictions you are obliged to notify the other party that the call is being recorded. For this reason, these machines repeatedly emit a tone to remind both parties that the conversation continues to be recorded.

(e) *Dictation* allows you to dictate messages for subsequent transcription. You by-pass the normal use of the telephone answering machine and use features exactly like those of an office dictation machine.

(f) *Remote Control* allows you to transmit a signal from any other phone by means of a small device. The machine will automatically respond and play back over the phone any messages that have been recorded. This is convenient if you are out of town, but expecting calls at your office.

As mentioned earlier, the telephone answering device has its limitations. Some callers find it very annoying to talk to an answering machine; others refuse to leave a message or the message is unclear. The impression could be created that you are very much a beginner in business and still struggling.

9. Interconnect phone purchase

Private telephone equipment companies are now able to compete using the main telephone circuits. Rather than renting or leasing your phone from your telephone company, you have the choice of purchasing your phone. You still have to pay the monthly service charges and long distance charges, but you do not have to pay the monthly equipment charges. Your decision is a matter of comparing the breakeven point in purchasing your phone over renting your phone.

e. SAVING MONEY ON LONG DISTANCE PHONE CALLS

There are many occasions when consultants wish to make long distance phone calls for which no reimbursement can be expected from the client, for example, in marketing efforts, prospective client contacts, or a fixed price contract where your costs are built into the contract. Some of the ways of saving money on long distance calls are mentioned below.

1. Direct distance dialing

By dialing a number directly rather than asking for operator assistance or third-party billing, you save quite a bit. The amount of the savings varies but can be obtained from your telephone company.

2. Reduced long distance rates

There are specific times, which vary in different regions, that long distance rates are one-third to two-thirds less than the regular daily rates. This saving can be considerable especially when the time zones allow you to telephone at the cheapest rate but still during the business hours of the long distance call recipient.

3. 800 service number

There are many companies, including prospective clients, that have "800 service." This system allows the caller to phone long distance free to the 800 number. An "800 service" directory which lists the firms that have 800 numbers can be purchased through the phone company.

4. Wide area telephone service (WATS)

Many businesses and governments have incoming and/or outgoing WATS service lines available. This system is similar to the 800 system, if they have an incoming system. If the company you are calling only has an *outgoing* WATS system, then you may prefer to phone and leave a message for a return call.

If a prospective client or other party phones you long distance, have a policy of accepting the phone call if at all possible in case it is not appropriate to return the phone call collect or not possible to return the call on a WATS line.

5. Some tips

If you are placing long distance phone calls on behalf of a client, ask the operator to call you back with time and charges. This will allow you to record the call in your record system so that the expenses can be passed on as direct expenses to your client and on the next bill. If you do not adopt this system, you won't be able to render an account to a client for various long distance phone calls until you receive your telephone bill.

To limit your overhead for long distance phone calls on behalf of the client, you may wish to ask the client (and confirm it in writing) for the authority to third-party bill to the client's phone number any calls pertaining to your contract or consulting project.

A technique for saving money on long distance phone calls that are being done for information purposes or for marketing purposes is to place a long distance phone call person-to-person at 12:30 p.m. in the time zone of the recipient. In most cases, senior people are not in their offices at this time; a message is left by your operator with the recipient company, giving your name and phone number and operator call back number. Also leave a message through the operator about the time and day that you will be in to receive the phone call. State the recipient's time to eliminate confusion. It is very rare for the recipient caller in government or industry to return your call on a collect basis. You can make sure that you are in your office or home when the incoming call is expected, and you won't have to pay the long distance phone charges.

4

LEGAL FORMS OF BUSINESS STRUCTURE

a. INTRODUCTION

There are basically three forms of legal structure: proprietorship, partnership, and limited company. You should seek competent legal and accounting advice before deciding on your business structure, as there could be distinct advantages or disadvantages to each depending upon your situation.

Many consultants start out as a sole proprietor, as that is the easiest way to start a business. If additional skill or personnel is required on a specific project, sub-consultants may be retained as independent contractors by the proprietor.

In a partnership of two or more consultants, it is common to have problems and dissolve. In the field of consultancy in particular, a healthy ego is essential to sell yourself and your skills. Because of this, conflict is likely to occur when two or more consultants share joint decision-making but have individual dreams and goals.

Forming a corporation is a third option. The corporation can be owned by just one person (similar to a proprietorship) or two or more people (similar to a partnership).

This chapter discusses the factors that you and your professional advisors should examine when making a decision about your business structure.

b. SOLE PROPRIETORSHIP

A sole proprietorship is a business owned and operated by one person. To establish a sole proprietorship, you need only obtain whatever local licenses you require and open your business. It is the simplest form of business structure and operation.

1. Advantages

Ease of formation: There is less formality and few legal restrictions associated with establishing a sole proprietorship. You can start almost immediately. There are no complex forms to complete and no documentation required between yourself and any other party. In most jurisdictions, all that is legally necessary to operate as a sole proprietorship is to register the business and obtain the proper licenses. Licenses can be required by various levels of government.

Cost: Registering the business and obtaining licenses involves minimal costs. There are no partnership or corporate agreements required because you are the sole owner. Legal fees are reduced accordingly.

Lack of complexity: A sole proprietorship is staightforward. Unlike other forms of business, there is little government control and, accordingly, fewer reports are required to be filed with government agencies and departments. The owner and the business are taxed as one.

Decision-making process: Decisions are made exclusively by the sole owner, who has complete authority and freedom to move. The owner does not have to obtain approval from partners or shareholders or a board of directors.

Sole ownership of profits: The proprietor does not have to share the profits with anyone. The profits generated by the business belong to one person. The sole owner decides how and when the money will come out of the business.

Ease of terminating/sale of business: Apart from legal responsibilities to employees, creditors or perhaps clients, you can sell the business or close it down at your will.

Flexibility: You are able to respond quickly to business needs in day-to-day management decisions as governed by various laws and common sense.

2. Disadvantages

Unlimited liability: The sole owner's personal assets, such as house, property, car and investments, are liable to be seized if necessary to pay for outstanding debts or liabilities. As mentioned earlier, the proprietor and the business are deemed to be one and the same in law.

Less financing capacity: It is more difficult for a proprietor to borrow money than for a partnership with various partners or a corporation with a number of major shareholders. A lender, when looking for security and evidence of outside resources, can turn to other people connected with the business rather than just the one person in a proprietorship. A partnership or corporation can give an investor some form of equity position, which is not available in a proprietorship.

Unstable duration of business: The business might be crippled or terminated upon the illness or death of the owner. If there is no one appropriate to take over the business, it may have to be sold or liquidated. Such an unplanned action may result in a loss.

Sole decision-making: In partnerships or corporations, generally there is shared decision-making or at least input. In a proprietorship, just one person is involved, and if that person lacks business ability or experience, poor decision-making can cause the business to suffer.

Taxation: At a certain level of profit there are tax disadvantages for the sole proprietor.

c. PARTNERSHIP

A partnership is usually defined as an association of two or more persons to carry on a business in common with a view to making a profit. The partnership is created by a contract, either verbal or written, between the individual parties.

1. Advantages

Ease of formation: Legal formalities and expenses in forming a partnership are few compared to incorporating.

Pride of ownership and direct rewards: Pride of ownership generates personal motivation and identification with the business. The profit motive could be reinforced with more people having a vested interest.

Availability of more capital: A partnership can pool the funds of a number of people compared to a sole owner who has only his or her own resources to draw upon, unless loans are obtained.

Combination of expertise and talent: Two or more partners, by combining their energies and talents, can often be successful where one person alone would fail. This is particularly true if the business demands a variety of talents such as technical knowledge, sales ability, and financial skills. It is important that working partners bring complementary skills to the business, thereby reducing the workload of each partner.

Flexibility: A partnership may be relatively more flexible in the decision-making process than a corporation, but less so than a sole proprietorship.

Relative freedom of government control and special taxation: Compared to a corporation, a partnership is relatively free from many restrictions and bureaucratic red tape.

2. Disadvantages

Unlimited liability: The major disadvantage of a partnership is the unlimited liability. This unlimited liability is much more serious than in a proprietorship because all the partners are individually *and* collectively liable for all the debts and liabilities of the partnership. Each partner's personal assets are liable to be seized if necessary to pay for outstanding business debts.

Unstable duration of business: Any change in the partnership automatically ends the legal entity. Changes could include the death of a partner, or the admission or withdrawal of a partner. In each case, if the business is to continue, a new partnership agreement must be written.

Management difficulties: As mentioned, when more than one owner assumes responsibility for business management there is a possibility that differences of style, priorities, philosophy, and other factors will arise. If these differences become serious disputes and are unresolveable, the partnership may have to be terminated, with all the financial and personal trauma involved. It is difficult for future partners to foresee whether or not personalities and methods of operating will clash.

Relative difficulty in obtaining large sums of capital: This is particularly true of long-term financing when compared to a corporation.

Partnership agreement problems: The larger a partnership becomes, the more complex the written agreement has to be to protect the rights and identify the responsibilities of each partner. This can result in additional administration and legal costs.

Difficulty of disposing of partnership interest: To withdraw capital from the business requires approval from all the other partners. This takes time and involves legal and administrative expenses.

3. Partnership agreement

A partnership agreement, sometimes called articles of partnership, is absolutely necessary in a partnership relationship. The agreement normally outlines the contribution of each partner in the business, whether financial, material or managerial. In general, it defines the roles of the partners in the business relationship. Some of the typical articles contained in a partnership agreement are shown in Table #3.

If you are considering a partnership relationship, complete the checklist headings and then see your lawyer and accountant. By the time you have completed the checklist with your prospective business mate, the engagement could be off.

4. Kinds of partners

An *ostensible partner* is active in the business and known as a partner.

An *active partner* may or may not be ostensible as well.

A *dormant partner* is inactive and not known or held out as a partner.

A *secret partner* is active but not known or held out as a partner.

A *silent partner* is inactive (may be known to be a partner).

A *nominal partner* (partner by estoppel) is not a true partner in any sense, not being a party to the partnership agreement. A nominal partner, however, holds himself or herself out as a partner, or permits others to make such representation by the use of his/her name or otherwise. A nominal partner, therefore, is liable to third parties as if he or she were a partner.

A *sub partner* is a person who is not a member of the partnership but contracts with one of the partners to represent that partner by participating in the firm's business and profits.

A *limited or special partner* risks only his or her agreed investment in the business assuming that statutory formalities have been complied with. As long as he or she does not participate in the management and control of the enterprise or in the conduct of its business, the limited partner is generally not subject to the same liabilities as the general partner.

TABLE #3
CHECKLIST OF ARTICLES IN A PARTNERSHIP AGREEMENT

1. Name, purpose, and location of partnership
2. Duration of agreement
3. Names and character of partners (general or limited, active or silent)
4. Financial contribution by partners (at inception, at later date)
5. Role of individual partners in business management
6. Authority (authority of partner in conduct of business)
7. Nature and degree of each partner's contribution to firm's consulting services
8. Business expenses (how handled)
9. Separate debts
10. Signing of checks
11. Division of profits and losses
12. Books, records and method of accounting
13. Draws or salaries
14. Absence and disability
15. Death of a partner (dissolution and winding up)
16. Rights of continuing partner
17. Employee management
18. Sale of partnership interest
19. Release of debts
20. Settlement of disputes; arbitration
21. Additions, alterations or modifications to partnership agreement
22. Non-competition in the event of departure

d. CORPORATION

A corporation is a legal entity, with or without share capital, which can be established by one or more individuals or other legal entities. It exists separate and distinct from these individuals or other legal entities. A corporation has all the rights and responsibilities of a person with the exception of those rights that can only be exercised by a natural person.

1. Advantages

Limited liability of shareholders: Shareholders' personal assets are separate from the business and cannot be seized to pay for outstanding business debts incurred by the corporation. There are exceptions, dealing primarily with the issue of fraud.

Flexibility for tax planning: Various tax advantages are available to corporations that are not available to partnerships or proprietorships. Tax planning must be undertaken with the help of a professional accountant.

Corporate management flexibility: The owner or owners can be active in the management of the business to any desired degree. Agents, officers, and directors with specified authority can be appointed to manage the business.

Employees can be given stock options to share in the ownership, which can increase incentive and interest.

Financing more readily available: Investors find it more attractive to invest in a corporation with its limited liability than to invest in a business whose unlimited liability could involve them to an extent greater than the amount of the investment. Long-term financing from lending institutions is more available since lenders may use both corporate assets and personal guarantees as security.

Continual existence of corporation: A corporation continues to exist and operate regardless of the changes in the shareholders. Death of a shareholder does not discontinue the life of the corporation. Continual existence is also an effective device for building and retaining goodwill.

Ownership is readily transferable: It is a relatively simple procedure to transfer ownership by share transfer unless there are corporate restrictions to the contrary.

Draw on expertise and skills of more than one individual: This feature is the same concept as in a partnership, where more partners (shareholders) contribute diverse talents. However, a corporation is not required to have more than one shareholder.

2. Disadvantages

Extensive government regulations: There are more regulations affecting a corporation than a sole proprietorship or partnership. Corporations must report to all levels of government.

Activities limited by the charter and by-laws: Depending upon the jurisdiction, charters can be very broad or can severely restrict a company's activities.

Manipulation: Minority shareholders are potentially in a position to be exploited by the decisions of the majority of the company.

Expense: It is more expensive to establish and operate a corporation due to the additional documents and forms that are required compared to a proprietorship or partnership.

3. Corporate purposes

Some jurisdictions require that the articles of incorporation include a statement of the purposes of the corporation. When you provide a list of the purposes of the corporation, make sure that you define them expansively. Do not restrict the activity of your corporation. A general clause should be included allowing the corporation to expand into any business activity permitted by law. A competent lawyer can assist you in preparing this document to enable you to maximize your corporate options.

4. Shareholders' agreement

A shareholders' agreement involves the same concepts of protection as a partnership agreement. Many of the provisions outlined in the partnership agreement are also included in the shareholders' agreement. There are additional provisions frequently covered in the shareholders' agreement, including:

(a) A restriction on transfer of shares

(b) A buy-sell provision that sets out the formula for buying or selling shares in the company

(c) A provision on personal guarantees of corporate obligations

(d) A provision on payback by corporation of shareholders' loans

(e) A provision giving all shareholders the entitlement to sit as a director or nominate a director as their representative. This protects minority shareholders from lack of managerial information and provides them with a directorship vote or veto on corporate decisions. If you intend to be a majority shareholder, you may not wish to volunteer this provision.

Many shareholders believe that corporate by-laws set out the recipe for resolving problems within the corporation and between the shareholders, directors, and officers in some magical fashion. In most cases, the by-laws only cover formulas for resolving disputes in a few circumstances. It is the shareholders' agreement that expands the protections to resolve fairly any disputes between shareholders.

If you intend to incorporate and have one or more additional shareholders in your corporation, it would be wise to obtain your lawyer's advice on a shareholders' agreement to protect your interests.

5. Maintaining the corporate protection

One of the advantages of operating through a corporate entity is the protection against personal liability for the debts and liabilities of the corporation. This is assuming, of course, that you have not signed personal guarantees.

However, there are situations that could cause you to be personally liable for corporate debts. Generally, if it can be shown that a fraud was perpetrated through use of the corporation, or the director totally disregarded the corporate formalities, the advantage of the "corporate veil" can disappear.

When a court treats the corporation as a sham and imposes personal liability on the shareholders or directors, it is said to "pierce the corporate veil." Here is a list of precautions to follow, to prevent personal legal attack.

(a) *Meetings:* A corporation acts only when its employees (officers, directors, and shareholders) act. If a corporation holds no directors' or shareholders' meetings, the corporation may not really exist. Therefore, every corporation should hold at least one shareholders' and one directors' meeting annually and have that fact documented.

(b) *Corporate name:* A business operating in the corporate form must let the general public know that it is a corporation with limited liability by attaching either "Inc." or "Incorporation," "Corp." or "Corporation," or "Ltd." or "Limited" to its name, depending upon the form you selected at incorporation. You must specify the corporate designation everywhere the company name appears.

(c) *Acting as agent:* When a shareholder/employee executes a document or engages in a transaction, the person must make it clear that it is being done on behalf of the corporation. That is, when you sign a check or contract, you should write your corporate office title (i.e., president, secretary, etc.) after your name.

(d) *Tax returns:* The corporation must file an annual tax return and observe the rules for withholding on payroll taxes. You must make sure that all periodic reporting requirements are satisfied and that there is never any failure to pay to the taxing authorities all sums paid by or deductions from the corporate employees. Any sales tax collected must be remitted within the appropriate period.

(e) *Adequate capitalization:* If a corporation is inadequately capitalized so that there is insufficient capital investment to meet the claims by creditors, the courts may impose personal liability on the corporation's share-holders or directors for its business obligations. You should, therefore, be careful that your "equity" in the corporation does not become too diluted by loans from yourself and from third parties. As an arbitrary rule of thumb, a debt to equity ratio not exceeding 8:1 is reasonable. However, what is truly "inadequate" depends on the extent of actual corporate liabilities and the extent of assets to satisfy those liabilities.

   The laws in Canada and the United States and within the individual provinces and states vary; these cautions may not be necessary or applicable in your area. Your lawyer can advise you properly.

(f) *Separate accounts:* Many shareholders of closely held corporations treat the corporation's assets as their own. They combine personal and corporate funds, use corporate funds to pay personal expenses, including medical bills and taxes, and generally disregard the corporate "formalities." By doing so, however, they run the risk that a court may also disregard the formalities and hold the person liable for the company's debts. The shareholders and directors, therefore, should maintain separate corporate and personal accounts, and use the company funds only for business needs.

(g) *Filing annual corporate forms:* Most jurisdictions require an annual report to be filed. The form requires that you list the shareholders, officers, directors and current business address of your company, as well as other incidental information. This document must be filed on time to avoid penalties and possible involuntary dissolution. This dissolution could mean that you would be held personally liable for debts of the corporation.

e. SUB-CHAPTER (SUB-S) CORPORATION (U.S.)

As a consultant you may wish to consider the advantages of a Sub-S corporation in the U.S. The purpose is to permit a small business corporation to treat its net income as though it were a partnership. One objective is to overcome the double-tax feature of taxing corporate income and shareholder dividends. Another purpose is to permit the shareholders to have the benefit of offsetting business losses incurred for the corporation against their income.

Only closely held corporations, that is with 10 or fewer shareholders may make the Sub-S election. All shareholders must consent to the Sub-S election, and only one class of outstanding stock is allowed. A specific portion of the corporation's income must be derived from active business rather than passive investments. No limit is placed on the size of the corporation's income and assets.

At some future point you may wish to revert to a full corporation for tax advantage reasons. This is permitted, but the corporation may not be able to re-elect the Sub-S vehicle for several years once the Sub-S election is reversed. This is to eliminate small corporations from changing frequently to maximize tax advantages. Since Sub-S forms of incorporation are not recognized in all states, you should obtain further information from your professional advisors.

5

SELECTING BUSINESS
AND PROFESSIONAL ADVISORS

Since you may be operating on your own, or with a few associates, you will need an extended management team to advise you in specialized areas where you lack knowledge, ability or interest. Your advisors are, in effect, your employees and associates, and should be considered an integral part of management decision-making.

Every business decision involves a legal decision or implication. Every business decision involves accounting, bookkeeping and, at times, tax considerations. The fatality rate of small businesses is enormously high. Statistically the odds are approximately ten to one that you as a small business person will not be in business three years after you begin your practice.

This chapter discusses the benefits of the effective use of business and professional advisors, how to selectively evaluate them, and how to use their skills to your advantage.

a. GENERAL CRITERIA FOR ADVISOR SELECTION

How well you select your professional and business advisors will have a direct bearing on your business success. Poor advisors or no advisors will almost certainly lead to your business downfall. Your main advisors are your lawyer and accountant, followed by your banker. You should see at least three different people from each of these three professions before you make your selection. It is important to have the comparative assessment.

The following general guidelines should assist you in the careful search and selection of your advisors.

1. Recommendations

One of the most reliable methods of finding an advisor is by a personal recommendation from your banker, your existing advisors or friends in business whose judgment and business sense you trust. Bankers and business advisors who deal on a regular basis with professional advisors are in a good position to pass judgment based on their business dealings. When lawyers, accountants or bankers refer each other, it implies a good working relationship and mutual trust.

Don't rely completely on any referral; make your own cautious assessment. You might also want to try the lawyer referral service in your area. For a nominal fee you can see a business or corporate lawyer for an initial consultation.

2. Credentials

In Canada all lawyers have an "LL.B." professional designation. In the United States, lawyers have either an "LL.B." or "J.D." professional designation.

Accountants in Canada have a professional designation such as "C.A." or "C.G.A." In the United States, look for the designation "C.P.A." The training requirements and public practice background of C.A.s, and C.P.A.s are similar if not identical.

Certification and credentials only ensure that the individual has passed a minimum standard of education. They do not ensure that the person is a dynamic, innovative or creative business advisor with a specific amount of experience relevant to your needs.

3. Clientele

Most professional advisors have a homogeneous client base. Some advisors have many small business clients, others emphasize personal clients, while others go after corporate business. An advisor with a good base of small to medium size commercial clients will probably be the most appropriate for your business needs.

4. Fees

Fees will often vary by the size of the community in which the professional practice is operated, the size of the practice, and the volume of business. You may find that advisors who charge fees in the middle range, edging toward the higher end of the scale, are often quality practitioners in high demand who are still aggressive and innovative in their business practice.

Advisors who are at the low end of the fee scale can be entrepreneurial types, but cut-rate pricing may also indicate a cut-rate, high volume approach to business which will not suit your objectives. Low prices are sometimes an indicator of low quality, low esteem or little experience.

Very high priced advisors tend to be more conservative, less aggressive and less willing to spend the necessary time with small business clients, as their priorities are the big firms. Fees vary and many professionals will negotiate them.

In a smaller or medium size community, a realistic hourly rate for a lawyer or accountant is approximately $50 to $75 per hour. Advisors in larger cities will be more expensive, perhaps $100 to $150 per hour. If you are given an estimate by your lawyer or accountant and that estimate is exceeded, it is not uncommon for your advisor to reduce the fee as a gesture of goodwill in order to keep your ongoing business. Lawyers in general are more agreeable to charging a fixed fee. In some jurisdictions a lawyer can charge a contingency fee. For example, a lawyer may sue on your behalf and recover $100,000 owing to you and receive a fee in the form of a percentage, say 35%, of that amount.

It is important to be very open when discussing fees and payment expectations.

5. Technical competence and industry knowledge

You must satisfy yourself that your advisor is competent in the areas of your greatest need. Ask him or her how much experience, and how comfortable, he or she is with your field.

A specific understanding of the problems, needs and issues of your type of business can enable your advisors to provide the exact assistance you require. This is different from technical skill competence. It has more to do with experience in a particular type of industry. If the advisor has provided guidance to other small business owners in similar situations, there is an increased possibility that the advisor will be able to provide you with more reliable assistance. For example, if you are a hospital consultant, a lawyer who specializes in or is very familiar with health or hospital law could be an asset to you.

6. Style and personality

A critical factor in the selection of advisors, beyond simple compatibility, is style. You can have greater confidence in the aggressive advisor who takes the initiative and offers advice before you request it. This style indicates an initiator rather than a reactor, a person who anticipates and performs before matters become serious. It also indicates a creator, an entrepreneur, and a person who can empathize with your problems and concerns. This kind of advisor is more likely to come up with creative solutions to problems, and be a complement to your planning function. This type of advisor will not only be a sounding board, but a true part of the management team.

7. Confidence

You should feel a sense of confidence when relating to your advisor, whether it be in the general sense or in dealing with a specific problem or issue. You should have a certain amount of personal compatibility with your advisor. If you don't, you will probably end up rejecting a fair amount of advice. In other words, if you do not feel that good chemistry exists with an advisor, seek a replacement as soon as possible. If you do not relate well to the advisor, you may hesitate to ask for advice, which could result in some poor management decisions.

Never allow your advisors to treat you in a condescending or paternalistic manner. You should consider them as equals with special knowledge offering a service in the same manner that you are offering a service to your clients.

8. Communication

You should select an advisor who communicates well, openly and free of jargon. Your advisor should explain the necessary concepts to you so that you understand the issues involved and the decisions that have to be made. Effective communication also means that your advisors forward to you any correspondence sent or received through their offices relating to your business.

9. Commitment

It is important to sense that your advisor is committed to your best interests and your success. An advisor who is involved with larger, more important or higher paying clients than you may become indifferent to your needs. You should be alert to this.

10. Availability

It is important for your advisors to be available when you need them. You are spending time and resources to develop a relationship that will enhance your business decisions. If your advisor is frequently out of town, or in the case of a lawyer, in court on a regular basis, you may not have the immediate access you need. Of course, if the advisor is of exceptional quality and ideally suited to your type of practice, some allowances should be made.

11. Length of time in practice

There is naturally a correlation between the degree of expertise and length of time in practice. You should therefore ask directly how many years of experience your advisor has in the area of your needs.

12. Ability to aid growth

A good professional advisor will have a history of assisting growth in other clients. The advisor would be able to anticipate growth problems in advance, and provide guidance to deal with them.

13. Small firm versus large firm

Choosing a small or large firm is in many ways a matter of your own personal style and the type of firm you relate to most comfortably. Larger firms tend to be in the central area of the city, which may involve parking problems. Their fees are higher. Generally, the larger firms do not have a small business orientation in their marketing and service priorities. The larger firms do have highly specialized advisors and a resource base of associate personnel. This degree of depth may or may not be necessary in your situation. It is not uncommon in larger firms to have small business clients passed over to junior associates or students in training as the more senior advisors handle larger clients.

Smaller firms generally deal with and relate to small business entrepreneurs. Selecting an advisor in a small or medium size firm of three to ten people provides you with a resource base if you need it. An advisor who is a sole practitioner may be very busy, too generalized in his or her areas of practice, and lack a referral resource base within the firm.

b. LAWYER

There are basically two types of lawyers that you should consider as your advisors. The same lawyer might be able to assume both roles.

You need a lawyer who specializes in small business. A lawyer who cares about small business clients assumes the same role and attitude toward your business health and survival as your physician to your personal health.

The other type of lawyer you need is one who specializes in contract law. You will need to have several "boiler plate" contracts prepared depending upon the type and style of service that you are providing. You can then modify these contracts on an individual client basis. There are times that you will need to have a specialized contract made up by a lawyer or have the lawyer review and advise you on a contract that has been prepared by the client.

If your business lawyer does not have the expertise in contract law, request that you be referred to someone within the firm or outside who does. For continuity and efficiency, you want to maintain your business lawyer for all matters that don't require additional expertise. You should be able to phone your lawyer as your needs arise, and feel confident that the unique aspects of your business are known and understood.

For your protection, you should retain a lawyer before you start up your business, as there are many legal pitfalls that can be encountered. There is a temptation to save money on legal fees in the beginning stages of the business when cash flow is minimal. Some people do their own incorporation to save on initial start-up expenses, but then continue the saving by never obtaining legal or accounting advice, an unfortunate example of false economy and bad judgment.

c. ACCOUNTANT

An accountant is the other essential business advisor on your management team. It is very important that you obtain a qualified accountant with the designations described earlier. A bookkeeper is not an accountant and, in most jurisdictions in Canada and the United States, there is no restriction from anyone using the name "accountant" and purporting to provide accounting services without any qualifications or training.

There are many essential services that an accountant can provide. Some of them are discussed below.

An accountant can advise on all start-up steps of a new business, including the tax and accounting considerations of various types of business organization. Normally an accountant will communicate with or coordinate work with your lawyer. The accountant considers such important matters as when your fiscal year-end should be and whether you should use cash or accrual method in keeping your books.

An accountant can advise on preparing a business plan for a loan application. This includes recommending the type of loan you should consider and how it is to be paid. Documents such as a profit and loss statement, a balance sheet, and a financial statement can be prepared by the accountant. He or she may refer you to a banker, which can have a positive effect on your loan application if the banker knows and respects the accountant.

An accountant can advise on all aspects of tax planning and tax-related business decisions which occur from time-to-time as well as file your tax returns.

An accountant can advise how to set up your office bookkeeping system. The accountant can have the bookkeeping done by someone in his or her firm, at a negotiated fee or you can hire an independent bookkeeper. Your accountant should be able to recommend some bookkeepers.

An accountant can analyze and interpret your financial information, point out areas that need control, and recommend ways of implementing the necessary change.

An accountant may be aware of various government grant programs that could be of interest to you.

An accountant can coordinate your personal and business affairs and advise you on investments, tax shelters, income splitting, and other matters.

An accountant can advise and assist you if you want to change your proprietorship or partnership into a limited company at some point. If the transfer is done correctly, you can minimize any negative tax consequences.

d. BANKER

Your relationship with your bank and banker is your financial lifeline. The process of selecting a bank and banker is a critical one, and substantial comparative shopping is necessary in order to obtain the optimal combination of personality and knowledge.

The qualifications of the banker should be considered along with the specific experience with your type of business, specific reputation for taking risk, and the demands that are made for security and for reporting results.

Find out the amount of the banker's loan approval limit. If your needs are less than the limit, the loan can be approved by that individual without further review by another loans officer. This means you only have to convince one person to approve your loan request, not additional anonymous people behind the scene. How well your relationship develops with the banker and how successfully your loans are approved will depend largely on the factors outlined in chapter 7 on how to obtain financing.

There are specific danger areas that can affect your banker's relationship with you. When the manager changes, there is always a period of risk and uncertainty. The new manager does not want to have any medium or high risk loans on the books to taint his or her record. During the first three or four months after a new manager takes over outstanding loans are reviewed and categorized within the criteria set by the new manager. This is the time when loans can be called or additional security requested or interest rates increased. You should develop a personal relationship with the manager when you take out a loan. If you hear that a new manager has taken over, make a point of quickly introducing yourself and briefly discussing your business in a positive way.

Bank policies change from time to time and your type of business could be looked upon as increasing in risk. For example, if real estate is in a slump in your region, a policy decision could be made by the bank to be very cautious about existing or pending loans related to real estate. If you are a real estate consultant, that decision could affect your loan. If you think the bank is concerned, prepare a realistic assessment of how you intend to deal with the situation in advance. You may have a diversified consultancy, not just related to real estate, or you may have other options available that you could explain to your banker.

Ask your accountant and lawyer which bank and banker they recommend. This is probably one of the most effective introductions. If the banker has an ongoing relationship with a professional who is advising you as a client, a less impersonal relationship will exist, and there is a better chance that decisions affecting your loans and your business will be made more carefully.

e. INSURANCE

It is important to select a professional insurance broker with experience and knowledge in the areas of insurance you require. An insurance broker can have various professional qualifications, and you may wish to find out what those credentials are. Insurance is covered in detail in chapter 10.

f. CONSULTANTS

1. Private consultants

You may wish to approach a practicing consultant for advice to assist you in your business. As previously discussed, consultants are not restrictively licensed like other professionals. To protect yourself, you should inquire about their expertise, qualifications, and length of experience. Obtain references and contact them.

Apply the general criteria for advisor selection. You will want to satisfy yourself that the consultant is personally successful. If the consultant has not been successful, how can he or she possibly offer advice that will help you? Consultant fees may range between $25 to $150 per hour or more, depending upon many variables.

2. Consultants subsidized by government

Both the Canadian and U.S. governments have consulting services available for small business.

(a) CASE (Counselling Assistance to Small Enterprises)

In Canada, the federal government, through the Federal Business Development Bank (FBDB), sponsors consultants in CASE. The counsellors are retired business experts who wish to remain active. They are able to identify areas of opportunity, solve problems, and help people manage more effectively. Businesses starting up, expanding, closing or just not making the kind of profit expected can benefit from the help of an experienced business person.

The requirements of the clients are matched with the background and expertise of available counsellors. The CASE coordinator selects the appropriate counsellor, reviews reports outlining recommendations submitted by the counsellor, and follows up on assignments. The hourly fee for the counsellor's time is nominal and includes meeting with the client, doing necessary research, and outlining recommendations in a written report to the client. The minimum charge of four hours is payable when the agreement is signed. Travel expenses of the counsellor are absorbed by the FBDB. Further information can be obtained from a local FBDB office.

The FBDB also sponsors small business management seminars and workshops. Contact your local branch to obtain further information and to place your name on their mailing list.

(b) SCORE (Service Corps of Retired Executives)

The American program is similar to the Canadian program, and is sponsored by the U.S. Small Business Administration (SBA). SCORE is composed of retired executives and active executives who share their knowledge, experience, and business counselling free of charge. Further information can be obtained from a local SBA office.

The SBA also sponsors small business management seminars and workshops. Contact your local branch to obtain further information and to place your name on their mailing list.

6

PREPARING YOUR BUSINESS PLAN

a. WHY PREPARE A PLAN?

Most consultants prefer to be a consultant first and a business owner second. But planning and good management skills are vital to business success. Those who do not plan run a very high risk of failure. If you do not know where you are going in your personal or business life, there is little prospect that you will arrive. A business plan is a written summary of what you hope to accomplish by being in business, and how you intend to organize your resources to meet your goals. It is an essential guide for operating your business successfully and measuring progress along the way.

Planning forces you to think ahead and visualize; it encourages realistic thinking instead of over-optimism. It helps you identify your customers, your market area, your pricing strategy, and the competitive conditions under which you must operate. This process often leads to the discovery of new opportunities as well as deficiencies in your plan.

Having clear goals and a well-written plan aids in decision-making. You can always change your goals, but at least with a business plan you have some basis and a standard comparison to use in evaluating alternatives presented to you.

A business plan establishes the amount of financing or outside investment required and when it is needed. It makes it much easier for a lender or investor to assess your financing proposal and to assess you as a business manager. It inspires confidence in lenders and self-confidence in yourself to know every aspect of the business when you are negotiating your financing. If you have a realistic, comprehensive and well documented plan, it will assist you greatly in convincing a lender.

Having well established objectives helps you analyze your progress. If you have not attained your objectives by a certain period, you will be aware of that fact and can make appropriate adjustments at an early stage.

Three or four hours spent each month updating your plan will save considerable time and money in the long run, and may even save your business. It is essential to develop a habit of planning and reassessing on an ongoing basis as an integral part of your management style.

b. FORMAT

The business plan format shown in Sample #4 is a starting point for organizing your own plan. The comments following the sub-headings should help you decide which sections are relevant to your business situations.

46

The business plan format normally consists of four parts: the introduction, the business concept, the financial plan, and the appendix.

The plan starts with an introductory page highlighting the business plan. Even though your entire business is described later, a crisp one- or two-page introduction helps capture the immediate attention of the potential investor or lender.

The business concept, which begins with a description of the industry, identifies your market potential within your industry and outlines your action plan for the coming year. Make sure your stated business goals are compatible with your personal goals and financial goals, your management ability, and family considerations. The heart of the business concept is your monthly sales forecast for the coming year. As your statement of confidence in your marketing strategy, it forms the basis for your cash flow forecast and projected income statement. This section also contains an assessment of business risks and a contingency plan. Being honest about your business risks and how you plan to deal with them is evidence of sound management.

The financial plan outlines the level of present financing and identifies the financing sought. This section should be brief. The financial plan contains pro-forma (projected) financial forecasts. These forecasts are a projection into the future based on current information and assumptions. In carrying out your action plan for the coming year, these operating forecasts are an essential guide to business survival and profitability. It is important to refer to them often and, if circumstances dictate, rework them.

The appendix section contains all the items that do not naturally fall elsewhere in the document, or which expand further on the summaries in the document.

SAMPLE #4
BUSINESS PLAN FORMAT

1. Introductory page
   (a) company name
      — include address and telephone number
   (b) contact person
      — consultant's name and telephone number
   (c) paragraph about company
      — nature of business and market area
   (d) securities offered to investors or lenders
      — outline securities such as preferred shares, common shares, debentures, etc.
   (e) business loans sought
      — such as term loan, operating line of credit, mortgage
   (f) summary of proposed use of funds

2. Summary
   (a) highlights of business plan
       — preferably one-page maximum
       — include your project, competitive advantage and "bottom line" needs

3. Table of contents
   (a) section titles and page numbers should be given for easy reference

4. Description of the industry
   (a) industry outlook and growth potential
       — outline industry trends — past, present and future — and new developments
       — state your sources of information
   (b) markets and customers
       — estimated size of total market, share and sales, new requirements and market trends
   (c) competitive companies
       — market share, strengths and weaknesses, profitability, trends
   (d) national and economic trends
       — population shifts, consumer trends, relevant economic indicators

5. Description of business venture
   (a) nature of consulting service
       — characteristics, method of operation, whether performed locally, regionally, nationally or internationally
   (b) target market
       — typical clients identified by groups, present consulting patterns and average earnings, wants and needs
   (c) competitive advantage of your business concept
       — your market niche, uniqueness, estimated market share
   (d) business location and size
       — location relative to market, size of premises, home or office use
   (e) staff and equipment needed
       — overall requirement, capacity, home of office use, part- or full-time staff or as required
   (f) brief history
       — principals involved in the consulting business or proposed consulting business, development work done, resumes and background experience of principals, resumes of key consulting associates if applicable

6. Business goals
   (a) one year
       — specific goals, such as gross sales, profit margin, share of market, opening new office, introducing new service, etc.
   (b) over the longer term
       — return on investment, business net worth, sale of business

7. Marketing plan
   (a) sales strategy
       — commission sales staff, agents, sub-consultants
       — sales objectives, sales tools, sales support
       — target clients
   (b) sales approach
       — style of operation and techniques
   (c) pricing
       — costing, mark-ups, margins, breakeven

(d) promotion
— media advertising, promotions, publicity appropriate to reach target market
— techniques of developing exposure, credibility and contacts
(e) service policies
— policies that your consulting practice will adopt with regard to credit and collection, bidding, nature of clientele, etc.
(f) guarantees
— service performance guarantees or other assurances will vary depending upon nature of consulting practice and type of contract or client
(g) tracking methods
— method for confirming who your clients are and how they heard about you

8. Sales forecast
(a) assumptions
— one never has all the necessary information, so state all the assumptions made in developing the forecast
(b) monthly forecast for coming year
— sales volume, projected in dollars
(c) annual forecast for following two to four years
— sales volume, projected in dollars
The sales forecast is the starting point for your projected income statement and cash flow forecast.

9. Costing plan
(a) cost of facilities, equipment and materials (as applicable)
— estimates and quotations
(b) capital estimates
— one time start-up or expansion capital required

10. Operations
(a) purchasing plans
— volume discounts, multiple sources, quality, price
(b) inventory system
— seasonal variation, turnover rate, method of control
(c) space required
— floor and office space, improvements required, expansion capability
(d) staff and equipment required
— personnel by skill level
— fixtures, office equipment
(e) operations strategy

11. Corporate structure
(a) legal form
— proprietorship, partnership or incorporation
(b) share distribution
— list of principal shareholders
(c) contracts and agreements
— list of contracts and agreements in force
— management contract, shareholder or partnership agreement, service contract, leases
(d) directors and officers
— names and addresses, role in company
(e) background of key management personnel
— brief resumes of active owners and key employees

(f) organizational chart
    — identify reporting relationships
(g) duties and responsibilities of key personnel
    — brief job descriptions — who is responsible for what

12. Supporting professional assistance
   (a) professionals on contract in specialized or deficient areas; would include lawyer, accountant, banker, insurance agent, etc.

13. Research and development program
   (a) product or service improvements, process improvements, costs and risks

14. Risk assessment
   (a) competitors' reaction
      — will competitor try to squeeze you out? what form do you anticipate any reaction will take?
   (b) list of critical external factors that might occur
      — identify effects of strikes, recession, new technology, weather, new competition, supplier problems, shifts in consumer demand, costs of delays and over-runs, unfavorable industry trends
   (c) list of critical internal factors that might occur
      — income projections not realized, client dispute or litigation, receivables difficulties, demand for services increases very quickly, key employee or consultant quits
   (d) dealing with risks
      — contingency plan to handle the most significant risks

15. Overall schedule
   (a) interrelationship and timing of all major events important to starting and developing your business

16. Action plan
   (a) steps to accomplish this year's goals
      — flow chart by month or by quarter of specific action to be taken and by whom
   (b) checkpoint for measuring results
      — identify significant dates, sales levels as decision points

17. Financial forecast
If a business has been in operation for a period of time, the previous years' balance sheets and income statements are required, preferably for the past two or three years.
   (a) opening balance sheet
      — The balance sheet is a position statement, not an historical record; it shows what is owned and owed at a given date. There are three sections to a balance sheet: assets, liabilities, and owner's equity. You determine your firm's net worth by subtracting the liabilities from the assets.
      — Your balance sheet will indicate how your investment has grown over a period of time. Investors and lenders typically examine balance sheets to determine if the company is within acceptable assets to liability limits.
      — see Sample #5
   (b) income and expense forecast statement (profit and loss)
      — The income and expense forecast can be described as the operating statement you would expect to see for your business at the end of the period for which the forecast is being prepared.
      — For a new business, the forecast would show what revenue and expenses you expect the business to have in its first year of operation.

— It is very useful, of course, to prepare a forecast for a period longer than one year. It is suggested that a detailed operating forecast be prepared for the next year of operation and a less detailed forecast for the following two years.

— Preparing an income and expense forecast for a new business is more difficult than preparing one for an existing business, simply because in a new business there is no historical record to go by. For this reason the preparation of this forecast is an even more essential, interesting and rewarding experience than doing it for an existing business, despite the time and effort required. The question will be answered by this analysis exercise, as to whether a profit will be made.

— The income statement (sales) is the most difficult because it is the most uncertain at the commencement of business. It is essential that a figure be projected on a conservative estimate.

— The main concern is to account for expenses accurately and in as much detail as possible. This will then provide a target or breakeven figure toward which to work.

— Some headings may not be appropriate for your type of consulting practice; other headings should be added.

— see Sample #6

(c) cash flow forecast

— A cash flow budget measures the flow of money in and out of the business. It is critical to you and your banker.

— Many businesses operate on a seasonal basis, as there are slow months and busy months. The cash flow budget projection will provide an indication of the times of a cash flow shortage to assist in properly planning and financing your operation. It will tell you in advance if you have enough cash to get by.

— A cash flow budget should be prepared a year in advance and contain monthly breakdowns.

— see Sample #7

(d) cash flow assumptions

When reviewing the cash flow plan, certain assumptions should be made:

— Sales: monthly sales (consulting service fees) that are expected to materialize

— Receipts: cash sales represent cash actually received; receivables collected represents the collection of amounts due for goods sold on credit; rental income is rent that will be collected in advance at the beginning of each month

— Disbursements: accounts payable to be paid in month following month of purchase

— Accounting and legal: to be paid upon receipt of bill, expected to be in the spring or after your fiscal year end financial statements have been completed

— Advertising: anticipated to be the same amount each month and paid for in the month the expense is incurred

— Automobile: anticipated to be the same amount each month and paid for in the month the expense is incurred

— Bank charges and interest: anticipated to be the same amount each month and monthly paid for in same month the expenses is incurred

— Equipment rental: to be paid for in monthly payments

— Income taxes: amount for taxes of the prior year and to be paid in the spring

— Insurance: annual premium to be paid quarterly, semi-annually or annually in installments of equal amounts

— Loan repayment: amount is the same each month and paid in accordance with the monthly schedule furnished by the lending institution

— Office supplies and expenses: to be paid in month following receipt of invoice and supplies to be purchased on a quarterly basis

— Taxes and licenses: to be paid for upon receipt of invoice, expected to be in January and July

— Telephone: to be paid for in month following the month the expense is incurred. Amount expected to be the same each month except in the last quarter when rates are expected to increase

— Utilities: expected to fluctuate with weather conditions and to be paid for in the month following the month the expense is incurred

— Wages and benefits: wages to increase at the beginning of the year. Amount considered to be the same each month and paid for in the month the expense is incurred

— Miscellaneous: expected to be the same each month and paid for in the same month the expense is incurred

— Bad debts: varies

(e) Breakeven analysis

— Your breakeven analysis is a critical calculation for every consulting business. Rather than calculating how much your firm would make if it attained an estimated sales volume, a more meaningful analysis determines at what sales volume your firm will break even. An estimated sales volume could be very unreliable as there are many factors which could affect revenue.

— The calculation of a breakeven point for every small business is one of the crucial pieces of information. Above the breakeven sales volume it is only a matter of how much money your business can generate; below the breakeven level of sales, it is only a matter of how many days a business can operate before bankruptcy.

— A breakeven analysis provides a very real and meaningful figure to work toward and might be required to be updated every few months to reflect your business growth.

— The breakeven point is where total costs are equal to total revenues.

— The calculation of total costs is determined by adding variable costs onto the fixed costs.

— Total costs are all costs of operating the business over a specified time period.

— Variable costs are those that vary directly with the number of consulting services provided or marketing and promotion activities undertaken. These typically include automobile expenses, business travel expenses, supplies, brochures, etc. Variable costs are not direct costs which are passed on to the client in the billing.

— Fixed costs are costs that do not generally vary with the number of clients serviced. Also known as indirect costs, these costs typically include salaries, rent, secretarial service, insurance, telephone, accounting and legal supplies.

18. Financing and capitalization
   (a) term loan applied for
      — the amount, terms and when required
   (b) purpose of term loan
      — attach a detailed description of the aspects of the business to be financed
   (c) owner's equity
      — the amount of your financial commitment to the business
   (d) summary of term loan requirements
      — for a particular consulting project or for the business as a whole

19. Operating loan
   (a) line of credit applied for
      — a new line of credit or an increase, and security offered
   (b) maximum operating cash required
      — amount required, timing of need (refer to "cash flow forecast")

20. Present financing (if applicable)
    (a) term loans outstanding
        — the balance owing, repayment terms, purpose, security and status
    (b) current operating line of credit
        — the amount and security held

21. References
    (a) name of present lending institution
        — branch and type of accounts
    (b) lawyer's name
        — lawyer's address and telephone number
    (c) accountant
        — accountant's name and address and telephone number

22. Appendix
    The nature of the contents of the appendices attached, if any, depends on the circumstances and requirements of the lender or investor, or the desire to enhance the loan proposal. It is recommended that the appendices be prepared for your own benefit and reference to assist your business analysis, and to be available if the information is required. The following list is a guide only. Some of the headings described may be unavailable or unnecessary.
    (a) personal net worth statement
        — includes personal property values, investments, cash, bank loans, charge accounts, mortgages and other liabilities. This will substantiate the value of your personal guarantee if required for security.
        — see Sample #8
    (b) letter of intent
        — potential orders for client commitments
    (c) description of personal and business insurance coverage
        — include insurance policies and amount of coverage
    (d) accounts receivable summary
        — include aging schedule of 30, 60 and 90 day periods
        — see Sample #9
    (e) accounts payable summary
        — include schedule of payments and total amounts owing
    (f) legal agreement
        — include a copy of contracts, leases and other documents
    (g) appraisals
        — fair market value of business property and equipment
    (h) financial statements for associated companies
        — where appropriate, a lender may require this information
    (i) copies of your brochure
    (j) testimonial letters from clients
    (k) references
    (l) sales forecast and market surveys
    (m) list of investors
    (n) credit status information
    (o) news articles about you and your business

SAMPLE #5
OPENING BALANCE SHEET (NEW BUSINESS)

DATE: _____

NAME OF COMPANY: _____

ASSETS

Current assets
Cash and bank accounts $ _____
Accounts receivable $ _____
Inventory $ _____
Prepaid rent $ _____
Other current assets $ _____

TOTAL CURRENT ASSETS   (A) $ _____

Fixed assets
Land and buildings $ _____
Furniture, fixtures and equipment $ _____
Automobiles $ _____
Leasehold improvements $ _____
Other assets $ _____

TOTAL FIXED AND OTHER ASSETS   (B) $ _____

TOTAL ASSETS (A + B = C)   (C) $ _____

LIABILITIES

Current liabilities (debt due within next 12 months)
Bank loans $ _____
Loans — other $ _____
Accounts payable $ _____
Current portion of long-term debt $ _____
Other current liabilities $ _____

TOTAL CURRENT LIABILITIES   (D) $ _____

Long-term debt
Mortgages and liens payable (attach details) $ _____
Less: current portion $ _____
Loans from partners or stockholders (owner's equity) $ _____
Other loans of long-term nature $ _____

TOTAL LONG-TERM DEBT   (E) $ _____

TOTAL LIABILITIES (D + E = F)   (F) $ _____

NET WORTH (C - F = G)   (G) $ _____

TOTAL NET WORTH AND LIABILITIES (F + G = H)   (H) $ _____

SAMPLE #6
INCOME AND EXPENSE STATEMENT FORECAST
(NEW BUSINESS)

(Name of business)

For the period: _____ months ending _____ , 19 _____

PROJECTED INCOME

SALES _____ $ _____

_____ $ _____

TOTAL SALES $ _____

OTHER INCOME $ _____

TOTAL INCOME   (A) $ _____

PROJECTED EXPENSES

Sales expenses
    Commissions and salaries $ _____
    Travel $ _____
    Advertising $ _____
    Automotive $ _____
    Other $ _____

TOTAL SELLING EXPENSES   (B) $ _____

ADMINISTRATIVE AND FINANCIAL EXPENSES
    Management salaries (or proprietor/partner draws) $ _____
    Office salaries $ _____
    Professional fees $ _____
    Office expense and supplies $ _____
    Telephone $ _____
    Rent $ _____
    Interest and bank charges $ _____
    Inventory $ _____
    Bad debt $ _____
    Other $ _____

TOTAL ADMINISTRATIVE AND FINANCIAL EXPENSES   (C) $ _____

TOTAL EXPENSES (B + C = D)   (D) $ _____

OPERATING PROFIT (LOSS) (A - D) $ _____

    Add: Other income
    Less: Provisions for income taxes $ _____

NET PROFIT (LOSS) $ _____

SAMPLE #7
CASH FLOW BUDGET WORKSHEET

	January Est.	Actual	February Est.	Actual	March Est.	Actual
Cash at beginning of month:	$_____	$_____	$_____	$_____	$_____	$_____
In bank and on hand	_____	_____	_____	_____	_____	_____
In investments	_____	_____	_____	_____	_____	_____
TOTAL CASH	$_____	$_____	$_____	$_____	$_____	$_____
Plus income during month:	_____	_____	_____	_____	_____	_____
Cash sales (include credit cards)	_____	_____	_____	_____	_____	_____
Credit sales payments	_____	_____	_____	_____	_____	_____
Investment income	_____	_____	_____	_____	_____	_____
Receivables collected	_____	_____	_____	_____	_____	_____
Loans	_____	_____	_____	_____	_____	_____
Personal investment	_____	_____	_____	_____	_____	_____
Other cash income	_____	_____	_____	_____	_____	_____
TOTAL CASH AND INCOME	$_____	$_____	$_____	$_____	$_____	$_____
Expenses during the month:	_____	_____	_____	_____	_____	_____
Rent (if applicable)	_____	_____	_____	_____	_____	_____
Utilities	_____	_____	_____	_____	_____	_____
Phone	_____	_____	_____	_____	_____	_____
Postage	_____	_____	_____	_____	_____	_____
Office equipment and furniture	_____	_____	_____	_____	_____	_____
Stationery and business cards	_____	_____	_____	_____	_____	_____
Insurance (health, fire, liability, theft, fire, etc.)	_____	_____	_____	_____	_____	_____
Answering service	_____	_____	_____	_____	_____	_____
Printing and supplies	_____	_____	_____	_____	_____	_____
Typing/secretarial service	_____	_____	_____	_____	_____	_____
Accounting and legal services	_____	_____	_____	_____	_____	_____
Advertising and promotion	_____	_____	_____	_____	_____	_____
Business licenses and permits	_____	_____	_____	_____	_____	_____
Dues and subscriptions	_____	_____	_____	_____	_____	_____
Books and reference materials	_____	_____	_____	_____	_____	_____
Travel: in town	_____	_____	_____	_____	_____	_____
Travel: out of town	_____	_____	_____	_____	_____	_____

SAMPLE #7 — Continued

	January		February		March	
	Est.	**Actual**	**Est.**	**Actual**	**Est.**	**Actual**
Conventions, professional meetings, trade shows	$_____	$_____	$_____	$_____	$_____	$_____
Continuing education	_____	_____	_____	_____	_____	_____
Entertainment	_____	_____	_____	_____	_____	_____
Contributions	_____	_____	_____	_____	_____	_____
Gifts	_____	_____	_____	_____	_____	_____
Salaries	_____	_____	_____	_____	_____	_____
Unemployment insurance	_____	_____	_____	_____	_____	_____
Pensions	_____	_____	_____	_____	_____	_____
Miscellaneous	_____	_____	_____	_____	_____	_____
Loan repayment	_____	_____	_____	_____	_____	_____
Other cash expenses	_____	_____	_____	_____	_____	_____
TOTAL EXPENSES	$_____	$_____	$_____	$_____	$_____	$_____
Cash flow excess or (deficit) at end of month	$_____	$_____	$_____	$_____	$_____	$_____
Cash flow cumulative (monthly)	$_____	$_____	$_____	$_____	$_____	$_____

SAMPLE #8
PERSONAL NET WORTH STATEMENT

Date: _____

Name: _____

Address: _____

GENERAL INFORMATION

Phone: Home _____ Business _____ Age _____ M or S _____

Dependents including spouse _____

Present employer _____ Position occupied _____ How long with this employer _____

Previous employer _____ How long _____

Landlord _____ Address _____ Monthly rental $ _____

SAMPLE #8 — Continued

Salary, wages or
commission per annum $ _____ Other income
per annum $ _____ Source _____

Guarantees on debts
of others: Name _____ Amount _____

_____

ASSETS

Bank accounts _____

Stocks at cost (market value _____) _____

Bonds at cost (market value _____) _____

Life insurance (cash surrender value)

    Beneficiary _____

Automobile — year _____

          — make _____ _____

Home — registered _____

      — building size _____ Lot size _____ _____

Other assets   _____

                           TOTAL ==================

LIABILITIES

Bank loan _____

Charge accounts _____

Policy loans on life insurance _____

Other loans _____

Installment purchases _____

Mortgages: Int. rate _____

   Term _____ Payments _____ _____

   Taxes _____ _____

Other liabilities   _____

                    SUB TOTAL _____

NET WORTH   _____

                    TOTAL _____

                               ==================

(Name of company)

SAMPLE #9
STATEMENT OF ACCOUNTS RECEIVABLE

AS AT _____ 19 ____

Date: _____

_____

(Name of company)

Names of debtors	Total (Omit Cents)	Current	31 - 60 Days	61 - 90 Days	Over 90 Days & Holdbacks	Remarks

1. Sub totals .... $_____

2. Aggregate of accts. under $ _____ $_____

3. Number of accts. _____ No. _____ No. _____ No. _____ No. _____ No. _____

4. TOTALS .... $_____

Percentage .... 100% _____ % _____ % _____ % _____ %

c. ESTIMATING YOUR START-UP FUNDS

1. Assessment of personal monthly financial needs

Personal expenses will continue in spite of the business, and therefore have to be taken into account when determining monthly cash flow needs. It is important to calculate personal expenses accurately so that appropriate decisions can be made in terms of funding and the nature of the start-up practice — whether it should start out on a part-time or full-time basis, using the home as an office or renting an outside office. See Sample #3.

2. Estimated business start-up cash needs

An estimate of the start-up cash required can be calculated by referring to Table #2. Naturally, each consultant's situation can vary considerably and therefore the worksheet is a guide only.

During your first few months you will probably not have enough sales revenue to finance your short-term costs. This usually occurs for one of three reasons: your sales are below projection, your costs rise unexpectedly, or you have not yet been paid for consulting work already performed (overdue accounts receivable). Many professionals experience accounts receivable problems during the early months of operation because clients tend to pay professionals after they have paid other outstanding bills. Your conservative cash flow analysis prepares you for this situation, and enables you to plan your cash needs.

d. SUMMARY

Before presenting your business plan to a lender or investor, have two or three impartial outsiders review the finished plan in detail. There may be something you overlooked or under-emphasized. After your plan has been reviewed by others, take your plan and financial statements to your accountant for review. You should also discuss with your accountant all the personal and business tax considerations that might be involved. You may wish to have your accountant come with you to the bank when you discuss your loan proposal. This is not uncommon and can create a very positive impression.

Discuss with your lawyer the security you are proposing. Your lawyer should explain fully before the plan is submitted the effect of your pledging collateral security and what the lender could do if you default. You should also seriously evaluate whether the security pledged is too excessive for the loan or risk involved and whether the risk is too great to pledge your personal assets.

Your familiarity with your business plan will increase your credibility and at the same time provide you with a good understanding of what the financial statements reveal about the viability of your business.

7

HOW TO OBTAIN FINANCING

Having completed your business plan and financial projections, you should now have a clear idea of your short-term and medium-term financial needs. You will want to be familiar with the types of financing available, the various sources, how to approach financial lending institutions, and the type of security that may be required. You should also be aware of the reasons that lending institutions or investors may turn down a request for funding. These matters and other issues are covered in this chapter.

a. TYPES OF FINANCING

There are two basic types of financing: equity and debt.

1. Equity

The money that *you* put into a company or business is equity. Initially all money must come from your own resources such as savings or personal borrowing from financial institutions, friends, relatives, or business associates. As time progresses, retained earnings in the business will increase your equity.

If you have formed a corporation, you can "buy" one or more shares and lend the rest of the money to the corporation as a "shareholder's loan." The advantages of a shareholder's loan are:

(a) Lenders consider these loans as equity as long as the money is left in the company.

(b) It is easier to repay the loan than sell shares back to the company or to other investors.

(c) Interest may be paid. For example, if you or your friends would like to earn a return on your investment, an interest rate may be established. The alternative is to pay dividends on shares when funds are available.

(d) Interest is tax deductible to the company.

2. Debt

A debt is a loan. It must be repaid, and the lender will charge interest on the money you have borrowed. With borrowed money, normally the principal and interest is paid back on a fixed monthly payment. You therefore have to include the principal and interest payments in a current business plan. Various forms of debt financing are discussed below.

(a) Short-term or operating loan (demand loan)

Short-term or operating loans are used for financing inventory, accounts receivable, special purchases or promotions, and other items requiring working capital during peak periods.

The main sources of short-term loans are commercial banks or similar financial institutions. Using a short-term loan is a good way to establish credit with a bank. This type of loan can be unsecured or secured by your personal or business assets.

Short-term loans are usually negotiated for specific periods of time; for example, 30, 60 or 90 days and frequently for periods up to a year or more. They may be repayable in a lump sum at the end of the period or in periodic installments, such as monthly.

Other characteristics of a demand loan include:

- Interest rate at time of signing may be lower than a term loan

- Fluctuating interest rate

- Repayment of the loan can be demanded at any time by the lender; usually only occurs when the account does not perform satisfactorily or in case of serious deterioration in the affairs of the business

- Can often be obtained more quickly than a term loan

(b) Line of credit

A line of credit is an agreement between you and the lender (a bank or similar financial institution) specifying the maximum amount of credit (overdraft) the bank will allow you at any one time for general operating purposes.

Credit lines are usually established for one year-periods, subject to annual renegotiation and renewal. Other characteristics of a line of credit include:

- Loan funds increase and decrease as you need the money or "revolves"

- Available from most banks

- Fluctuating interest rate

- Interest rate at time of signing may be lower than a term loan

- The lender uses accounts receivable, the money owed to you by customers, and inventory as the security. For accounts receivable, the lender may lend between 50% and 75% of the value, not including amounts over 90 days. For inventory, a lender may lend up to 50%

- Can often be obtained more quickly than a term loan

- Repayament of the loan can be demanded at any time by the lender or the line of credit can be reduced; usually this only occurs when the account does not perform satisfactorily or in a case of serious deterioration in the affairs of the business, or reduction in the value of the security provided

- The amount of credit granted is based on the lender's assessment of the creditworthiness of the company, its principals and the credit requested, among other factors.

(c) Term loans

A term loan is generally money borrowed for a term of one year up to fifteen years. A term loan is usually amortized. In other words, the regular loan payments include principal and interest and are for a fixed aggregate amount over the life or term of the loan agreement.

Term loans are commonly used to provide funds for the purchase of an existing business, to help finance expansions or capital expenditures, and to provide additional working capital for a growing business.

While the majority of term loans are secured by collateral such as fixed assets, or other chattels (cars, building, land, equipment, etc.), the lender places great importance upon the ability of the borrower to repay his or her indebtedness out of the business' earnings over the life of the loan.

The main characteristics of a term loan are:

- It may be repaid over a period of time generally related to the useful "life" of the assets; for example, car — 3 to 5 years; land and building —after 3 years.

- The lender will only give you a percentage of the value; for example, car — 80%; building — 75%. The other 20% or 25% of the cost of the asset must come from the equity you have in the company or new funds from shareholders or yourself.

- The company must be able to show the lender that future sales will generate enough cash to repay the loan.

- There are different lenders for different types of term loans. One consideration in the approval of your proposal is "leverage" or "debt to equity ratio." This is the ratio of the money you owe to the money you put in the business. Generally, the lender's assessment of this ratio is discretionary; but if you are a new business, or just building up a reputation, it is unlikely that the lender will want to go beyond 2:1 or even 1:1. Consequently, this may place an additional restriction on the amount that you can borrow.

- Interest rate at time of signing is slightly higher than a demand loan.

- Your payments, principal plus interest, are all the same.

- Repayment period of loan is specified and agreed upon in advance.

- It could take a longer time to obtain a loan approval than a demand loan.

(d) Trade credit or supplier financing

This is the most often used form of short-term financing. This means that a supplier will not insist on immediate payment for purchase of merchandise.

Terms can be arranged between both parties as to when payment will be made —generally 30 to 90 days.

(e) Renting or leasing

Renting or leasing assets is an alternative form of financing. Leasing companies will consider arranging a lease with option to purchase on virtually any tangible asset. Renting premises, as opposed to buying a building, is also a financing alternative. Assets such as typewriters, office furniture, personal computers or word processors, automobiles and telephone equipment, are examples. The advantages of leasing are:

- It frees up equity capital for investment in areas of greater return.

- It frees up borrowing power for the more critical areas of the business.

- There is no down payment requirement with leasing.

- Rates are usually fixed for a set term.

- The full payment is an allowable expense.

- Purchase options can be exercised at a later date at a pre-determined price.

There are also disadvantages. You should discuss the tax and financial considerations with your accountant before you make your decision.

b. SOURCES OF FINANCING

1. Equity

The most common source of equity capital is personal funds from savings. In exchange for the funds provided to the company, the owner obtains all the shares of the corporation or ownership of the business.

Equity can be further increased from the savings of friends willing to invest, or even from relatives. However, many small business people have created problems by bringing in friends or relatives as investors.

Conflicts generally occur if the business is not doing as well as everyone initially imagined, or if the terms and conditions of such loans are not clearly spelled out, or if the lenders or investors insist on becoming involved in day-to-day operations.

Any agreement should be documented in writing between the parties and signed in advance to eliminate any misunderstanding. Agreement should be reached on the rate of interest to be paid, when the loans will be repaid, any options you have to pay them back early, and the procedures that all parties will follow if the loans become delinquent. Consult competent legal counsel in advance to protect your interests.

An equity investment can be in the form of stockholder loans, or common stock or shares in the company or a combination of loans and shares. The investment structure will vary in each situation.

Generally speaking the advantage of money being invested as shareholder loans is that it can be paid back to lenders without tax, other than personal tax and interest you receive before the loan is paid off.

If the money is in the form of shares, it is much more difficult to withdraw since shares must be sold to someone else, and may be subject to capital gains tax.

Long-term debt investors may therefore place restrictions or conditions on when and how the company can pay off shareholder loans, redeem shares, or possibly even pay dividends on shares. These restrictions or conditions are imposed to protect the long-term debt invested.

The advice of a tax accountant is recommended since your personal tax situation and that of other potential equity investors could have a bearing on whether the shareholders' investment should be in the form of loans or purchase of shares.

2. Debt

Commercial banks are a major source of capital for new and continuing small ventures. Additional organizations that provide financing include insurance companies, pension companies, real estate investment, trust, commercial and mortgage banks, and even trust companies and credit unions.

(a) Small business administration (U.S.)

You may wish to consider the small business administration (SBA) in the U.S. The SBA was created by the federal government to assist entrepreneurs. Since 1953, the SBA has expanded to include many activities including finance and investment.

The SBA is organized in 10 regions and each region is subdivided, providing branch offices in many areas. SBA guidelines defining who qualifies for small business assistance vary, depending on the general classification of the enterprise. As the lender of final resort, the SBA tries not to compete with or replace the private banking system but to supplement it. There are three types of loans available from the SBA: guaranteed loans, immediate-participation loans and direct loans.

Since the SBA's loan regulations do change from time to time, you should verify current conditions by contacting your nearest branch of the SBA (listed in the telephone directory under U.S. Government) or write to: Small Business Administration, Washington, D C 20416.

(b) Federal Business Development Bank (Canada)

In Canada, the Federal Business Development Bank (FBDB) was established by the federal government especially to help those companies that could not obtain financing elsewhere. To obtain FBDB financing, the amount of your investment in the business must generally be sufficient to ensure that you are committed to it and that the business may reasonably be expected to be successful.

FBDB financing is available as loans, loan guarantees, equity financing, leasing, or any combination of these methods in whatever way best suits the particular needs of your business. If loans are involved, the interest rates are usually at slightly higher rates than chartered banks.

If you wish to obtain further information, contact your local branch of the FBDB or write to: Federal Business Development Bank, 901 Victoria Square, Montreal, Quebec H2Z 1R1.

c. COMPETITION BETWEEN LENDERS

There is considerable competition between banks and other financial institutions. Make comparisons between at least three different financial institutions to assess the most favorable loan package available.

All aspects of financial dealings are negotiable. Obtain the lending terms in writing before you sign. Have your outside advisors, such as your accountant or lawyer, review the terms. In addition, you may want to obtain the advice of your associates. Don't rush into a relationship with a financial institution without reasonably exploring all the other alternatives.

d. TIPS ON APPROACHING YOUR LENDER

When you approach a financial institution, you must sell the merits of your business proposal. As in all sales presentations, consider the needs and expectations of the other party — in this case, the loans officer. A loans officer will be interested in the following.

(a) Your familiarity with the business concept and the realities of the marketplace as reflected in your detailed business plan.

(b) Your ability to service the debt with sufficient surplus to cover contingencies, including carrying interest charges, and eventually repay the debt in full as demonstrated in your cash flow forecast and projected income statement.

(c) Your level of commitment as shown by your equity in the business or cash investment in the particular asset being purchased.

(d) Your secondary source of repayment, including security in the event of default, and other sources of income.

(e) Your track record and integrity as shown in your personal credit history, your business plan and business results or past business experience.

(f) Your approach. During the loan interview remember you're doing business the same as you do when you're with a client. Don't be subservient, overly familiar or too aggressive. Keep in mind that a lender is in business for the same reason you are — to make a profit. Keep the profit motive in mind during the interview. Don't try to appeal to a lender's social conscience. It won't work, since loans aren't granted for their social impact.

(g) Your judgment in supplying information. Be sensible with the number of documents you provide at the outset. You do not want to overwhelm the loans officer with too much material. For example, the introductory page, summary and financial plan sections provide a good basic loan submission if the amount requested is small. You should have all other documents prepared and available if requested.

(h) Your personal appearance. You should present yourself in a manner that projects self-confidence and success.

(i) Your mental alertness. What times during the day are you at your mental peak? This should be the time that you arrange for an interview with the loans officer.

(j) Your consideration in allowing sufficient lead time for approval. The lender needs a reasonable time to assess your proposal. Also, the loan may have to be referred to another level within the financial institution for review.

(k) Your credit rating. It's a good idea to review your credit rating periodically, as there may be errors to correct in your file. Note your positive and negative points, so you can discuss them when raised by the lender.

If your request for financing is approved, find out everything you need to know about the conditions, terms, payment methods, interest rates, security requirements, and any other fees to be paid. No commitment to accept the financing should be made until all this information is provided and understood and its impact on the proposed business analyzed. Ask your accountant and lawyer to assist you in the loan application in advance and review the bank's approval. Make certain you get the approval particulars in writing.

e. WHY LOANS ARE TURNED DOWN

If a request for financing is not approved, find out why. Use the lender's experience to your advantage. Lenders handle many requests for financing, and have experience in the financial aspects of many businesses, even if they do not have direct management experience.

If there is something specifically wrong with the financing proposal, see if it can be corrected and then re-apply. If not, use this knowledge when approaching other potential lenders or on future occasions when seeking funds.

Some of the causes of a loan rejection could be the following:

(a) The business idea was considered unsound or too risky. A lender's judgment is generally based on past performance of other businesses similar to the one you are proposing.

(b) Insufficient collateral. A lender must be satisfied that there are sufficient assets pledged to meet the outstanding debt if your business does not succeed financially. If you are just starting a business, a lender generally requires you to pledge personal assets, such as your home, car and other securities, against the loan. If you are borrowing funds under a corporate name, your personal guarantee will generally be requested and in some cases your spouse's guarantee as well, depending upon the circumstances. You may therefore not have sufficient security required for the amount of loan you are requesting or for the degree of risk, in the lender's opinion, that might be involved.

(c) Lack of financial commitment on your part. A lender will be reluctant to approve loan financing for business ventures if you are not fully committed. The lender does not want to foreclose or repossess and then have to sell assets to collect your money. The lender will therefore want to know how much personal financial capital you have made available to the business venture in order to assess your commitment to repay the loan. If you have not made any financial commitment and yet have security that you wish to pledge, the security alone may not be sufficient.

(d) Lack of a business plan or a poor business plan. A lender could reject your loan application if you have not prepared a detailed business plan or do not understand its significance.

(e) The purpose of the loan is not explained or is not acceptable. It is important that the specific use of the funds being borrowed be outlined in detail. It is also important that the purpose and amount of funds being requested be reasonable and appropriate. For example, it could be considered unreasonable for you to calculate a large draw or salary from your business in the first six months. If you intend to use the loan to pay off past debts or financial obligations, it may not be approved since the funds would not be directly generating cash flow for your new business venture.

(f) Your character, personality or stability can effect a lender's decision. It is important to appear confident, enthusiastic, well-informed, and realistic. If your personality is not consistent with the personality required for your type of business in the eyes of the lender, it could have a negative effect. If you are going through a separation or divorce proceedings or have declared personal bankruptcy or had business failures in the past, these factors could have an adverse impact on your loan application.

f. TYPES OF SECURITY A LENDER MAY REQUIRE

Lenders primarily lend money to businesses that exhibit a strong potential to repay the loan. Nevertheless, they want to be covered in case of a default. Sometimes your signature is the only security the lender needs when making a loan. The kind and amount of security depends on the lender and on the borrower's situation. The most common types of security or collateral are: endorser, co-maker, guarantor, promissory note, demand loan, realty mortgage, chattel mortgage, assignment of accounts receivable, postponement of claim, pledging of stocks and bonds, and assignment of life insurance.

1. Endorser

Borrowers often get other people to sign a note in order to bolster their own credit. These endorsers are contingently liable for the note they sign. If the borrower fails to pay off the loan, the lender expects the endorser to make the note good. Sometimes the endorser may be asked to pledge assets or securities as well.

2. Co-maker

A co-maker is a person who takes on an obligation jointly with the borrower. In such cases, the lender can collect directly from either the maker or the co-maker.

3. Guarantor

A guarantor is a person who guarantees the payment of a note by signing a guarantee commitment. Both private and government lenders commonly require a personal guarantee from officers of corporations as security for loans advanced to the corporation. If the corporation defaults in its financial obligations, the lender has a choice of suing the guarantor or the corporation or both for the monies outstanding. Try to negotiate a limited guarantee to cover the shortfall in the security, if other securities have been pledged. Be very careful not to sign a personal guarantee for the full amount of the loan if at all possible. Recover your guarantee as soon as the business has paid off its obligation or can carry the debt on its own security. Resist having your spouse sign a personal guarantee of your debts. Your personal guarantee is often all you have left to negotiate with on another occasion.

4. Promissory note

A promissory note is a written promise to pay a specified sum of money to the lender, either on demand or at a specified future time.

5. Demand loan

A demand loan involves a written promise to pay the amount of monies outstanding to the lender upon demand.

6. Realty mortgage

A lender may require a mortgage against your property for the advancement of funds. It could be a first, second or third mortgage against your property, or a collateral mortgage to a guarantee or demand note.

7. Chattel mortgage

A chattel mortgage is on specific property, such as a car or boat, other than land and buildings. The title of the chattel remains in the name of the borrower, but a lien against the chattel is placed in favor of the lender.

8. Assignment of accounts receivable

A borrower may have to assign the business receivables to the lender to secure an operating line of credit or other loan. The borrower still collects the receivables, but in a default, the lender will assume collection. The assignment is supported by submitting monthly a list of the business receivables.

9. Postponement of claim

If there are any loans from shareholders, the lender may ask for an agreement that the company will not repay the shareholders until the lender has been repaid in full.

10. Pledge of stocks or bonds

The possession of stocks and bonds may be transferred to the lender, but title remains with the borrower. The security must be marketable. As a protection against market declines and possible expenses of liquidation, banks usually lend no more than 75% of the market value of "blue chip stock." On federal government or municipal bonds, they may be willing to lend 90% or more of their market value.

The lender may ask the borrower for additional security or payment whenever the market value of the stocks or bonds drops below the lender's required margin.

11. Assignment of life insurance

A lender may request that the borrower assign the proceeds of a life insurance policy to the lender up to the amount outstanding at the time of death of the borrower. Another form of assignment is against the cash surrender value of a life insurance policy. Banks generally lend up to the cash value of a life insurance policy.

8

KEEPING RECORDS

A consultant must keep accurate and thorough financial records covering all income received and expenses incurred. Records help in producing income, controlling expenses, planning growth and cash flow, keeping tax payments to a legal minimum, and complying with the multitude of regulatory requirements. This chapter explains the basic concepts and procedures of keeping records and outlines some of the issues you will have to discuss with your accountant and bookkeeper.

a. ACCOUNTING AND BOOKKEEPING

Accounting is the process of analyzing and systematically recording, in terms of money or some other unit of measurement, operations or transactions of the business. To capture these facts and figures, a system is necessary. Such a system usually consists of bookkeeping records which may be set up in journals, ledgers or other records.

A professional accountant can help design a system for recording the information each consultant needs in his or her particular circumstance. Some tips on selecting an accountant are outlined in chapter 5.

Bookkeeping is the process of classifying and recording business transactions in the books of account. A bookkeeper keeps the various records, journals and ledgers current and accurate.

Many consultants are not inclined or do not know how to maintain the books. A part-time bookkeeper can be employed to keep the books either at your home or place of business, or at the bookkeeper's office. It is highly advisable that a professional accountant establish a system for your books. You can then hire a bookkeeper recommended by your accountant or a business associate you trust.

Make sure the bookkeeper is competent to handle your specific type of records, as some bookkeepers specialize in certain areas. The costs of a book-keeper are considerably lower than that of a professional accountant, and normally range between $10 to $20 per hour. Bookkeepers are not qualified to provide tax advice. Only an experienced tax accountant is able to provide you with the necessary tax planning information.

Different kinds of bookkeeping systems are discussed below.

1. Separate record-keeping

It is essential that your business books and records be kept separate from your personal books, records, and bank accounts. This is not only required by tax regulations, but is sound business management.

Separate records will allow you to control cash flow, budget for expenses, and draw up financial statements. A separate bank account for the business has the following advantages:

- Financial statements can be drawn and taxable income computed easily.

- When all income is deposited into the business account the income journal is maintained by the bank in the form of complete records of all receipts.

- Applications for financing for business purposes can be prepared more accurately with business records.

- All business expenses can be proven from one source.

- Personal draws can be budgeted carefully and completely controlled. Funds can be taken from the business account periodically and deposited into the personal account as draws or salary.

2. Double-entry and single-entry bookkeeping

Double-entry bookkeeping is usually the preferred method for keeping business records. Transactions are entered first in a journal, then monthly totals of the transactions are posted to the appropriate ledger accounts. The ledger accounts include five categories: income, expense, asset, liability, and net worth. Income and expense accounts are closed each year; asset, liability, and net worth accounts are maintained on a permanent and continuing basis.

Single-entry bookkeeping is not as complete as a double-entry method. This system, however, is relatively simple and records the flow of income and expense through a daily summary of cash receipts, a monthly summary of receipts, and a monthly disbursements journal such as a checkbook.

Your accountant will advise you about the appropriate system for your needs.

3. One-write accounting system

"One-write" is an accounting system where all the sales you make are automatically, through carbon paper, posted to a sales journal and monthly ledger card (for sending out statements) on the receivables side, and all the checks are posted to the proper expense journal on the payables side. The one-write system is also effective for showing the "aged" balance of receivables. In other words, it shows who owes you how much for 30, 60, 90 or over 90 days.

You may use either the receivable or payable system or both. It makes record-keeping very simple for you and your accountant, and is particularly useful if you write 50 or more checks and statements each month. If you are using the one-write system for payables, it automatically posts the checks written to a cash disbursement journal and all you need to do is summarize the sheet every 25 checks.

If you are interested in accounting systems, contact the suppliers under "accounting systems" in the yellow pages of the telephone directory.

4. Cash or accrual basis for records

Cash basis record-keeping is a method of recording transactions so that revenues and expenditures are reflected in the accounts in the period the related cash receipts or disbursements occur.

Accrual basis record-keeping is a method of recording transactions so that revenues and expenses are reflected in the accounts in the period they have been earned and incurred, whether or not such transactions have been finally settled. There are advantages and disadvantages of each system based on your circumstances. Tax advice will assist you in making the correct choice.

b. BASIC ACCOUNTING RECORDS

As previously discussed, informal records consist of evidence of business transactions such as sales slips, invoices, checks, etc. These informal records are then gathered into a more formal structure. For accounting purposes, these formalized basic records are referred to as "books of original entries" or as "journals."

1. Sales journal

A sales journal is a daily register of both cash and charge sales. The sales, both cash and charge, may be recorded by numbered invoices and accounted for. The total is then entered as the day's sales in the sales journal.

2. Cash receipts journal

This journal often combines the function of a sales journal along with a record of all transactions resulting in money coming into the business. When combined, this journal is referred to as a "sales and cash receipts journal".

In the cash receipts journal, all cash sales, charge sales, collections on account, and total deposits to the bank are entered. This is usually done in conjunction with the cash receipts journal. Referred to as a "daily summary of sales and cash receipts," it is both a summarizing vehicle as well as a form of reconciliation between cash on hand, cash receipts, charge sales, and total sales.

A sales and cash receipts journal briefly describes the transaction, whether it is a cash sale or a charge sale, whether the cash receipt came from a source other than a sale, and the amount of the total deposit.

In summary, the journal will show:

(a) Cash sale

(b) Bank deposit

(c) Receipts on account from a client

(d) Other receipts

3. Accounts receivable ledger and control account

These records are separate. The accounts receivable ledger contains separate cards or sheets for each charge client and records the sale with the invoice number or reference, the date, and the amount of the sale. When payments are made, the amount of the payment is deducted from the balance owing and is cross-referenced to the cash receipts journal.

The control account records in total all the charge sales and all the payments by charge customers which are detailed individually in the accounts receivable ledger. At any given time, the sum of all the individual charge account balances in the subsidiary ledger will equal the total net balance in the control account.

The accounts receivable aging schedule accompanies the accounts receivable ledger. This is a record of each charge customer that shows the balance owing and the age status of the charge — normally current, 30, 60, or 90 days.

In summary, each client has a ledger sheet that details: name, address, telephone number, credit information, date of sale, invoice number, date of payment, receipt number, balance owing.

Periodically the individual balances are added up (usually once a month), and the totals are reconciled to the accounts receivable balance in the general ledger.

4. Accounts payable journal

This journal is usually a subsidiary journal to the cash disbursements journal. The accounts payable journal records invoices for purchases, the amount and date, and when the invoice has to be paid. This journal's purpose is primarily a control over the payables. It allows you to correctly determine outstanding liabilities and when these obligations must be met.

5. Cash disbursements journal

This journal records, daily, all cash outlays for purchases, expenses, payroll, cash withdrawals, and loan payments. The payee or account is referenced, the check number is given, the amount is specified, and the purpose of the disbursement, by amount, is shown under the proper heading for each day. The purpose could be payroll, inventory purchased, accounts payable falling due, tax payments, etc. Any disbursements such as interest charges or withdrawals are also recorded.

6. Payroll journal

This journal consists usually of two records. The first is the record for the individual employee; it shows the pay period, the gross amount earned, the deductions (income tax, unemployment insurance, pension plan) made at source, and the net earnings. The second record is the "payroll summary" which, for the pay period, gives the total gross earnings, deductions, and net salaries paid to all employees. The total of the employees' salaries appears as an entry in the cash disbursements journal.

7. General ledger

The general ledger is the final book of entry in an accounting system. This record is required to complete even the most basic of bookkeeping systems. Every entry from the preceeding journals and ledgers is listed in the general ledger. The general ledger must always be kept in balance; that is to say, all debits and credits must be equal, so that the net additions and subtractions equal zero. The general ledger is to be used for preparing financial statements. Because it is the book of final entry, and a permanent record, none of the pages should ever be thrown away.

As it is important to understand the principles behind the bookkeeping records, it is recommended that you take various bookkeeping courses that are available through the FBDB (Canada), SBA (U.S.), community colleges, school board continuing education classes, and other educational facilities. Also see *Basic Accounting for the Small Business,* another title in the Self-Counsel series.

c. NON-FINANCIAL RECORDS

Administrative records can improve efficiency and profit. Non-financial records such as personnel records, tax records, and service records should be maintained.

1. Personnel records

Personnel records consist primarily of policies, benefits, and other matters pertaining to the general administration of the employees or consultants as a whole. Personnel records can also consist of individual records on each employee. These records contain all documents and correspondence relating to an employee from the time of applying for employment to termination. Individual employee records also include a summary of personal data, education and training, work history, and job and wage record.

2. Tax records

Tax records record details of sales taxes, income taxes, business taxes, and employee income tax deductions. Most businesses are regulated by a combination of federal, state/provincial, and municipal/county governments. The information for these records is obtained from different aspects of the business operations. For example, payroll deductions and service are obtained from the payroll records, and information on sales taxes collected comes from either the sales journal or the daily summary of sales and cash receipts.

Tax records detail assessments, rates, calculations, and remittances both by amount and date. Tax records also let you know when remittances must be made to avoid late filing penalties.

3. Service records

Service records are all the records associated with the provision of a service. Most importantly, these records are used to record, for each client, the cost of material, labor and overhead. These calculations are then used to determine a price when bidding on a contract or presenting a proposal, or assessing the profitability of a particular activity or product.

Service records can also keep track of employee efficiency to control non-chargeable time and to identify activities that are not performed to expected standards.

d. OFFICE SYSTEMS

Office systems should be implemented to reduce exposure to liability and to increase business awareness and sound decision-making.

1. Handling new matters

It is important that a form be developed to gather administrative information in a standard, consistent, and uniform manner to reduce the likelihood of an error or omission. The form should provide date and deadlines, as well as information that might give rise to potential conflicts of interest. You should have separate forms for prospective clients and new assignments. See Samples #10 and #11.

2. Time records

Maintenance of effective time records is critical in documenting what was done by the consultant or sub-consultant. Such records must be made as business is transacted.

Accurate time records are extremely important to ensure that clients are promptly charged, and that you have accounted for all billable time expended. It is easy to forget time expended if you don't write it down immediately. Time records also reflect the expenditure of time for the benefit received, and whether or not your efficiency and profit are improving or certain activities or clients should be reconsidered. See Sample #12.

SAMPLE #10
PROSPECTIVE CLIENT SHEET

Name _____

File # _____

Telephone _____

Address _____

_____

_____

LEAD

Date of inquiry _____

Person making inquiry _____

Source of referral _____

Nature of initial inquiry _____

Consultant contacted _____

Follow-up planned _____

Dates of:

Phone conversations _____

Meetings _____

Correspondence _____

Total time expended on client prior
to any proposal preparation _____

Status _____

PROPOSAL

Presentation date of proposal _____

Time required to complete proposal _____

Cost estimate _____

Consultant with primary
responsibility for assignment _____

Disposition of proposal _____

ASSIGNMENT

Starting date _____

Consultant(s) assigned _____

Primary client contact _____

Total billing _____

Completion date _____

SAMPLE #11
NEW CONSULTING ASSIGNMENT SHEET

File # _____   New client ( )
Consultant in charge _____   Old client ( )

Client _____ Date opened _____
Address _____
_____ Phone _____
Contact person(s) _____
Cross index _____
Assignment _____

. . . .

Type of work:

( ) Feasibility study   ( ) Marketing study   ( ) Research
( ) Grant acquisition   ( ) Organizational study   ( ) Speaking engagement
( ) Management study   ( ) Personnel/labor study ( ) Training
Other _____

. . . .

Fees (costs additional):

Person/Class	Rate	Per	
			Range quoted $_____ to $____
_____	_____	_____	Minimum quoted $____
_____	_____	_____	Time value $____

Other fee arrangements (method of payment) _____
Costs (projected)   _____
Total fees and costs   _____

. . . .

Source of client contact _____
Promised completion date _____ Expected completion date _____
Opened by _____

. . . .

CLOSING INFORMATION
Assignment completed on _____
Time value $_____   Total fee rec'd $_____   Variance $_____
Client available for reference: Yes ( )   No ( )

SAMPLE #12
TIME AND SERVICE RECORD

Date	Client No.	Client name	Service	Service Code	Loc'n Code	Time Hours	Time Decimal Conv.	By
				TOTAL TIME:			

Service codes

1	ADV	Advice	7	ENT	Entertain	13	REV Review
2	AP	Appear	8	INT	Interview	14	SEC Secretarial
3	AUD	Audit	9	INV	Investigate	15	TCF Phone call from
4	CON	Confer	10	OF	Office	16	TCT Phone call to
5	DIC	Dictate	11	PR	Promotion	17	TVL Travel
6	DR	Draft	12	RES	Research	18	TR Train

Local code

A In Town
B Out of Town
C Client's Office
D Other

Decimal Conversion:

6 mins. = .1 hour	36 mins. = .6 hour
12 mins. = .2 hour	42 mins. = .7 hour
18 mins. = .3 hour	48 mins. = .8 hour
24 mins. = .4 hour	54 mins. = .9 hour
30 mins. = .5 hour	60 mins. = 1.0 hour

If there is a legal dispute, your time record and service documentation could make the difference between winning and losing. Keep your time records in a detailed fashion as if you had to introduce them as evidence into court. The odds are that at some point in your consulting career you will have to do so.

Consider using a "daytimer" type of system for time keeping. Carry it with you at all times and transfer all notations to your daily time record docket sheet. You should get into the habit of recording all your daily activities in your daytimer, whether client related or not so that you can graphically analyze how your time is spent. For example, make a note of hours spent on client entertainment, marketing, professional development, and research each day.

3. Standard form engagement letters or contracts

You should have your lawyer help you develop letters of agreement and contracts that you can use with modification in each particular situation. It is important that the services to be performed and fee to be rendered are clearly outlined in a written contract.

4. Billing, credit, and collection

Monthly or interim billing should be done wherever possible. This means bills can be sent close to the time the work was done. It also keeps your cash flow even and enables you to spot fee disputes while there is still time to remedy the problem. An effective record-keeping system for credit and collection is also needed. This system can include a standard credit application form, client account record, etc. This subject is covered in detail in chapter 12.

5. Calendars

Important dates and deadlines should be entered into an effective calendar system, which will provide a double-check on entries, adequate lead time for performance of tasks, deadlines, limitation dates, secretarial administration of the system, input by associates and sub-consultants as appropriate, and follow-up to ensure that the performance has occurred.

6. Filing systems

An effective filing system should be developed to eliminate the possibility of misplacement of client materials. A filing reference system should be designed for speedy retrieval of client information.

9

HOW TO LEGALLY MINIMIZE PAYING TAX

It is very important to obtain professional advice on tax planning. An accountant who specializes in tax should be retained before you start your business to advise you on all the various considerations. Tax legislation is changing constantly, and varies by jurisdiction.

This chapter gives an overview of some of the key areas to consider when discussing your new business with your professional advisors. Your advisors will review the business plan that you will have prepared, your personal financial circumstances, and your anticipated profit, and recommend the correct approach for your needs.

a. TAX AVOIDANCE AND TAX EVASION

The distinction between tax avoidance and tax evasion should be made clear. Tax avoidance is the principle by which the consultant plans his or her transactions within the law using all available tax planning benefits to minimize the liability for paying income taxes.

Tax evasion is an action that is outside the law, and normally implies the receipt of monies without declaring them as income. Tax evasion is criminal in nature and can result in serious consequences including jail.

b. CASH OR ACCRUAL METHOD

Consultants have a choice about the method of accounting for financial transactions. Based on your individual situation, one method may be more attractive than the other. The cash basis of accounting is a method of recording transactions in which revenues and expenditures are entered in the accounts during the period in which the related cash receipts or disbursements occur.

The accrual basis of accounting is a method of recording transactions in which revenues and expenses are entered in the accounts during the period in which they have been earned and incurred, whether or not such transactions have been finally settled.

Tax planning is particularly difficult for cash basis consultants, because expenses are generally deductible in the period paid, and income is generally taxable as it is received. For accrual basis consultants, the problem is simplified in that cash does not need to exchange hands for the recognition of income, at least not within the tax period. For either type of method, the intent is that income and expenses be matched within like periods.

An example of tax planning for the consultant who reports on a cash basis is found in the timing of bill payment. Toward the end of the year, the cash basis consultant should maximize allowable deductions by paying all bills applying to that tax year, before the year closes. Accordingly, it is not wise to request advance payments from current clients before the year is closed.

c. FISCAL YEAR-END

The choice of fiscal year may depend on consideration of financial savings for accounting fees, tax deferral in the first year, and administrative convenience.

It is prudent to select a fiscal year distinct from the calendar year if you intend to retain accountants for annual audit or tax purposes. January through April is the busiest time for accountants, and you are likely to have better service and more attention paid to your financial affairs when your corporate fiscal year ends, for example, in July rather than in February.

If you experience seasonal changes in business volume, it may be wise to tailor a fiscal year-end along seasonal lines.

Ask yourself if you are particularly busy at a certain time of the year. For example, if you are a consultant who specializes in education, you will likely be busiest in the winter and relatively free during the summer months. If you are a consultant to the retail business, you may be the busiest during the period of time leading up to the holidays.

In these cases, you might benefit from structuring the fiscal year-end so that the highest concentration of income occurs in the beginning of the fiscal year. By doing this, you have the remainder of the year to plan for taxes, take care of business development for the next fiscal year, and regulate cash flow effectively.

d. CORPORATIONS, PROPRIETORSHIPS OR PARTNERSHIPS

The tax implications of a proprietorship and a partnership are the same. The net income or net loss from the proprietorship or your share of the partnership are declared on your personal income tax filings. Depending on your level of taxation, you could be paying more tax than if you were incorporated.

Your particular situation will determine whether or not it is best to incorporate for tax reasons. Factors to consider include your salary draw level, value of benefits a corporation would absorb, tax bracket, and projected growth patterns. The immediate and long range tax liability of the individual is a governing factor.

Remember, that in the U.S. an exception to the normal corporation exists which allows the consultant to have the advantages of a proprietorship and a corporation. The features of a Sub-S corporation are briefly discussed in chapter 4. Your accountant can better advise you in detail.

e. MAXIMIZING DEDUCTIBLE EXPENSES

It is very important for consultants to have a record-keeping system that keeps track of all expenses relating to the consultant's overhead as well as expenses that are directly payable by the client. For a specific project, you may have given a fixed price contract incorporating expenses that otherwise would be passed on to the client for separate payment.

Expenses are allowed if they are related to the operation of the business, are reasonable, are "ordinary" and "necessary," and if they are for items to be used within a period of one year. Your accountant can advise you in your situation.

If you are going to incur expenses that would be useful for more than one year, generally that expense cannot be fully deducted within the year the money is spent. The depreciation formula for expenses such as typewriters, desks, autos, etc., may be claimed for the useful life of the asset.

To ensure that you account for all expenses, keep all payment stubs, receipts, and vouchers, and maintain a record of entertainment and automobile expenses. The tax department can disallow claims for expenses without verification that the expense was indeed incurred and that it was related to your business and the generation of income.

Some of the areas you should discuss with your accountant to obtain advice and guidelines are discussed below. The examples given are general guidelines only. It is critical that you receive expert tax advice in advance on these and other expense deductions related to your consulting practice. As mentioned earlier, tax regulations and interpretations are constantly changing and tax court decisions alter the law on an ongoing basis. Only a tax accountant can properly advise you on the appropriate deductions in your individual situation.

1. Home office

It is quite common for consultants to operate out of their homes to keep overhead costs down. An office in the home is deductible, but the guidelines are very strict.

(a) The office must be necessary to the conduct of the business.

(b) A room or area must be used 100% of the time exclusively for the business.

(c) Deductions are allowed on a square foot percentage or other reasonable basis.

(d) Any deductions for an office in the home that are being claimed must be disclosed on the consultant's tax return.

It is important to keep an accurate account of home office expenses, as the potential for abuse in this area is well known. Deductible expenses are made on a percentage basis. For example, if 15% of the home's living space is used completely for the conduct of business, 15% of the following expenses are deductible:

    (a) Interest paid on home mortgage

    (b) Rent of home or apartment, home owner's or tenant's fire insurance

    (c) Property taxes

    (d) Reasonable expenses such as maintenance

    (e) A portion of the telephone charges might also be deductible. Expenses related to the telephone should be itemized as applicable to business use rather than estimated as a percentage of the total. An alternative is for the consultant to install a corporate business telephone in the home office.

Your tax consultant can advise you about home office expense deductibility. It is necessary to maintain careful documentation of home office expenses to support deductions claimed on an income tax return.

2. Automobile

This is a potential problem area if one car is being used for both business and pleasure. A full deduction for business use is difficult to claim if you are using it personally at any time. A ledger record of business usage is essential.

A complete log should be kept of all mileage pertaining to business with a description about the purpose of the trip. In addition, a record of all tolls and parking expenses, repairs, purchases, and insurance payments should be kept. In some cases an estimate of business use for a jointly used car may be allowable if it seems reasonable in the circumstances. Because an estimation may be disallowed, good management requires accurate record-keeping.

If you have two cars, one for business use and one for personal use, it is easier to establish a case for full deduction of all the expenses related to one car.

3. Entertainment

It is difficult to claim a deduction for entertainment unless an accurate record is kept showing the date, amount, location of entertainment, who attended, connection to business, and the purpose of the meeting. As this area is one of potential abuse, it is looked at very carefully on an audit and may be disallowed. It is important, therefore, to mark on the back of the receipt the necessary information immediately after the entertainment function and before you forget.

4. Travel

This is another area in which potential abuse occurs, and it is therefore scrutinized very carefully. Travel that is strictly for business is deductible. This normally includes the cost of transportation; lodging of a reasonable nature; meals; transportation while away, such as taxis, rental cars and buses; tips; personal services, such as laundry; and telephone costs.

A personal trip cannot be written off as a business expense. Some consultants believe that a personal trip may be "converted" into a business trip if business is conducted while away from home. The key criterion is whether or not the trip was primarily personal in nature. If it was primarily personal in nature, this could exclude deductibility of any business expenses.

A careful distinction must be maintained where business expenses and personal expenses are combined. For example, a spouse may accompany a consultant on a business trip. The consultant is only able to deduct the portion of the expenses that relate directly to business. The primary purpose of the trip must be for business, not pleasure. All expenses pertaining to the spouse's share of travel, lodging or meals would not be deductible.

There are limitations on the number of business conferences and conventions that can be taken outside the country each year and be deductible. You must obtain specific advice on these points.

5. Bad debts

Income is recognized only as the cash is collected. Therefore, cash basis taxpayers cannot deduct bad debts for uncollected fees. However, the consultant can deduct returned checks as bad debts. If you are an accrual basis taxpayer and want to deduct bad debts, two important tests are required to determine if the debt can be declared "uncollectable." The criteria are the record of your attempt to collect the debt and the length of time the debt has been outstanding.

6. Insurance

Insurance premiums for all business related insurance policies are fully deductible. If coverage extends to both personal and business protection, only the business portion can be deducted.

7. Professional development

All the expenses related to professional development are deductible if they are directly related to your business and generating income, and if they are reasonable. Again, detailed documentation is required to support the deduction.

10

INSURANCE

Proper risk management means planning for potential problems and attempting to insure against them. You should be familiar with the numerous types of insurance available, the method of obtaining the insurance, the best way to reduce premiums, and the pitfalls to avoid.

a. OBTAINING INSURANCE

Insurance companies market their services chiefly through the methods discussed below.

1. Agencies

These are normally the smaller individualized operations that place home, car or other common types of insurance with several insurance companies to which they are contracted. In some cases, small agencies, to earn their commission, are under an obligation to place a certain volume of insurance with each company they deal with. Therefore, it is possible that you might be sold policies offered by companies which may not suit your needs and may not necessarily be placed on a competitive basis.

2. Insurance brokers

Insurance brokers claim to have complete independence from any insurance company and more flexibility than the common agencies. In comparison with agencies in general, brokers from the larger companies are more knowledgeable and flexible in the types of coverage and policies available, and they specialize in certain areas. Also, a broker should have no vested interest in placing insurance with any particular company, and will therefore attempt to get you the best price and the best coverage to meet your needs. You should make specific inquiries to satisfy yourself.

As in all matters of obtaining professional advice or assistance, you should have a minimum of three competitive quotes and an opportunity to evaluate the relative strengths and weaknesses of each. If the brokers are using the same insurance base for the best coverage and premiums, then all three brokers should recommend to you, in theory, the same insurance companies for the different forms of coverage you are requesting.

3. Clubs and associations

Ask your local Better Business Bureau and Chamber of Commerce about their group rates for insurance. These two organizations frequently have various types of insurance coverage available at a reduced group rate.

b. PLANNING YOUR INSURANCE PROGRAM

It is important to consider all criteria to determine the best type of insurance for you and your business. Your major goal should be adequate coverage, avoiding both over- and under-insurance. This is done by periodic review of risk, and by keeping your agent informed of any changes in your business that could potentially affect your coverage.

The following principles will help in planning an insurance program:

(a) Identify the risk to which your business is exposed.

(b) Cover your largest risk first.

(c) Determine the magnitude of loss the business can bear without financial difficulty, and use your premium dollar where the protection need is greatest.

(d) Decide what kind of protection will work best for each risk:

- Absorbing risks

- Minimizing risks

- Insuring against risks with commercial insurance

(e) Insure the correct risk

(f) Use every means possible to reduce costs of insurance:

- Negotiate for lower premiums if loss experience is low

- Use deductibles where applicable

- Shop around for comparable rates and analyze insurance terms and provisions offered by different insurance companies.

(g) Risk exposure changes, so a periodic review will save you from insuring matters that are no longer exposed to the same degree of risk. Conversely, you may need to increase limits of liability. Reviews can help avoid overlaps and gaps in coverage, and thereby keep your risk and premiums lower.

(h) If you are pleased with a particular broker who can handle your various forms of insurance, it is preferable to be selective and have just one broker company. An advantage of the larger broker firms is that they have a pool of insurance professionals expert in various areas as resource people for you.

(i) Attempt to keep your losses down in every way. Although your business may have adequate coverage, losses could be uninsurable, exempt from coverage, or have a large deductible. Problems with insurance coverage could seriously affect the survival of your business.

c. TYPES OF BUSINESS AND PERSONAL INSURANCE

The types of insurance you might need will vary widely as the risks vary widely according to the type of consulting practice you have. The following overview of insurance policies is provided to make you aware of what exists, and what might be appropriate in your situation. As mentioned earlier, these types of insurance are not necessarily recommended. Only you can make that decision after an objective assessment of your needs following comparative research in a competitive insurance market.

1. General liability

Most liability insurance policies encompass such losses as:

    (a) Money you must legally pay because of bodily injury or damage to the property of others.

    (b) All emergency, medical, and surgical expenses incurred from the accident.

    (c) Expenses for investigation, your defense, settlements and a trial.

A general liability policy covers negligence causing injury to clients, employees, and the general public. The policy is normally written up as a comprehensive liability policy.

2. Products or completed operations liability

This policy offers protection against a law suit by a customer or client who used your product or service and, as a result, sustained bodily injury or property damage from it.

3. Errors and omissions liability

This coverage protects you and other professionals against litigation arising from losses incurred by your clients as a result of an error or omission in your advice to them.

4. Malpractice liability

This insurance protects you from claims arising from any losses incurred by your clients as a result of negligence or failure on your part to exercise an acceptable degree of professional skill.

5. Automobile liability

This coverage includes other people's property, other automobiles, persons in other vehicles, and persons in the insured automobile.

If you are using your car for business purposes, exclusively or occasionally, it is important that you have your premium cover business use. It is possible that your current motor vehicle insurance policy has just a premium based on personal use. Problems could occur if there were an accident and it was discovered that your car was indeed used for business purposes.

6. Fire and theft liability

You probably already have fire and theft insurance if you are working out of your home as a consultant. If you are working in an office or an apartment, it is important to make sure that you have satisfactory coverage.

7. Business interruption insurance

The indirect loss from a fire or theft can be greater than the loss itself. If your premises or files are destroyed, you can lose revenue. Certain expenses must still be met. Such a situation could put a severe strain on working capital and seriously affect the survival of the business.

Business interruption insurance is designed to cover the period between the time of the loss and the return to normal operating conditions. The insurance policy could also include the costs of temporarily renting other premises.

8. Overhead expense insurance

Consultants whose business income would cease if they were temporarily disabled by illness or accident may take out insurance to cover the cost to them of their fixed business expenses or overhead which have to be met even when they are unable to earn income.

9. Personal disability insurance

You could possibly be disabled for a short or long period of time. This insurance pays you a certain monthly amount if you are permanently disabled, or a portion of that amount if you are partially disabled, but capable of generating some income.

10. Key person insurance

The death of a key person could seriously affect the earning power of your consulting practice. For example, if you have an associate, or partner or sub-consultant who is critical to a particularly large project or your business as a whole, life insurance should be considered.

If the key person dies, the loss may result in a decrease of confidence by your existing or potential clients, leading to a loss of future contracts, loss of competitive position, loss of revenue, and the expense of finding and/or training a replacement. The amount and type of insurance will depend upon many factors, as designing an evaluation formula for a key person is difficult.

Proceeds of the key person policy are not subject to income tax generally, but premiums are not a deductible business expense.

11. Shareholders or partners insurance

If it is your intention to have a partnership in your consulting practice or a shareholder in your corporation, you may wish to consider shareholder or partnership insurance. Normally this type of insurance is part of a buy-sell agreement which allows for a deceased shareholder's or partner's interest to be purchased by the surviving partners or shareholders of the corporation.

In the absence of a buy-sell agreement funded by life insurance, the death of a partner could cause the immediate dissolution of the partnership in law. Unless there is an express agreement to the contrary, the surviving partner's duty is to liquidate the business, collect all outstanding accounts, pay off all debts, and account as trustee to the personal representative of the deceased partner for the value of the deceased's interest in the business.

In the case of a corporation, the deceased shareholder's interest would be considered an asset and would go to the beneficiary outlined in the will if a will existed. Naturally, the introduction of a new shareholder who owns an interest in the company, especially a majority interest could have a very traumatic effect on the shareholders and the company's continued operation.

In summary, the procedure is that each partner shareholder applies for a life insurance policy on the life of the other. The applicant is the beneficiary and pays the premiums on his or her partner's life insurance policy. When a partner dies, the funds from the insurance are received tax free by the beneficiary (the partner). These funds are then used to purchase the deceased partner's share of the business. The surviving partner retains control of the business, and the heirs of the deceased get cash for their interest.

12. Business loan insurance

In many cases your lender will be able to provide you with insurance coverage for the outstanding amount of your loan and then incorporate the premium payments into the loan. In the event of your death, the outstanding balance of your loan is paid off.

13. Term life insurance

This type of insurance insures a person for a specific period of time and then terminates. The most common period is five years. If the insured dies within the term of the policy, the insurance company pays the full face amount to the heirs. The costs of premiums are based on life expectancy for the person's age during the five-year period. Term life does not have a cash or loan value.

Because term life insurance can be written for various time periods, and because of inexpensive premiums, it is valuable to the businessperson. Such term policies are often used to provide collateral security for loans to the firm or for personal obligations. There is generally a reduced rate of approximately 10% for non-smokers.

It is highly advisable to have term insurance in the amount of at least your personal financial obligations and business financial obligations for which you have a direct or contingent liability. This area is frequently overlooked.

14. Medical insurance

It is important to take out sufficient medical coverage for your needs. If you are doing any consulting assignments outside the country, you should have extended coverage that pays for medical bills that may be incurred by injury or illness while you are out of the country.

15. Group insurance

You may be eligible for group insurance rates if you have four or more employees. The policies of insurance companies vary, but medical and dental plans are available for small groups.

16. Workers' compensation insurance

If you have a number of employees, you should make certain that you are covered by workers' compensation insurance if you are eligible. With this coverage, the insurer pays all costs that the employer is required to pay for any injury to the employee. The insurer also covers the employees for all benefits and compensations required by the appropriate laws.

If you have failed to pay your employer's portion of the insurance coverage, or have failed to meet your responsibilities adequately to your employees in terms of safety, is is possible that you as the employer could be held liable for any injury to the employee as determined by the common law as well as under workers' compensation laws. Employee coverage and the extent of the employer's liability vary considerably.

11

PROFESSIONAL LIABILITY

Consultants have the same degree of potential for law suits against them as other professionals, such as physicians, accountants, and lawyers do. The claims made against the consultant could be that the consultant was responsible for a wrongful act or omission or professional misjudgment. Professional liability claims may be brought by the client or by third parties, such as investors, creditors or lenders.

If the consultant is doing business as a proprietorship or partnership, liability extends to the consultant personally. It may also extend to the consultant's estate after death. Liability can also extend to persons who were the consultant's partners at the time of the alleged negligence. Claims may be made by the client long after the error or omission occurred. The statute of limitations in many jurisdictions will not begin until the claimant discovers or should have discovered, or knows or has reason to know of your alleged mistake.

As a consultant, you must weigh the degree of risk involved in your specific area of practice. Obtain expert legal and insurance advice about the proper methods of protecting yourself.

a. CONTRACT AND TORT LIABILITY

It is not uncommon for a consultant to be sued for both breach of contract and tort liability.

1. Contract liability

A claim made against a consultant by a client could be based on the allegation that the consultant failed to perform the services described in the contract in a reasonable and prudent manner. This liability involves only those who are parties to the contract, and it applies whether there is a verbal contract, implied contract or written contract.

For the client to succeed in the claim against the consultant, all of the following elements must be proven:

- There was a valid contract between the client and the consultant. This contract, as mentioned earlier, could be verbal or in writing.

- The consultant materially failed to perform his or her obligations under the contract.

- The client suffered damages as a result of the consultant's breach of obligation.

In actions brought under a breach of contract, it is irrelevant in most jurisdictions whether the consultant's breach was innocent, negligent or willful. The client need only prove that a material breach of contract occurred and that damages resulted. There are, of course, numerous defenses a consultant can raise depending on the particular circumstances. The amount of monies assessed against the consultant would be an attempt to restore the client to the position held if the contract had not been breached.

A consultant can be sued for breach of contract, for example, if the precise duties and responsibilities or services required under the contract were not met exactly as detailed in the contract. This is a good reason to make certain that a contract is written, not verbal. In a verbal contract it is difficult to establish exactly what the terms of the agreement were.

Another example is a consultant who signed a fixed price contract for a service to be provided by a certain date. If the consultant miscalculated the fixed price and abandoned the project before it was completed, he or she could be sued. This is not uncommon among new consultants unfamiliar with the skill required in preparing a fixed price proposal.

2. Tort liability

Tort liability is a violation of civil law rather than a breach of contract. Liability in tort is incurred toward the public at large. Any third party who has suffered through the direct or indirect actions of the consultant can make a claim against the consultant even if no contract existed with the consultant and the claimant had never met the consultant. For example, if a consultant submits a report with recommendations to a client and the client follows the recommendations, expends a large sum of money and subsequently loses the money, the clients creditors and investors and lenders could attempt to sue the consultant for losses suffered (damages) due to negligent advice of the consultant. It would have to be shown that the consultant knew or reasonably should have known that others would be seeing the report with recommendations, and they would be relying on that report before investing or lending money.

For the claimant to succeed in a claim against the consultant, all the following elements must be proven:

- The consultant owed the claimant a duty of care.
- The duty or standard of care was breached.
- Measureable damages resulted from the breach.
- There was a direct connection between the breach of duty and the damages that occurred.

In a suit based on tort, evidence introduced into court must establish that the consultant departed from the local custom and standard of practice. If a consultant is found to be negligent, the court will attempt to compensate the claimant for the damages incurred.

b. REASONS FOR CLAIMS

1. Counterclaims

In many instances when a consultant sues a client to collect overdue fees, the client will counterclaim. The client may have a valid reason for not paying the fee, but very often the countersuit is intended to create delay and act as a leverage mechanism for settlement.

2. Conflict of interest

A consultant could be liable if it can be shown that the consultant had a vested interest in the outcome of the recommendations. For example, a client requests a computer consultant to review existing hardware and make recommendations for replacement. The consultant recommends replacement equipment. At some later point the client learns that the consultant received a kick-back from the distributor of the product line for recommending a very large order. The client could sue the consultant for the undisclosed profit; and, if it could be shown that the recommended hardware system was not the appropriate system in the circumstances, additional liability on the consultant's part could be present.

3. Conflicting interest of clients

A consultant could be working for two clients who are in competition with each other. If it can be shown that confidential information was disclosed or the benefits of assistance to one client was at the expense of the other client, then possible liability of the consultant could be present.

4. Delegation of part of contract to employee or sub-consultant

The primary consultant is responsible for the work of employees or agents under the primary consultant's control. If the client maintains that the consulting work was not done, or not done properly by the employee or sub-consultant, legal action can be taken against the primary consultant.

5. Third party damages

If a third party such as a creditor, investor or lender suffers damages as a consequence of the recommendations of the consultant to a second party, a third party can sue in tort.

6. Unclear expectations by client

It is possible that a client has unclear or unrealistic expectations of the work to be performed by the consultant and the benefit to the client. This lack of clarity can be a basis for dispute if the performance was not perceived to be related to expectations.

c. HOW TO AVOID PROFESSIONAL LIABILITY AND PREVENT LOSSES

Although the possibility of being exposed to legal liability cannot be totally prevented, it can be substantially minimized by implementing effective administrative systems and procedures.

Many professionals concentrate on the technical aspects of their profession. Good management is equally important. Consideration must be given to proper staffing, training, credit and collection, and office procedures, such as keeping diaries, checklists and properly written records of every aspect and phase of the consulting business. As well, it is important to stay within the limits of your training, experience, and expertise. Do not take on work that is beyond your capability.

Some good management techniques that can help keep you out of trouble are discussed here.

1. Client control

Clients who habitually try to avoid paying fees by claiming that errors have been made, or clients who frequently resort to litigation can be costly for your business. Make sure that you have control over the areas for which you are responsible. In other words, do not assume responsibility for matters that your clients control.

You should implement a pre-screening process to select clients. Ways of pre-screening are covered in chapter 16.

2. Cost estimates

Avoid giving firm cost estimates for activities arising from your services if possible. Depending upon the type of consulting practice you have, you could be locked into a situation where a fixed cost has been given and the project suffers an overrun. Architects and engineers especially should avoid giving firm billing cost estimates.

3. Carefully drafted contracts

It is most important that a consultant operate with written contracts with clients. The contracts should be drafted carefully and based on competent legal advice. Contract ambiguities and misunderstandings are a major source of professional liability claims. Letters of understanding or contracts should be sent out to the client for acknowledgment and signature and returned by the client.

4. Free opinions

Be careful not to provide free opinions without knowing all the facts. You could be put in a position of being liable, even though you were not officially retained

95

and had not received any fees. If it can be shown that someone relied on your advice and subsequently suffered because of your advice, you could be held liable.

5. Law

Make sure you understand the law pertaining to your specific work in the jurisdiction where the law would be interpreted. For example, if you are performing consulting assignments outside your home jurisdiction, different laws may apply that could create problems for you.

6. Sub-consultants

Sub-consultants should be carefully selected. Check to see that they carry adequate professional liability insurance. Make sure your insurance covers any work performed by a sub-consultant.

7. Records, systems, and procedures

Effective systems for your files, records, billing and office procedures are essential for any business. See chapter 8 for specific ideas on how to keep your records straight.

8. Continuing education

It is important that the consultant develop more expertise and training on an ongoing basis through various professional development and continuing education courses. This shows a professional attitude and desire for knowledge and current information.

9. Quality control

The consultant should set up some system for monitoring the activities and performance of employees or sub-consultants. If a system is in place, this will show that you have developed a high standard of care in the operation of your business.

10. Communication

Effective communication helps eliminate many client problems. This topic is covered in chapter 16.

d. PROFESSIONAL LIABILITY INSURANCE

The procedures outlined in the previous section, if implemented, should substantially reduce the risk of professional liability. However, professional liability insurance is necessary since the risk cannot be completely removed. Professional liability coverage should indemnify the consultant for losses and costs involved in the defense of claims.

The liability insurance coverage is limited to claims "arising out of the performance of professional services" including errors, omissions and negligent acts. If you provide a service outside the specified designation for your specialty, the insurance coverage could be voided.

There are two types of professional liability insurance coverage — claims made and occurrence. A claims made policy insures only against claims made during the policy period. Occurrence coverage provides protection against claims occurring during the policy period, even if the claims arise long after the occurrence and the policy period.

There are many provisions in the policy that should be thoroughly explained, and if you are not completely satisfied, alternative coverage should be considered. The seven most important factors that have to be reviewed in selecting or analyzing a professional liability insurance coverage are:

(a) Declarations

(b) Exclusions

(c) Insuring agreements

(d) Definitions

(e) Limits of liability

(f) Deductibles

(g) Policy conditions

Your premiums can be reduced in a variety of ways, some of which are discussed here.

1. Increase deductibles

The greater the deductible, the less expensive the policy premium should be. Check to see if the policy deductible applies to each separate claim or just once a year.

2. Comparing prices

There is competition in the marketplace for professional liability coverage. Make certain that the reduced premium presented to you does not reflect less attractive provisions in the policy that you may not understand. Professional advice should again be obtained from independent sources to satisfy yourself as to the nature of the coverage that you are getting. It is a prudent investment to have a lawyer who specializes in insurance law, review the proposed insurance terms and conditions.

3. Changing the type of coverage

Claims made policies are generally less costly than occurrence policies. The reason, as discussed earlier, is because the claims made policy covers just claims made during the policy term. The risk therefore to the insurance company is reduced compared to occurrence coverage.

In occurrence coverage the risk of the insurance company is considerable as a claim can be made against the insurance company many years after the negligence occurred and after your policy expired. The cost of settling a claim long after the event could be much higher than a settlement today. It is this risk and uncertainty on the part of the insurance company that is passed on to you in the form of higher premiums for occurrence coverage.

e. PRACTICING WITHOUT INSURANCE

Some consultants choose to conduct their business without any professional liability insurance. If the degree of exposure and risk is very low, this might be a viable alternative. If the consultant has very few personal assets and is effectively judgment proof, then personal bankruptcy may be an alternative in the most extreme circumstances if a claim is made.

Incorporating a company and conducting the consulting practice through the company should add some protection in a law suit if the company lacks any assets. The danger of operating a consulting business that has a risk element but no professional liability insurance is the uncertainty if problems occur. A client or third party could sue the consultant personally as well as the corporation and, until the trial, you would not know what the outcome would be. In the meantime you would have to incur the costs and pressure of the process. In other words, conducting a business through a corporation is not an automatic guarantee of personal protection. The other uncertainty is the nature and amount of damages that your advice caused your client or third parties. It may be very difficult to project at the time you are conducting a consulting assignment what the financial damages could be if your advice is in error.

If you do intend to practice without professional liability insurance, it is most important that you receive expert legal advice to maximize your protection in advance.

12

CREDIT, BILLING, AND COLLECTION

Many consultants starting out in businesses are more interested in performing their skilled service than developing a clear credit billing and collection policy. In many cases a consultant has had no previous business experience and does not realize the pitfalls that can occur.

A system rigidly followed is essential to your survival. It does not take many bad debts to completely eliminate the profit of the business for the whole year. In more serious cases, you could go out of business if a substantial debt owing by a client is not paid.

A number of common mistakes occur with beginning consultants. First, the consultant, wanting to build up a clientele and reputation as quickly as possible, takes on many clients, performs the service and incurs expenses, but allows the client to defer payment. Second, the new consultant may be too busy or too inexperienced to monitor receivables carefully. Third, unpaid bills are not followed up quickly with appropriate steps to collect funds. The effect of this sloppy approach can be disastrous.

This chapter outlines the pitfalls to be aware of and the procedures to adopt when reviewing your collection policy. If you develop the correct system for your needs, it will enhance your cash flow and profit and minimize stress, client problems, and bad debts.

a. DISADVANTAGES OF EXTENDING CREDIT

When you extend credit, the understanding is that the client intends to pay, is capable of paying, and that nothing will occur to prevent the client from paying. You assume that most clients are honest and acting with goodwill and in good faith. Many of these assumptions may not be accurate.

There are a number of potential disadvantages to extending credit.

Extending credit may take a great deal of your time, and the administrative paperwork — checking references, monitoring and following up on slow paying clients — may be tedious.

The expense of credit checking and collection could be more than you wish or are able to pay. Expenses could consist of credit reporting agency fees and memberships, collection costs, legal fees, and time lost that you could otherwise spend generating revenue.

You will need to increase your working capital requirements to keep your business in operation because receivables from your clients may or may not be paid when you expect or need it. You will be paying interest on the additional working capital that you may have to borrow to offset your decreased working capital.

b. ASSESSING THE CLIENT

It is important to be very careful about extending credit. Apply the following general guidelines to your business.

(a) Develop a clear credit policy for your business after consultation with your accountant and lawyer. Experienced professional advice is essential before you extend credit.

(b) Develop a credit application information sheet that has all the necessary information for your files.

(c) Consider joining a credit bureau as well as a credit reporting agency such as Dun and Bradstreet. Check into the past debt payment profile of your potential client in advance.

(d) Obtain references from your client if appropriate, and check the references. Ask about the client's length of time in business.

(e) Ask the client if consultants have been used before and the method of payment that was negotiated.

(f) Consider carefully the amount of credit being extended. The greater amount of money unpaid, the greater the risk for you.

(g) If the work you do is highly specialized, and you have very little competition, you have a lot of leverage in the nature of credit that you would be extending.

(h) If the client is a large institution or government, ask about the customary length of time for accounts rendered to be paid. Specify in your contract the exact terms of payment; government payments in particular can be delayed by bureaucracy for two or three months or longer.

(i) If the client requests deferred fees, you run a risk of default or other problems. Sometimes clients request a deferment of fees or payment because it is a large project, the client is suffering cash flow difficulties, or other considerations. If you are faced with a decision about deferral of fees, you should consider charging interest on the total amount, charging higher fees, requesting a sizeable retainer fee before you start the project, or obtaining collateral to protect yourself if your total fees are substantial.

(j) Consider the future benefit of a relationship with the prospective client. If there is a possibility of future contracts or sources of contacts with other prospective clients, you may wish to weigh the benefits against the risks.

c. AVOIDING CLIENT MISUNDERSTANDINGS ON FEES

Communication is vital to minimize client misunderstanding on fees. Many consultants feel uncomfortable discussing money matters during the first interview with the client. Or sometimes consultants become so involved in the client's problem that the fee is not discussed. It is important that the amount of money you expect is understood and agreed upon by the client before you commence work.

Three ways to eliminate misunderstanding on the issue of services performed for fees are through communication, written contract, and invoice.

1. Communication

Communication is a critical element to a satisfactory client relationship. It is important that the subject of fees be discussed openly at the time of the initial interview and resolved so that the client feels satisfied with the final bargain. Ask potential clients if they have hired consultants in the past, and the nature of the contract relationship that existed.

The interview should be followed by a letter of confirmation outlining the essence of the discussion about fees, among other matters. Progress reports should be sent to the client from time to time if the circumstances warrant it; copies of correspondence concerning the client should be sent to the client. If appropriate, try to involve the client with the project in some way so he or she feels a bonding to you in the project, and sees and appreciates the work you are doing on an ongoing basis. This should minimize the risk of a client disputing your fees for services.

2. Written contract

A written contract must be signed before work is commenced. The contract can take various forms as outlined later in chapter 18. Basically, a letter of agreement or formal contract explains the nature of fees involved and the method of payment — whether it is payment upon receipt, net 10 days or net 30 days.

Be very wary about financing a client; if at all possible, have payment upon receipt. This should assist your cash flow and minimize risk of late payments. The contract should also state the interest that will be added to the outstanding debt if it is not paid within the terms of the contract. The contract should spell out in detail the exact services that you will be performing for the fee.

In certain circumstances a stop work clause could be inserted in the agreement to the effect that if payment is not made within the terms of the contract that, at the option of the consultant, all work will stop.

Finally, the contract must be signed by the client decision-maker in authority. It is preferable that this individual be the same person with whom you negotiated the contract.

3. Invoice

To minimize misunderstanding on invoiced amounts, it is advisable to provide a detailed breakdown of the charges for services and expenses for the particular phase of the contract. If appropriate, reference should be made on the invoice to the contract agreement on fee structure and method of payment.

d. MINIMIZING RISK OF BAD DEBTS

There are several effective techniques to minimize the risk of bad debts. As discussed previously, most consultants cannot afford to have one or two non-paying clients without seriously affecting the viability of the business. The following general guidelines may not all be appropriate in a given client situation. Your judgment in each individual situation must dictate the appropriate approach.

1. Advance retainer

A client can be asked to pay a retainer or deposit of 10 to 25% or more of the total contract amount prior to the work being performed. This can be justified on the basis that you are very busy, and if you are going to schedule in a commitment to that client, it is your policy to require a advance commitment retainer.

This is also an effective technique for a potentially high risk client who has a reputation for non-payment or late payment, or who constantly argues about bills. This approach can also be considered when dealing with a new client who has not used consultants before.

2. Pre-paid disbursements

Depending upon the length of the job and the type of client, you may wish to request pre-paid disbursements if the disbursements are going to be sizable. You do not want to carry the client for out-of-pocket expenses at the risk of your own cash flow. You also do not want to run the risk of a non-payment or dispute of the overall account. As mentioned earlier, it is one thing to lose your time, it is another thing to also be out-of-pocket your own funds.

3. Progress payments

It is common for consultants to request funds by means of invoicing at specific points in the project. The stages at which progress payments are to be paid would be outlined in the contract.

4. Regular billing

Statements can be sent out on a weekly or monthly basis, depending on the circumstances. It is important to outline in the contract, if appropriate, your policy on the timing of billings. That way the client will not be taken by surprise. This also provides you with the advantage of knowing at an early stage in the consulting project if the client is going to dispute your fees, and at this point you can either resolve the problem or discontinue your services. It can be very risky to allow substantial work to be performed before rendering an account, or waiting until the end of the project.

5. Billing on time

Generally a client's appreciation for the value of your services diminishes over time. This is a common problem. It is important, therefore, to send your bill while the client can see the benefit of the service you have provided. Present your final bill at the completion of the project.

6. Accelerated billing

If you sense that the client may have problems paying the bill or other factors cause you concern, accelerate your normal billing pattern. You want to receive payment on your account before difficulties can appear.

The risk of rendering an account that states "net 30 days" is that the client is not legally overdue in payment to you until after 30 days. If you become aware of client financial problems, it is difficult to commence legal action or garnishee before the 30-day period has expired.

7. Withholding vital information

If you have documents, records, reports, and other material related to the client and the project, you may feel it appropriate, if circumstances warrant, to withhold returning all the necessary material to the client until your account has been paid, or other appropriate arrangements made.

8. Holding up completion of important stage of project

If client problems occur, you may wish to stop providing your services and resources at a critical stage until the matter has been resolved to your satisfaction.

9. Personal guarantee of principals of a corporation

Depending on the project and client, you may want to have the principals behind a corporation sign a formal contract as personal guarantors. Another variation is to have the contract in the name of the corporation and its principals as co-covenantors of the contract.

10. Monitor payment trends of clients

Record and monitor the payment patterns of clients so you can watch for trends that may place your fees at risk.

11. Follow-up of late payments

If you see an invoice is more than a week or 10 days overdue, begin the various steps of your collection system immediately.

12. Involving client in assignment

As mentioned previously, try to involve the client in some fashion during each step of the project. By making your client aware of your services, benefits, time and skill, you should minimize problems that could occur because of an unbonded or remote relationship.

e. BILLING FOR SERVICES

Billing requires a system that is carefully designed and effective. It is important to have a third party review your billing procedures before you open your business. Examine your billing procedures on an ongoing basis, especially during the first year, to make sure they are effective. This also gives you an opportunity to review your fee arrangements to make sure you are bringing in the appropriate cash flow for the time you are spending. As mentioned previously, it is important to monitor each client's file to see general trends in your client billing patterns.

Proper records must be maintained that detail the time and expenses incurred so that the bill can be prepared at the appropriate time. You should have an established procedure for regular billing so outstanding accounts are rendered on a regular basis, thereby minimizing collection disputes or bad debts.

When rendering a bill, make sure you send the account either directly to the appropriate person who has the authority to pay your account, or deliver the bill personally to the client. Your style, the client, and the circumstances will determine the most appropriate approach.

You may choose to send a general bill to your client outlining briefly the services performed, the number of hours, the expenses, and the total fee. A note on the bill might say, "detailed particulars are available upon request." See Sample #13 for a general bill and Sample #14 for a detailed bill.

Your bill should be rendered on your consulting firm's stationery showing your name, address, and telephone number. Always use stationery, not a blank piece of paper with your name typed on it. Prepare three copies of the bill. Send the original and a copy to your client and keep a copy for your files.

The wording on your bill should include the following:

(a) The date the bill is mailed

(b) The name and address of the person billed

(c) The phase of the project that has been completed

(d) A detailed outline of the services performed

(e) The consultants or other resource personnel who performed the services

John Smith & Associates

Consultants

123 Main Street
Anytown, Anywhere
(000) 123-4567

Date:
File reference:
Invoice number:
Terms: Net cash

TO: Superior Conglomerate Ltd.
     789 Jones Street
     Anytown, Anywhere

RE: South Branch Computing System Analysis

PROJECT CONSULTANT: John Smith

For professional services provided between July 15 and July 30, 198-:

Review, analysis and recommendations pertaining to
computing system:

26 hours @ $100 $2,600.00

Direct Expenses:

Photocopies, long distance telephone calls, and
automobile mileage   157.50

TOTAL FEES AND DIRECT EXPENSES DUE UPON RECEIPT $2,757.50

Detailed particulars supplied upon request.

Thank you.

Yours truly,

John Smith & Associates

DETAILED INVOICE

John Smith & Associates

Consultants

123 Main Street
Anytown, Anywhere
(000) 123-4567

Date:

File reference:

Invoice number:

Terms: Net cash

TO: Paul Roberts, President
Superior Conglomerate Ltd.
789 Jones Street
Anytown, Anywhere

RE: South Branch Computing System Analysis

PROJECT CONSULTANT: John Smith

Professional Services:

July 15	Attendance at South Branch site to review operations (4 hours)	$ 400.00	
July 17	Meeting with Mr. Roberts to discuss findings (3 hours)	300.00	
July 19	Attendance at South Branch site to analyze operations (5 hours)	500.00	
July 22	Preparation of report and recommendations (8 hours)	800.00	
July 26	Meeting with Mr. Roberts to review recommendations (3 hours)	300.00	
July 30	Prepare final report of recommendations (5 hours)	500.00	
Total professional services (28 hours @ $100)			$2,800.00

Direct Expenses:

Photocopies of 5 progress reports (400 pages @ 20¢)	80.00	
Long distance telephone call of July 20 to Mr. Roberts	17.50	
Automobile mileage (200 miles @ 30¢)	60.00	

Total Direct Expenses: $ 157.50

TOTAL FEES AND EXPENSES DUE AND PAYABLE
UPON RECEIPT $2,957.50

Thank you.

Yours truly,

John Smith & Associates

(f) The date services were performed, and the total hours worked

(g) Total charges for services

(h) Expense column separated and listed underneath the services column
and then totalled

(i) Total of fees and direct expenses payable by client

(j) The date charges are due and payable (if appropriate, make a reference
to "as per letter of agreement (or contract) dated (month/year)"

(k) Use "thank you" or some other positive and appreciative closing remark

(l) Your signature and title

f. WHY CLIENTS PAY LATE

If you have established appropriate precautionary measures and a credit and
billing policy, you should have very few overdue accounts. Overdue accounts will
occur, though, in any practice and understanding your options should minimize
your problems in this area.

There are several common reasons why a client might be late in paying for
consulting services. The client could be indifferent to your deadlines. Some
clients have a sloppy attitude about paying accounts due and are accustomed to
being pressured or reminded frequently before they finally meet their
obligations.

Institutional or government payment procedures sometimes involve a two
or three month wait for accounts to be paid. This type of information is easily
available by asking the right questions before you begin. Your account may be
lost in the maze and require personal attention.

A client may deliberately delay payment in order to save money at your
expense. You save the client interest on working capital if he or she can use your
money for free. This is why you should have an interest factor for overdue

accounts built into your initial contract as well as showing on the statement. If the overdue interest is high enough, that should act as an incentive for the client, to pay on time. If this is in the contract, the client cannot argue that there was no agreement on overdue interest. Rendering a statement with the interest factor noted on it is not in itself evidence of an agreement between the parties on the amount of interest on overdue accounts.

A client may prefer to give priority to other creditors, where pressure to pay is greater.

The client may not have the money. This does not necessarily mean that the client is going out of business, but is cash poor at the moment. The technique to handle this problem is discussed in the next section.

g. COLLECTING LATE PAYMENTS WITHOUT LEGAL ACTION

Because of the expense, time wasted, stress, and uncertainty of legal action, it is preferable to collect as much as you can from clients yourself. Some steps that you may wish to consider are:

(a) Send out a reminder invoice with a courteous comment that the invoice is "overdue and that perhaps it was an oversight or the check is already in the mail."

(b) The alternative to the above is to telephone the accounts payable department or the client directly to ask when the payment can be expected. Courteously ask if there was possibly a misunderstanding, or if they need further information or clarification on any matter. Make sure that you note in the client file the date and time, the person you spoke to at the client's office, a summary of the conversation, and when payment can be expected.

(c) If you have not received payment within a week of the preceeding step, send a letter stating that the account is in arrears and that it is to be paid on the terms of the contract. The alternative is to again telephone the client and ask about the reason for the delay.

(d) Another technique is to ask when the check will be ready. Say that you will be around to pick up the check or will arrange for a courier service to pick it up as soon as they telephone your office to advise that it is ready.

(e) If the client has still not paid, stopping work on the project is another option.

(f) If the client refuses to pay, then legal steps may be required immediately depending upon the size of the bill, the importance of the client, the reasons for non-payment, and the costs of legal action. Alternatively, you may decide to compromise with a client and settle for a reduced payment.

(g) If the client is unable to pay because of cash flow problems or other financial difficulties, you have to assess your options. If the client is not disputing the bill and wishes to have credit, there are basically three options:

- Installment payment plan: the client would agree upon definite dates for payment and would send you the amounts owing upon receipt of statements from you.

- Post-dated checks: you would receive post-dated checks from the client for the agreed period, and in the agreed amount.

- Promissory note: the client would sign a promissory note agreeing to the total amount of the debt and the date on which the debt would be paid. The note should be signed by the principals if the client is a corporation. Interest on the full amount of the debt should be built into the promissory note. It is negotiable whether or not interest is added onto the other two payment plans.

For more ideas and information on debt collection, see *Collection Techniques for the Small Business*, another title in the Self-Counsel series.

h. LEGAL STEPS IF ACCOUNT REMAINS UNPAID

If it is apparent that the client has no intention of paying you, or is objecting to your bill, or is unable to pay you, then legal action must be considered. It is critical that legal action be commenced as quickly as possible after it becomes apparent that you will not be paid by other arrangements. At this stage you are not interested in keeping the client for present or potential future business. You just want to salvage the best of a bad situation. There are basically three legal options available.

1. Collection agency

You may wish to assign the debt to a collection agency for which you will be charged between 25% to 50% of the amount collected. This is better than writing the account off as a total loss. Different agencies have different styles of collection, and one agency may achieve better results with your bad debts than another. If your client pays you directly during the period of the contract with the collection agency, you are obliged to pay the commission to the collection agency. Collection agencies are listed in the yellow pages of the telephone directory.

2. Small claims court

Small claims court is a relatively quick, informal, and inexpensive method of taking your client to court. If you are successful and obtain a judgment against your client, that does not necessarily mean you are going to collect on the judgment. There are additional steps you will have to take, such as garnisheeing the client or filing a judgment against the title of any properties owned by your client. Your client could turn out to be judgment proof.

3. Lawyers

Lawyers can be very effective in the collection of debts if you act promptly and select a lawyer who is experienced in the law and tactics of collecting. Lawyers generally bill on an hourly basis, and the more time expended on attempting to collect a debt, the more money it will cost you without any assurance that you will be successful at trial. If you are successful at trial and do obtain a judgment, your client could be bankrupt or judgment proof in terms of assets. As mentioned previously, the litigation process can be very protacted, uncertain, stressful, and expensive.

i.   BAD DEBTS AND TAXES

Keep an accurate record of any bad debt accounts and the procedures you went through to attempt to collect. Generally you will be allowed to deduct bad debts from your other income, but this is a matter that should be discussed with your accountant as the laws and circumstances can vary.

13

SETTING FEES

There are many ways to set fees: by the hour, by the day, by the month or by the project. The most common fee arrangements (approximately 85% of them) are a daily rate (per diem), fixed price, and fixed price plus expenses.

This chapter discusses in detail how to determine the fee structure most appropriate for your situation and how to give an accurate quote to a prospective client.

a. DAILY BILLING RATE (PER DIEM)

The daily billing rate has three components: labor, overhead, and profit.

1. Labor

The labor daily rate is obtained by taking the average of your most recent annual salary, your current annual salary, a recent job offer annual salary or the prevailing annual salaries in the marketplace for your type of work, and dividing the number by 261. The number 261 is the number of days in the year excluding weekends. For example, if your annual salary is $46,800, the daily labor rate is $46,800 divided by 261 days, equalling $180.

2. Overhead

Before calculating your daily overhead rate, it is important to understand a number of concepts pertaining to overhead and daily billing.

(a) Fixed and variable expenses

Fixed expenses are those expenses for overhead that are constant and do not change based on your volume of workload. Variable expenses are expenses that can change based on volume of workload; they include extra secretarial time to administer various aspects of your office operation, additional postage for promotional or marketing purposes, additional phone calls for promotional or marketing purposes, etc.

(b) Indirect and direct expenses

Indirect expenses are expenses you incur as overhead and the cost of doing business, and are not directly attributable to a specific client. Direct expenses are expenses incurred on behalf of a specific client, and are charged directly to that particular client. These expenses can vary considerably from one consulting project to another. Some examples of direct expenses frequently encountered in consulting are:

- Computer time
- Printing and photocopying
- Postage
- Other consultant's time
- Long distance telephone calls
- Out of town living expenses such as meals, lodging, tips, etc.
- Air travel
- Car rental
- Parking and tolls

When quoting a daily rate, it is a common practice to state "plus expenses" after the daily rate. This includes all the direct expenses that have been outlined, plus any other direct expenses you might incur. If you are quoting your fee on a fixed price basis, direct expenses are incorporated within your estimate cost sheet.

(c) Calculation of overhead

Sample #2 in chapter 3 gave a checklist for determining your monthly overhead. Multiply that figure by 12 to get your annual overhead for the purpose of these calculations. Divide that figure by 168 to get your daily overhead. The number 168 represents the average number of billable days per year you have available. Although there are approximately 21 days a month of potential billable days, the norm is that one-third of that time is used for such non-billable functions such as vacation, sick leave, professional development, administration of the practice, and marketing. Studies have shown that approximately 15 to 20% of an experienced consultant's time is spent on developing and implementing various marketing plans.

The overhead rate is expressed as a per cent of your labor rate by dividing your daily rate for labor by your daily rate for overhead. For example, if $180 is your daily labor rate and your daily overhead rate is $130, the per cent factor is 72.2%, rounded out to 72%. This percent is a guide to the efficiency of your practice as well as a factor you would use for the overhead estimate in a fixed price contract.

3. Profit

Profit is the reason you are in business. It is your reward for taking business risks and the responsibility and pressures of ownership. It is above and beyond your salary for labor. Profit for consultants generally ranges from 10 to 30% of your salary, plus benefits, plus overhead. The amount of profit you decide to build in will depend on many factors, including your expertise, the demand for your services, and the competition in the marketplace.

To calculate your daily billing rate (or per diem), the formula is as follows:

Daily labor rate	$180.00
Daily overhead rate	130.00
Total daily cost	310.00
Profit (15% of $310)	46.50
Total daily billing rate	$356.50
(Rounded out to next highest $25)	$375.00

It is usual for consultants to calculate their daily or hourly billing rate rounded out to the next highest $25 amount. Recent studies have shown that the daily billing rates for all types of consultants range between $300 and $1,200 per day with an average of approximately $700 per day. There are many factors that will determine your rate, such as the economy, competition, experience, repeat business possibilities, and your financial needs.

In the example above, the daily billing rate would be quoted at $375.

When calculating per diem time, normally all time spent on the client project is billed out, including all time recorded for phone calls and travel. Your client should be advised in advance in writing that these charges will be passed on as direct costs. Many consultants prefer to charge the client directly for the time expended on travel on an hourly or per diem basis. Other consultants prefer not to charge directly for travel time. They may work on a client's project while travelling and charge out their work to the client as if working in the office. Another approach is to charge a higher billing rate for work the requires travel. For example, if your normal billing rate is $50 per hour, you may charge $65 per hour for work that requires travel, in addition to a minimum rate of a half-day or a full day for travel regardless of how much time is spent. You have to develop guidelines that meet your client's needs as well as your own.

b. HOURLY RATE

The hourly rate is calculated by dividing the daily rate by eight hours. Some consultants divide by seven hours or nine hours, depending upon their style of operation, but the average is eight hours. For example, a daily billing rate of $375.00 divided by 8 is $46.80 or, rounded out to the next highest $25 amount, $50. You quote your fee as $50 per hour.

Most consultants have a minimum number of hours (such as four hours) for any work contracted on an hourly basis. In addition to a minimum number of hours, some consultants prefer to add an extra factor onto the billing rate of 10 to 20% for the inefficiency of this type of fee arrangement. For example, at 20% extra, the hourly billing rate of $50 plus $10 equals $60 per hour. You should also charge travel time in addition to your hourly rate or minimum charge, depending on the circumstances.

c. CALCULATING A FIXED PRICE QUOTATION

1. Determining a fixed price estimate

Another method of quoting fees is to calculate a flat rate for the entire project. To calculate a fixed fee, a number of factors are determined, such as direct labor (that is, the cost of any consultants or secretarial or clerical staff), overhead (which is the per cent you have previously calculated of the total direct labor cost) and all direct expenses related to that specific consulting project.

The last factor in the formula of calculating a fixed rate estimate is the profit factor. In each situation you determine what you believe to be a fair profit for the risk, the time involved, the skill, the competition, your need for the job, and the ongoing work that might arise from this project. The profit is a per cent of the total of the preceeding expenses; that is, direct labor, overhead, and direct expenses. You then have calculated the total fixed price to quote to your client. Normally, your costing sheet is not shown to the client, only the total price. An example of a fixed price costing sheet is shown in Sample #15.

A fixed fee arrangement is often preferred by a client, as the total cost of the project can be budgeted and planned. The risk is the consultant's. If you have a budget overrun, you could lose a lot of money or go out of business. If you are very efficient and accurate in your costing of the fixed price and the management of the project, you could obtain the reward of an underrun which means a higher profit margin.

A fixed fee should only be used when you have effective cost control of the project, and are able to estimate your time and costs with a high degree of accuracy and experience. It is very risky to propose a fixed price contract for projects with which you have little experience, especially if the assignment is a unique or complex one.

If you are very experienced in a certain area, you would probably prefer a fixed price contract due to the efficiency of your mode of operation. In other words, because of your expertise and efficiency, you might not make as much on an hourly per diem basis as you could make by negotiating a fixed price.

2. Tips on preparing fixed price estimates

Because of the risk involved in a fixed price contract, many consultants avoid that type of fee arrangement if possible. In many cases though, a client requires a fixed price because that is their style of operation, or a government contract might be involved which frequently entails a fixed price arrangement. In order to minimize the risk of an overrun, that is, costs exceeding your revenue, and to increase your confidence in the preparation of estimates, the following guidelines are provided:

(a) A precise and specific definition of the project must be obtained. This is either obtained from the client, for example, in government projects where considerable detail is provided for costing purposes; or, the consultant must obtain as much information from the client as required to enable a detailed reconstruction of the entire project requirement. This involves having a checklist of questions that you ask the client to

SAMPLE #15
FIXED PRICE COSTING SHEET

DIRECT LABOR		
Senior consultant (15 days at $300)	$4,500	
Senior consultant: B. Smith ($525 per day) 3 × $525	1,575	
Junior consultant (7 days at $150)	1,050	
Secretarial (12 days at $60)	720	
TOTAL DIRECT LABOR		$ 7,845
DIRECT EXPENSES		
Air fares (5 x $191) (3 x $30) (1 x $61)	$1,106	
Automobile mileage (550 x .22)	121	
Entertainment	375	
Postage	190	
Printing and photocopying	550	
Rental cars	430	
Telephone	210	
Miscellaneous	470	
TOTAL DIRECT EXPENSES		3,452
SUBTOTAL		11,297
PROFIT (15%)		1,695
TOTAL FIXED PRICE		$12,992

ensure you have not forgotten any of the key components of the contract.

(b) It is helpful to draw a functional flow diagram (FFD) showing the interconnecting parts and stages of the project. This could be the same functional flow diagram you include in your proposal, or a less detailed one.

(c) Once you have determined the various skills and roles required of you for the project, list them all in order of sequential priority of the activities or stages. After you have listed each of the areas, do a break-down of the stages within each of those areas. If you need more detail to assess the amount of time and direct expense, continue breaking down each of the sub-components into the various parts.

(d) Use a bid sheet when pricing a project. Each function of the project should be outlined and the direct labor and direct expense costs allocated.

(e) The advantages of the detailed costing, apart from a higher degree of accuracy, is the ability to be more flexible with your client. For example, if your client rejects your first fixed price proposal as being outside the budget allotted, you could reduce your estimate by reviewing your costing sheet in areas that still allow you to perform the overall project. You maintain your credibility with your client by not discounting your prices because of pressure from the client or your financial need. You are adjusting the price downward as a direct outcome of reducing the expense and time you will be putting into the project.

(f) Before you submit your bid to a client, make sure you have a person experienced in bidding in the area that you are doing your consulting work. Have your detailed costing sheet reviewed to find any areas you may have missed or that could be improved.

d. FIXED PRICE PLUS EXPENSES

A fixed price plus expenses fee arrangement is quite common; it is used when a fixed price is desired by both parties but expenses cannot be calculated with certainty. For example, you may have an estimate for the number of trips required, but there could be factors outside your control which could affect that financial outlay and therefore your costing. You should estimate the direct expenses for the benefit of your client, but the contract would clearly state that the client is responsible for all direct expenses.

e. CONTINGENCY FEE

In a contingency fee arrangement you do not receive any income unless you perform the objective successfully. The normal procedure is that you obtain a percentage of the final benefit that the client receives. For example, if you are skilled at appealing on behalf of a client a property reassessment tax, and you save your client considerable money, then you receive a portion of the saving.

The advantage to the client of this arrangement is the lack of risk — if taxes are not reduced, no fee is paid to the consultant. It is therefore an effective marketing device for clients who would otherwise not want to commit themselves to a consultant. From a consultant's viewpoint, considerable money can be made, much greater than the profit earned under the traditional consulting fee arrangements.

Many professional associations consider contingency fees unethical because of the risk of conflict of interest for the consultant. For example, if a consultant is retained to find a key executive for a client and performs an executive search, the final recommendation could be a biased one to obtain the commission payment.

f. PERCENTAGE FEE

A percentage fee is a common arrangement for engineers and architects on construction projects. Normally a uniform percentage is applied to the cost of the project. Percentage fees are not dependent on a successful result of the performance of a service, which makes them different from contingent fees.

g. PROJECT VALUE FEES

There are times when a consultant has unique and effective skills in a given situation, and thereby saves the client considerable money. The client is usually charged a substantially higher fee than a normal hourly rate. It is not uncommon for lawyers to apply this method. For example, a lawyer, through skill and experience and tactical negotiating techniques, might purchase a business at a considerable savings to the client. The lawyer may have spent only 15 hours at $150 per hour on the file, but saved the client $2 million. Because of the "value" obtained by the client the lawyer charges a substantially higher fee — possibly five or ten times more than the actual time spent.

h. RETAINER FEES

A retainer relationship, involves a consultant being "on call" either for continuing services, or to ensure that he or she is available when needed. The retainer is normally a fixed amount of money paid to the consultant every month. The consultant keeps track of the time spent and a running balance of the account, and bills for any excess. An account is rendered every month for extra time spent over and above the monthly retainer.

Another type of arrangement might involve not submitting additional accounts until the end of the retainer period, at which time any overage would be made up. A third variation could be that you are committed in your retainer arrangement to providing a certain amount of service every month. If you underestimated the amount of the monthly time involved, you would be then paid the extra time per month.

If you have an "on call" arrangement with the client, and therefore you are unable to commit yourself to other projects, the client would pay the fixed amount every month for the privilege of having you on call, whether or not your services were used. This could be whatever you negotiated; for example, 25 to 50% of your average monthly billable time. In addition to the on call retainer, when you perform services for the client you would bill out at your hourly or daily rate, depending upon the nature of your arrangement.

i. EQUITY FEES

If a client is having difficulty in a business venture and you have skills in obtaining financing or business management, a fee could be negotiated in the form of equity or percentage of the shares in the company. This is normally negotiated when the client lacks the financial resources to pay for your time. The risk for the consultant and the business is a high one so the equity arrangement would have to be very attractive to justify the risk, depending upon the situation.

The problem with an equity fee arrangement is that it changes your role from a consultant to a part owner. You could lose your ability to be an objective consultant due to your vested interest in the outcome of your advice. It would be prudent, due to potential conflict of interest, to remove yourself from the situation by either selling out your interest once you have received it, or resigning as a consultant.

j. UTILIZATION RATE

The utilization rate tells you how efficient you are; that is, the cost/benefit factor. It tells you the percentage of your total working hours that you bill to clients. To determine the utilization rate, divide the number of billable hours by the number of total working hours available. For example, if you assume a 40-hour work week and allow two weeks' vacation, you would have approximately 2,000 total work hours available each year. If you divide 1,000 hours of billing to clients each year by 2,000 you have 50% utilization rate. If you consult part-time at 12 hours per week and you bill for 4 hours each week, then your utilization rate is 33.3%.

Your utilization rate quickly informs you how much of your time clients are directly paying for and how much you must absorb as overhead. The fewer hours you bill, the more you must charge per hour, or reduce your overhead; the more hours you bill, the less you need to charge to maintain your profit level. You can see how important it is to keep an accurate record of how all your time is spent when operating a consulting practice, so that you can accurately and graphically see how efficiently (or inefficiently) you are operating.

k. VARYING YOUR FEES

The fees you quote a client can vary depending on various factors. As mentioned earlier, you should consider factors as: your experience, the ability of the client to pay, the future benefit of ongoing work the client might provide, your need for cash flow, and the different regional areas for which you are submitting a consulting proposal.

If you are submitting a proposal outside your region, you should check out the cost of doing business in that area. Is it more or less expensive than your own region? Check on your competitors and their rates within the region you are considering. If the local rates are higher, consider raising your rates to meet local schedules. If the rates are lower, consider reducing your rates, but only with a very clear analysis of the benefit and profit. The rates might be too low to be attractive. It is important that you go through these steps, as a prospective client will be able to detect inadequate preparation if your costing does not reflect local variances and customs.

l. INCREASING FEES

From time to time you will want to increase your fees. This could be based on your regular monthly, quarterly or other review of your cash flow statements, profit and loss statements or projected needs. Your utilization rate, as described earlier, is also a factor.

If you are considering increasing fees, it is tactically a good idea to do it at a fixed time every year, such as January 1. You should also attempt to notify your clients at least three months in advance, in writing, of your intention to increase your fees. Include a brief explanation about the reasons, such as an increase in costs, if appropriate. Invite the client to contact you if there are any questions. It is important, for obvious reasons, to keep the increase competitive.

m. INCREASING PROFITS WITHOUT INCREASING FEES

There are many ways you can increase your profits apart from raising fees. Naturally clients are not always going to appreciate your reasons for increasing your fees, so through careful tactics other effective methods could be used to increase your profits. Some methods you may wish to consider are as follows:

- Keep your overall fixed overhead down. Review all the ways of saving costs on space, telephone, and personnel discussed earlier.

- Use company cars, space, and supplies wherever possible.

- Obtain the client's agreement to supply necessary support services such as secretarial and clerical, mail rooms, postage, delivery service, and other support services and personnel. This will keep your administration costs down.

- Obtain approval to charge authorized purchases pertaining to the project to the client.

- Keep an accurate record of all out-of-pocket expenses incurred pertaining to the client's project, document them, and bill for them properly.

- Arrange with the client to pay you in advance for entertaiment or travel expenses you anticipate. That way you can use the client's money and provide an accounting for any extra funds.

- If you are consulting on an hourly basis, attempt to arrange to be at your client's office or project for a full day if possible, rather than a portion of the day.

- Transportation costs and time of travel are not always accurately reflected in the adjustments with the client. Naturally you would attempt to spend the minimum number of hours at a higher hourly rate, but these factors may not cover your commuting time.

- Determine a minimum fee requirement. The time and costs of a proposal, and the administrative work required by a project, will dictate a minimum fee and profit before you make a proposal.

- Avoid giving away free consulting. There are techniques to avoid giving away your time, which is worth money. This will increase your effective utilization rate and therefore increase profits. The various ways of avoiding free consulting are covered in chapter 17.

- Increase your rates for work requested outside of regular business hours. A premium fee should be charged for work performed on the weekends or evenings or part of a day. This suggestion also applies when clients ask that their project be given priority over other projects.

- Consider obtaining advance payment on account for projected initial or total disbursements if they are considerable. The deposit can be collecting interest for your benefit. As discussed previously, you should consider negotiating in advance for a sizable deposit if your services are in demand and you are expending time for the client at the expense of other client work you could do.

- Review your credit policy regularly. If you extend credit, make sure your receivables are promptly collected; otherwise you will be paying more interest to the bank on your operating line of credit loan.

- Attempt to minimize bad debts by adopting the various procedures suggested in chapter 12, with modifications for your own situation and after your lawyer's advice. Eliminating bad debts is a very effective way of increasing your profits.

- Consider negotiating a bonus with a client for meeting contract needs. For example. if you complete a project for less than the amount allocated in the budget, you could negotiate a percentage of the saving. If your client has deadline schedules, you could agree to give the project priority, which would involve considerable overtime and other disruptions for you and negotiate a bonus for the number of days you are ahead of the deadline.

- Consider negotiating a "value of the project" fee or a contingency fee arrangement if the circumstances and the nature of your consulting practice make this approach feasible. You could therefore increase your profit without spending additional time by receiving a higher return due to your skill, knowledge of the industry or tactical or negotiating abilities.

14

DETERMINING MARKET OPPORTUNITIES

Before determining market opportunities and identifying clients with accuracy and success, various matters have to be considered.

You have to be very certain in your own mind of your area or areas of specialization. It is impossible to target your market without this basic information. Review the exercises in chapter 2 to determine your specific skills, talents, and attributes, and attempt to visualize the market that was suited to your abilities. It is important to avoid the tendency to be too restrictive in your view of the market for your services. Look for a wide spectrum to apply your services in vertical and horizontal markets and in both the public and private sector. Identify common themes and processes. Know why there is a demand for consulting services, so you can aim your marketing at those concerns when targeting prospective clients.

Thorough research is required to educate yourself and stimulate your mind on the wide range of possibilities. Read selected newspapers, magazines, and trade journals on a regular basis, and look for consulting opportunities created by political, economic, and social changes affecting your area of expertise and interest.

The next chapter discusses marketing techniques in more detail. This chapter is intended to provide a brief overview of the private and public sector markets and the possibility of market opportunities.

a. PRIVATE SECTOR OPPORTUNITIES

There are numerous opportunities in the private sector. By being aware of the issues and problems and solutions in your service area, it will be easier for you to identify and think of opportunities every time you are exposed to information through personal communication, television, radio, newspaper, magazines, trade journals or books. The habit of training yourself to be aware of marketing opportunities at all times is essential.

It is important to understand the motivating factors that will cause a potential client to want your services. You might be very aware of the needs of your service within your specialty area, but a client who does not recognize that your service is needed will not be receptive to your offer of assistance.

There are many reasons that motivate a client to retain a consultant, but three of the basic reasons are: to obtain information, to save time, and to save money. If you can visualize the ways you can save a client time and money, and provide the most current and accurate information in the client's area of interest and need, market opportunities in the private sector will be considerable.

1. Individuals

Individuals buy the services of consultants in a wide variety of fields. A walk through the yellow pages of your telephone directory should provide a good example. Advice on how to save money or how to make money is fairly common. In this instance, the target market is anyone in the higher earning bracket, including executives and professionals. Some examples of consultants in this area are tax consultants, financial consultants, investment consultants, and real estate consultants. Other consulting areas include interior design and fashion.

2. Small businesses

Small businesses provide an excellent client base for a new consultant. The failure rate of small businesses is very high. Lack of knowledge by the small business owner/operator in important areas of small business management is often a factor. If your skills include small business management and how to make money or save money for a small business owner, you can find a market. There are numerous books available on small business management that will provide ideas for you. Some are included in the Bibliography.

Various techniques can be used to attract small business clients. You can offer a fee based on percentage of savings or profits that occur as a result of your advice. Naturally, you would have to have a measurable basis for showing the positive benefits that your advice has created. A percentage fee is a good marketing device. It shows confidence in yourself, and it is a difficult offer to refuse as your payment is based on performance.

Another need of small businesses is to raise funds, either through the venture capital market, commercial banks or government grants and loans. Most small businesses go through growing pains. Wherever business growth occurs, problems occur, and wherever problems occur, a need exists for solutions.

3. Medium size businesses

There is a high demand for consultants in medium size businesses. Companies often hire experts as required instead of hiring staff. Staff involves the related costs of training, benefit packages, and long-term commitments for possibly short-term needs. Businesses are vulnerable to economic changes, and their survival is based on keeping overheads low and making a profit. Any areas of need you can identify to increase efficiency and productivity and sales, and decrease overhead and losses will create a demand for your services.

Medium size businesses, as well, are constantly going through various stages of growth with all the predictable problems involved.

The advantage of dealing with a medium size business is that projects tend to be more lucrative. There is also a greater chance of repeat business. Another advantage is that the decision-makers are generally more sophisticated, better able to see the need more readily, more accustomed to dealing with consultants, and able to respond more quickly on proposals.

4. Large companies

It is more difficult to obtain contracts from larger companies. Many large companies prefer dealing with large consulting firms or well-known consultants with considerable experience and contacts.

Because of the money available in larger businesses, consulting opportunities do exist, particularly in the area of temporary technical assistance. It is common for consultants to large companies to have developed their experience and confidence with smaller companies and medium size companies before marketing the larger companies.

b. PUBLIC SECTOR

Government is a major user of consulting services. Marketing opportunities are available in various forms in the public sector. You can submit a solicited or unsolicited proposal and attempt to get the contract directly. You can indirectly benefit from government by sub-contracting with other companies who have been awarded the main contract. An additional way of making money through government is as a grants consultant assisting organizations or businesses to obtain grants or subsidies.

If you are considering government as a source of business, you should be aware of the various ways of obtaining contacts or information to assist you. You should also have an understanding of the way the government approval system operates.

1. Making contacts and obtaining information

There are various steps you can take to obtain the necessary information and make the necessary contacts to assist you in your government dealings.

(a) Read government advertisements and publications pertaining to your areas of interest. Appendix 1 is an extensive summary of Canadian and U.S. government sources of information.

(b) Place your name on the government mailing list. There are numerous government departments and you can request that your name be placed on each list to receive all relevant information, including proposed procurements and contracts awarded relating to your field.

(c) Attempt to have your name placed on the government sourcing list as a consultant in various specialty areas. When the government is looking, your name should come to their attention. There are various computerized sourcing lists throughout the departments of government; make sure that your name is on all the ones that relate to your areas of interest.

(d) Contact government contract officers. Most government contracts are awarded at the department or agency level where the specific needs are best known and money has been allocated. The phone book has listings for various branches of government. The public library has updated lists of all the key government departments, individuals, their titles and phone numbers. Once you have obtained the correct department, ask to speak to the contract officer who can provide you with further background.

(e) Visit government departments and agencies. After you have submitted your resume to various government departments, you may wish to meet the person in charge of contracts approval and introduce yourself. This may or may not be appropriate or possible, depending on your geographic location and government policy. Keeping contact with the key person who could award a contract shows your interest in keeping your name current. It also demonstrates initiative and confidence. On the other hand, it could cause irritation or you could have a personality conflict.

(f) Contact large consulting firms that are the recipients of government contracts and require additional consulting assistance for those contracts.

(g) Contact other companies that have recently received a government contract. You can obtain government award publications, or view them in the public library. These are published weekly and announce all the contracts that have been awarded, who received the contract, and the amount and nature of the services to be performed. With this information, you can determine what sub-contracting opportunities might be available in your area of specialty, and immediately contact the companies concerned.

(h) If you have friends or acquaintances who work in government, tell them you are looking for consulting assignments in your specialty. You should also provide them with your resume and brochure if possible. They might be in a position to inform you if they hear of an agency in need of your services. You might therefore hear of a need before the department has advertised for services or selected a consultant. You can then submit an unsolicited proposal.

2. Understanding the government approval system

The government approval system is very formal and bureaucratic in its operation. Most government contracts are from solicited proposals, whereas in the private sector, submitting an unsolicited proposal is the most common method. The general procedure for government approval is given below. The procedure is the same for any level of government (i.e., municipal, state/provincial, federal).

(a) A government department head or agency requiring consulting service assigns personnel to an internal search to see if the service can be performed in-house.

(b) If no civil service employee is available to perform the work, a request for proposal is advertised, proposals are received, and the consultant is eventually selected. It is quite common that consultants are "pre-selected" before the closing date of the advertisement. This is because the consultant may already be on the source list and be known as best suited for the project. The advertisement is a required government formality.

(c) The government department drafts a contract and submits it to the consultant for review and signature.

(d) The signed contract is reviewed and approved again by the government's legal department.

(e) A contract is forwarded to the chief administrative officer of the division for approval.

(f) The contract and specifications are forwarded to a government purchaser for approval.

(g) The contract and fee schedule are forwarded to the government controller to verify that funds are available and have been set aside to honor the payment commitment.

(h) Notification of formal approval is sent to the consultant to begin the consulting services within the terms of the contract.

(i) Work begins and is completed.

(j) Payment is received at the end of the project or throughout the project, depending on the terms of the contract. Many government departments are slow in paying due to their bureaucratic nature and requirements within the system for approval before payment. As this may cause cash flow difficulties for you, you should make arrangements for progress payments if at all possible. If necessary you can get a bank loan for your cash flow needs based on the strength of a government contract.

c. GRANT CONSULTING

A grants consultant attempts to obtain grants, loans or subsidies for a client. The federal government and its various agencies award large sums of money to eligible applicants. The process followed by a grants consultant is as follows:

(a) The consultant learns as much as possible about the sources of funding, the amount of funding, the procedures required, and the key contact people. The consultant contacts the approval officer and obtains information on the appropriate or desired detail and format for successful applications.

(b) The consultant determines the potential target market and the names of the firms and individuals who could be future contacts.

(c) A personal letter with brochures is sent to the key people, followed by a telephone call and meeting, if possible.

(d) The consultant identifies the specific needs of the organization or company in the interview process. The interview process is similar to that described in chapter 16.

(e) The consultant advises the organization of the availability of government funds, and the consultant's expertise in obtaining them. Most organizations and businesses do not have people who realize that money is available or know how to effectively submit an application to obtain it. The consultant performs the analysis and all the necessary detail for documentation, and prepares the application for signature by an authorized representative of the organization or company.

(f) The consultant normally takes an administration fee which is a negotiated percentage of the amount awarded. The client therefore has an incentive to deal with the consultant, because the consultant's fee is based on performance only and paid from the funds received.

(g) The consultant could also be responsible for coordinating the implementation of the program on which the funding was based, if applicable.

(h) Once a grants consultant has succeeded with one group, marketing to all other organizations similar to that group can be effectively performed.

See Appendix 3 for a list of publications available on current government funding.

15

MARKETING YOUR CONSULTING SERVICES

a. INTRODUCTION

Marketing is an essential process for success in the consulting business. Marketing is a process that involves a wide spectrum of activities, ultimately directed at convincing prospective clients that their needs can be met and their problems can be solved through your specific services. Marketing is the stimulus that creates an awareness and demand for your services. Selling is a part of the marketing program. It is intended to result in a consulting assignment by means of personal interaction begun at the initial interview and maintained during and after the assignment.

The dynamics of the marketing/selling stages have to be clearly understood and carefully cultivated by the consultant. For example, when you are marketing yourself, you have to carefully calculate the image that you want to project when you are packaging your product, that is, yourself, and your services. You and your marketing efforts must project authority, confidence, friendliness, candor, expertise, competence, and leadership.

Many consultants fail, or maintain a marginal income because of poor marketing. Consultants frequently do not appreciate the necessity of marketing, do not know how to market, do not like to market, do not want to market or do not take the time to market.

This chapter will help you understand the various techniques required to build your image as an expert or authority, thereby creating a demand for your services. The next chapter will cover some of the personal selling techniques involved in the first interview. Once your marketing plan has stimulated the interest, the next step is to close the contract.

b. MARKETING PLAN

A summary of the factors that go into your marketing plan follows:

  (a) Define your skills and services. This is covered in chapter 2. You should have a clear idea now of the nature of services you will be offering potential clients. You may have decided on just one particular area of interest and specialty, or you may have decided on several areas that you will promote as unique areas, either to the same client or to different categories of clients.

  (b) Targeting prospective clients. Identifying possible client consulting opportunities is the next step in the marketing plan. This was covered in the last chapter.

(c) Make the public and potential clients aware of your services and create a demand. The various techniques required for this step are covered in the next section.

(d) Respond to inquiries with direct client meeting. Naturally, once interest has been shown by a prospective client due to your effective marketing, your next step is to quickly follow up on the lead, personally see the client, if possible, attempt to ascertain the client's precise needs and determine how to remedy the problem.

(e) Prepare a proposal. This step follows the preceeding one, confirms the client meeting and outlines what you intend to do, how, for how much, and when. You can only write a convincing proposal after you have had an opportunity to ascertain the client's needs and the benefits that you can provide.

(f) Perform the project. This is the purpose of the whole marketing exercise — to end up with a client so you can provide your service, generate revenue, and make a profit.

(g) Follow-up is the final step in the marketing plan. If you did not obtain a contract after your previous attempts to market, you should maintain some follow-up procedure in case the client needs your services in the future. Possibly there were budget restraints the first time.

If you were able to obtain a contract and provide a service, you should have a follow-up routine for that client to encourage repeat business. It is important to keep communication open with the client in various ways for goodwill and possible referral business.

c. MARKETING TECHNIQUES

The following suggestions describe traditional as well as unusual ways of marketing consulting services. Many of the techniques cost little or nothing except for your time. Whether you use just a few of the techniques or all of the techniques depends on your style, your priorities, the nature of your service and your type of clientele.

1. Newspaper

Most consultants do not use newspapers as a source of advertising for their services. It is looked upon as unprofessional by many. Most clients select a consultant by reputation. But it depends on the nature of your consulting business. For example, if you specialize in small business cash flow problems, and in your region there are small businesses with problems, you might put a tasteful, professional advertisement in the display ads in the business section or in the classified section to stimulate interest.

2. Advertising in trade or professional journals

The advantage of advertising in these publications is the very specialized market you reach as the readers could all be potential prospects. Therefore, the cost/benefit feature of this form of advertising can be low. You should attempt to get all the trade and professional journals related to your areas of skill and services, and familiarize yourself with the format and the nature of journal ads.

3. Directories

There are many excellent reference guides to technical, professional, and trade organizations and associations. Your public library might have the *Encyclopedia of Associations* and *The National Trade and Professional Associations Directory*. Many of the organizations listed in the directories publish annual directories of their memberships.

Of the organizations that have directories, approximately half of them will include your name in their directory free of charge as a consultant in that area of interest. Most of the other organizations have paid advertising available, which could be of benefit if the target group is read by a prime segment of your market.

For additional sources of information on directories, refer to the Bibliography and Appendix 1.

4. Brochures

Brochures are a very important part of marketing your practice. There are many ways to use a brochure.

(a) Leave the brochure with a prospective client after a face-to-face meeting.

(b) Mail the brochure after a written or formal request for further information.

(c) Send the brochure in a direct mail campaign targeted to prospective clients.

(d) Distribute the brochure at a seminar or presentation you are giving.

(e) Send the brochure out the next day to those attending a seminar or presentation as a form of follow-up communication.

Keep in mind that your brochure is probably the first contact a prospective client has with you and the services you offer. The reaction to the brochure may be positive or negative, depending upon its format, content, and quality. Following are some tips on preparing a brochure.

(a) As the first impression of the brochure is critical, it is important that the layout, graphics, and paper be of first quality. You want to stimulate a desire in the recipient to retain you as a consultant, or at least to inquire further.

(b) Use an 8½″ x 11″ size of paper that will have three folds and six panels. Obtain advice from typesetters and graphic artists and printers before you finish your draft. Seek out comparative opinions and quotes until you are satisfied with the quality and cost offered.

(c) The phrasing of the text should reflect a confident, positive, dynamic yet professional tone. Have the spelling, grammar, syntax, and style of your text reviewed by someone with skills in that area.

(d) The text should be concise, clear, and brief. Text in point form can be easily read. Refrain from using large or complicated words. Keep the words simple and direct. Focus on the benefits that a prospective client will receive from your services. Draft the text from the viewpoint of the client's needs.

(e) Provide information on the history of your business, the nature of your business, your clientele, and the type of services you perform. Explain why a particular service might be required. Explain or list the benefits that you can give to provide the service and meet the need or resolve the problem. Think of previous clients who benefitted from your advice and assistance.

(f) List your academic and professional achievements and experiences.

(g) Do not list your associates unless you have a long-standing relationship or know that they will be staying with you for an extended time. Refer to the resource base of talent your firm offers. You may wish to itemize the skills that are provided by key associates.

(h) If appropriate, a number of testimonials from clients, or a list of important clients, could be included in the brochure.

(i) Many consultants prefer not to have their photograph in the brochure, as a matter of personal choice and style. The reaction of a potential client to your photograph could be negative or positive based on your picture alone. The design of the brochure should be consistent with your stationery and business cards.

(j) Before you have the brochure printed, have a number of your friends, relatives, and business associates look at the draft copy of the brochure and obtain their candid feedback.

5. Direct mail

Direct mail can be a very effective means of making potential clients aware of and interested in your services. There are several advantages to direct mail: the cost is flexible, the sales message can be personalized to the needs of that particular target group, and the letters can be individually addressed to specific persons on a word processor. An important cost/benefit aspect is the controlled circulation to a very select audience.

An integral part of direct mail marketing is the development or rental of a mailing list. There are many sources of rental lists. The major ones are Standard

Rates and Data Service, and Dun and Bradstreet. Both these companies have extensive mailing lists available for the United States and Canada. The lists include names, addresses, and postal/zip codes broken down into specific categories and regions.

Mailing lists are generally rented for one-time use, and are "seeded" by means of fictitious companies or individuals to ensure you do not use the list more than the time contracted. For further information, look under "direct mail" in the yellow pages.

The various directories of organizations related to your specialty may also rent or sell mailing lists. The advantage of this type of mailing list is that prospective clients may be members of the organization that publishes the directory. You would therefore be targeting your services to your specific trade or interest market.

There are brokers who represent all the major direct mail marketing companies. For a fee, they will determine the best mix of mailing lists for your purposes, depending upon the amount of money you are prepared to budget for the purpose. The broker will obtain the best rates for you and charge you a fee.

It is important to keep a record of all contacts you make, and record the names and particulars. All clients should be added to your mailing list.

It is difficult to estimate with certainty, but approximately 1 to 4% of direct mail marketing ultimately ends up as consulting assignments. Many factors will determine your response rate, such as the type of consulting service you provide, the economic climate at the time, the cyclical or seasonal demand for your type of service, and the techniques and format you use in the direct mail approach.

There are various stages involved in direct mailing, all of which are equally important to obtain the desired objective. The basic steps are as follows:

(a) Your first mailing should be within the regional area you can realistically service. It is also an opportunity to test market and analyze the effectiveness of your mailings without spending a large sum of money.

(b) Your mailing should consist of a personalized cover letter (on a word processor if available) and sent directly to the key person who is the decision-maker. Use quality letterhead stationery to create a professional impression. Depending upon the circumstances, you might also enclose your business card. Enclose a copy of your brochure with your letter. Outline briefly the services you offer and the benefits that will be obtained by the prospective client. State that you will contact the client in 10 calendar (or business) days to answer any questions and discuss the matter further at that time.

(c) Keep an accurate filing system of all prospective clients you intend to follow-up. List all pertinent information on the card so you can review it and familiarize yourself with it before you contact the client. Note the date in your daily diary or calendar to remind you to contact the prospective client on that date.

(d) Follow-up with a telephone call 10 days after you mail the letter. This will create a positive impression with the client with regard to your administration and professionalism. Follow the phone call with a visit to the prospective client if circumstances allow. The next chapter outlines other procedures and techniques to follow before, during, and after the first meeting with the prospective client.

(e) If the response to your mailing is poor, thoroughly review all your techniques and format. This includes the direct mail target group, cover letter, brochure, telephone techniques, and meetings.

(f) Constantly revise, refine, and upgrade your mailing list with new prospects.

(g) Send out mailings on a quarterly basis (or more often), as your finances, marketing plan, and other circumstances dictate. This will remind people of your services and expertise, and the repetition ultimately does have an effect. When sending out repetitive mailings, consider enclosing a newsletter, which you could easily prepare, and copies of any articles or other papers pertaining to the industry that is your target base. You may want to have a tear-off feature in the newsletter offering a free subscription to the newsletter if a request is sent to be kept on the mailing list. This way you should be able to track the response. Over time, a large portion of qualified prospects should respond to regular and consistent promotional efforts.

6. Contact network

You need to develop a contact network for future prospects and mailing list purposes. It is a very effective way to acquire clients by referral. Studies have shown that a high percent of a consultant's clientele comes from referrals through a contact network or from satisfied clients. A contact network is a collection of relatives, associates, and acquaintances who will facilitate your prospects of being accepted by an organization or individual who needs your services.

You already have many and you can cultivate many more. A partial list includes past and present clients, employees, professional colleagues, business associates, bankers, lawyers, accountants, friends, neighbors, and relatives. Also included are contacts you develop in associations and religious, professional, trade, business or other organizations. If you sit down and list everyone you know who comes to mind as a potential contact, the list will be longer than you think.

Developing the contact network is the most effective and inexpensive way of increasing your exposure and credibility. Continually update your network by adding leads and other contacts to your mailing list.

7. Membership in professional, trade or business associations

Joining a group and then actively participating in meetings and other functions is an effective means of developing leads. Attempt to attend meetings on a regular basis and get involved in discussions. Evaluate a group or association on the basis of potential consulting prospects who are active in the association. You want to look for members who are likely to give you consulting opportunities. Because of the time commitment involved to develop your reputation within an organization, you must be very selective in your membership. Limit your memberships to one or two. You may wish to consider such civic or trade organizations or associations as the Chamber of Commerce, Rotarians, Kiwanis, or associations directly related to your service area. Obtain a list of all the members of the organization and review the list thoroughly. Most lists provide the name, position and company, type of business or profession of the member, and address.

8. Donating your services

You may wish to donate some consulting time and commitment to a worthwhile nonprofit organization as a gesture of goodwill. Naturally, you have to be very cautious about the time involved relative to the potential benefit, but your services without charge can enhance your image and result directly or indirectly in referrals.

9. Attending public and professional meetings

Consider attending meetings covering a subject directly or indirectly related to your field of expertise. You want to see and be seen. Plan to contribute your opinion, if appropriate, in a well-planned, concise, and intelligent fashion. Prospective clients could be attending the meeting. Attempt to identify and talk to people you believe are worthwhile contacts. There are many meetings held on an ongoing basis, such as city council meetings, federal commissions, public hearings on specific areas of concern, and appeal board meetings.

10. Lectures

Many organizations or associations need speakers for breakfast, luncheon or dinner meetings, conferences or conventions. Look in the yellow pages of your telephone directly under "associations" to obtain various names. Also, review directories of associations available at your local library. Two publications, in particular, are: *National Trade Professional Associations and Labor Unions of the U.S. and Canada* and *Directory of Associations of Canada*.

When you contact the program chairperson, offer your services for free, and advise him or her that you have a number of prepared talks you believe would be of particular interest to the membership. Mention that your subject areas are topical and interesting, and your talk can be between 10 and 30 minutes long. This is the normal range of time required for a speaker. Ask about the mix of membership and the number of members who normally attend meetings. Attempt to get in advance a list of members to review so that you can direct your comments more accurately toward your group.

It is helpful to have ready two or three 10 to 20 minute presentations with supporting material. You will then be available on short notice for any presentation.

The object of the presentation is not to make money, but to obtain contacts and increase your credibility and exposure for future consulting opportunities. Those who attend the presentation will probably tell their friends or acquaintances about you if your presentation is interesting. Make sure you tell the audience that you are a consultant. During your presentation you can give a number of examples or anecdotes based on your experiences. This will reinforce your image as an expert. People will remember you better by the examples or stories that you relate.

Books related to public speaking and effective presentations are listed in the Bibliography. You may also wish to consider Dale Carnegie courses, Toastmasters membership or public speaking workshops to enhance your communication ability.

11. Teaching

There are many opportunities to offer your services as a teacher for school board adult education classes or university or community college continuing education courses. You generally get paid for your time, but ideally the students who attend the course will be potential clients or will recommend you to friends or associates. Make sure that you teach adults only to maximize the potential benefit. You are primarily looking for credibility, exposure, and contacts. The preparation required to teach a course also keeps you current on your subject area.

12. Seminars and workshops

Depending upon your area of expertise and the size of your target market, you may wish to consider offering your own seminar or workshop. You can offer the seminar free, or at a nominal charge. The people who attend are excellent potential clients. You should try to select a subject that allows you to provide a practical overview of important tips and ideas within your specialty area. You can promote your seminar through your direct mail list. Allow four to eight weeks lead time to ensure that people can schedule in your seminar.

Other items to consider are the length of the seminar, the location, the time, whether day or evening, when refreshments would be served, if any, and the number of people you can accommodate. Make sure your announcement states that it is limited, advance registration only.

In your announcement you can request that registration be made by telephone one week in advance of the seminar. This will give you some idea as to the response, and assist you in the preparation of your material.

You may also wish to consider the free advertising possibilities in the local newspaper and other monthly or weekly publications. If you allow yourself enough lead time, you should be able to conduct the seminar at a cost of $100 to $500. Depending upon the number of people and the amount you are charging, you could break even on the seminar.

If you have a deadline for registration one week before the seminar, and not enough people appear to be interested, you can try to negotiate a cancellation arrangement with the hotel facility by paying a portion of the room rent, or possibly nothing at all if the hotel is able to rebook the facility.

Make sure you distribute your brochures, newsletters, and any other appropriate material at the seminar. Develop a seminar evaluation form with questions that will provide a good source of biographical information on the participants, opinions of you and your seminar topic through means of rating scales, and space for additional comments. Provide a coupon on the seminar evaluation form for participants to complete if they wish to be kept on your mailing list for newsletters. Also have a space on the form for asking what particular areas of interest or concern a participant might have. This should assist you in developing other seminars, or improving the existing one.

When a person phones in to register prior to the seminar, as well as on the day of the seminar, make sure that you get the full company name, address, phone number, and name and position of the person attending. You will want this information for your mailing list. For further information on conducting seminars and workshops, refer to the books outlined in the Bibliography.

13. Free media exposure

There are many devices for obtaining free media exposure. Exposure provides credibility for you, and develops an awareness in the public that you are an expert or authority in one or more areas. If a seminar or presentation is offered, either through your own company or through some other organization, consider preparing a news release. Send it in advance to the appropriate radio, television, newspaper or magazine contact person. Determine who the contact person is and call in advance so he or she will be expecting your letter or news release. It also gives you an opportunity to introduce yourself and to make sure that the approach you are adopting will obtain the desired free exposure.

Ask the contact person what format is preferred for the information they require. Spell out in your letter, and in your conversation, why you feel the topic of the presentation is of interest to the readers, viewers or listeners. The subject matter may be topical or controversial.

14. Radio and television talk shows

The previous point dealt primarily with announcements of upcoming presentations. An extension of that exposure is to appear in person on a radio or television talk show. The same approach applies as in free media announcements. Locate the appropriate contact person and sell them on the benefits to the listeners or viewers of you being interviewed on the program. If possible, try to be on the program a week before your seminar or presentation, in order to stimulate attendance. If the talk program is too distant from the seminar date, the listener may forget about it.

15. Letters to the editor

It is easy to get published in the "letters to the editor" section of a magazine or newspaper. Write a letter that is topical and relevant and reflects a controversial or divergent opinion. Refer to an earlier article if you are reacting to something previously published. Mention in the letter that you are a professional consultant in the field and have expertise in the subject area.

16. Writing articles

Writing is an effective way of developing exposure, credibility, and contacts. Once you have developed the format, style and discipline, you should be able to write three or more articles a year for various publications. All publications are looking for articles; many do not pay very much, if anything, for unsolicited articles — but they do frequently get published.

To locate magazines that have your target audience, look at a publication by Standard Rates and Data Service entitled *Business Publications Rates and Data*. You should be able to find this publication in your library or university, or through a local advertising agency.

Write an article about your area of expertise that you believe would be of particular interest to the readership of the publication. Use examples and stories in your article. The subject matter could deal with new trends, the effect of pending legislation, technical information, or any other angle that will enhance your image as an expert.

Contact the publishers of the magazines or journals and obtain free copies so you can review them and familiarize yourself with their style and length. If your article is accepted for publication, request a by-line and a brief biographical comment at the end of the article. Say that you are a consultant in your area of expertise, and invite questions or comments about the article. Not all publications will permit this.

There are numerous books on writing style. Some of them are listed in the Bibliography. Have your article reviewed by at least one, if not two, friends or relatives who will candidly comment. Submit a good quality 5" x 7" glossy photograph of yourself and a biography with the article. Submit the article one at a time to the editors of several trade journals and business magazines whose readership constitutes your potential target base. If your article is published, obtain extra copies from the publisher to distribute in your next direct mailing or presentation.

There is an additional benefit to writing articles. The research process is an excellent way to develop contacts and credibility. For example, you could carefully select 20 or 30 people to interview for background information for the article. These people could include key potential clients. Have a script ready before you phone them, ask open-ended questions, listen carefully and note their answers. Ask follow-up questions to their responses. This should show that you are knowledgeable and an intelligent communicator. When you contact the prospective client to be interviewed over the telephone, introduce yourself as a consultant writing an article. You can ask their opinion on such matters as the effect of pending legislation, unique problems they encounter in their field of interest, and major opportunities or trends they perceive.

Research implies analysis, and your analysis should be thorough. The telephone conversation can be followed by a letter on your stationery thanking people for their cooperation and assistance. Depending upon the responses to your questions, you may see that many consulting opportunities exist with the people contacted. They may have mentioned some of their problems. At a comfortable time in the future, you may wish to contact these sources and follow up with a personal letter and brochure. Depending upon the circumstances, you might feel it appropriate to say you will contact them 10 days later to ask whether you may be of service. Subtlety is essential.

17. Writing a book

Having a book published is another marketing technique to establish yourself as an expert in your field. There are a number of limitations though. You have to find a publisher for your book or publish it yourself, which can be quite expensive. Your book could be obsolete by the time it is published, as approximately one to one and a half year lead time is required before publication. The time you would have to spend on the book might not be justified in terms of the cost/benefit due to loss of income or potential income. It could be far more beneficial to spend the time writing articles rather than a book. Regular articles also keep your name in front of the public and reinforce your image as a specialist.

18. Have articles written about you

Every field of consulting has news value. By carefully cultivating relationships with editors and reporters, you could be looked upon as being an expert in your area. They might invite your opinion and quote you in an article on the topic. You could also have articles written about you, if you can demonstrate the newsworthy feature, topical benefit, or uniqueness. Attempt to look for news angles that could have a direct or indirect effect on the public at large or your target group in particular. Look at economic, social, political or legislative factors. Over time you could build up a reputation as an authority that will generate inquiries from prospective clients.

19. Announcement columns

Many professional, trade, or university alumni publications have sections devoted to announcements of interest about their members. Make a point of regularly updating information provided to these publications whenever you can find an excuse to justify it, if your style allows. Such things as having given a presentation, expanding the services that you provide, or announcing new associates or distinctions can get your name inserted. If you are giving a seminar or workshop, give yourself enough lead time for an announcement to be inserted, if possible, in these publications. Various publications of a daily or weekly nature frequently may have a free announcement section available.

20. Newsletters

Newsletters are a very common way for consultants to promote themselves. It is a subtle form of advertising that can give you credibility, as well as providing advice to readers. Most newsletters are distributed free, since they are used as a marketing device. Once you establish a reputation and a large mailing list, economics and demand may justify charging a fee for a subscription.

The important features of a newsletter are effective use of colors and layout, a professional appearance, and well-written articles on interesting subjects. Most potential clients who will receive your newsletter are very busy; unless the newsletter captures the attention and is easily readable, it will not serve the purpose that you intend. The newsletter should have tips, news and ideas, and possibly a question and answer column. The length should be two to six pages on regular 8½ x 11 size paper, and published on a regular basis, such as monthly, bi-monthly, quarterly or semi-annually. The frequency of your publication will depend on your finances and time.

A newsletter is distributed in the same manner outlined earlier for brochures. When sending out brochures with covering letters in response to an inquiry, you should also include a recent copy of your newsletter. As in the case of direct mail marketing and brochures, you should address the newsletter to the key people in target organizations.

16

THE CLIENT INTERVIEW AND CLIENT RELATIONS

Your efforts at marketing have now been successful. The prospective client is aware of your services and a meeting has been arranged, requested by you or the prospective client. This will provide an opportunity for mutual assessment. The initial interview is a critical step before preparing a proposal and obtaining a contract. There are many important techniques that you will have to understand and adapt for your particular needs. This chapter covers the matters you should consider before, during, and after the client interview.

a. PURPOSE OF INTERVIEW

The purpose of the interview is primarily fact finding, followed by an analysis of the client needs and problem identification. After these steps, you are then able to prepare a proposal. The meeting, of course, has other purposes, such as assessing the prospective client's personality, ability to pay, and expectations. It also provides an opportunity for an interchange of ideas and mutual assessment. As negotiating skills are involved, you may wish to refer to the section on negotiating in the Bibliography. *How to Read a Person Like a Book* is of particular interest on non-verbal communication.

b. BEFORE THE MEETING

If the client contacted you, you know a need exists and the client has some confidence in you. You should not have an interview over the telephone if at all possible. You want to have a face-to-face talk. Do not quote your rates over the phone, as they could be misinterpreted and the prospective client may not wish to continue to the next stage of the interview. If you are asked about your rates, attempt to defer an answer until the time of your meeting by stating that your rates vary depending on various factors such as estimated time involved, the type of work required, and whether the client is a profit or nonprofit organization. None of these factors can be ascertained accurately before an interview. In addition, there are different forms of fee structure that can be negotiated. This response should satisfy any inquiry.

The initial interview is normally free, as a goodwill and marketing technique. Naturally, it depends on the circumstances. Once a specific date and time has been set for the interview, confirm it in writing beforehand so no misunderstanding occurs. If the consultation is to be without charge, state that. Send your brochure with the letter. Your brochure should describe your background, past experiences, nature of service and references, if you think that is appropriate.

There are specific steps to take to prepare for the interview.

Review the client's circumstances so you are familiar with them before the interview. Find out everything you can about the company, industry, and problems affecting the industry. Learn the client's jargon and way of doing business. You can obtain considerable information from business publications, annual reports, trade journals, newspapers, and other clients in similar industries.

Try to find out about the client's likes and dislikes, hobbies, memberships, sports, recreation, and travel. Look for clues of personal interest or accomplishment when you are in the client's office. If you can find common links, a basis for friendship can be quickly established.

Prepare specific questions to ask during the interview. Concentrate on client needs and problems. Some of the basic questions to ask include:

(a) Has the client used a consultant before? How long ago? What was the experience like? What was the purpose?

   If the client has not used a consultant before, you may need more time to convince the client, and there may be more problems to be aware of in working with the client. If the client has used a consultant before, and the relationship was a positive one, you should find out what particular aspects were considered favorable. If a previous consultant relationship was not satisfactory, you should find out the reasons for that from the viewpoint of the client.

(b) Has the project been attempted previously? If so, who attempted it and why was it abondoned? The assignment might be impractical or impossible to complete to the client's satisfaction.

(c) If a client had a past relationship with a consultant, what type of financial fee arrangement was negotiated? It is not necessary for you to know the dollar amount, just the type of contract. You can then ask if that type of arrangement was satisfactory. That will provide you with guidelines on the type of fee arrangement to present in your proposal. Naturally, you want to offer the same type of fee arrangement a client feels comfortable with. If you prefer a different type of fee arrangement, you will have to discuss the benefits of that with the client during the interview, if possible.

(d) What specific measureable results and benefits must be obtained for the client to feel satisfied? The nature of the change, what form it will take, and how long it will take must be clarified. It is essential that the expectations of the client be specific, measureable, attainable, and realistic.

(e) Has a time period for the proposed project been discussed, and is that possible within your time schedule and other commitments? Has the subject of the cost of the project in general terms been discussed? What was the client's tentative reaction? If the type of payment has been discussed, what are the terms?

(f) Has a discussion taken place about the client's responsibilities in matters such as availability of the client's personnel, equipment, and work area, etc.? Does the consultant report to a committee or to one person? Access to information resources is required in order to complete the project. Can that access be obtained and how? Has the client been effectively convinced of the consultant's role as an agent of change? Does the client demonstrate appreciation and respect for the consultant?

(g) Is travel involved?

(h) Do you feel confident that you are qualified and able to help the client?

(i) Do you feel comfortable that a clear understanding exists of the client's problem or need?

Try to understand and anticipate client fears or concerns in advance and deal with them. A client may have underlying biases about you as a consultant that could affect the interview and its outcome. By knowing in advance the fears that might exist, you can counter them directly during the interview and proposal stages. Studies have shown that the following anxieties often exist. They are listed generally in order of priority.

- A consultant may be incompetent.

- The client may be continually dependent upon the consultant once the first relationship begins.

- The consultant might assume or interfere with managerial control during the project.

- The consultant's fees are excessive relative to the services provided.

- The consultant may not be able to complete the project in time.

- The need for a consultant is an admission of failure on the part of management.

- The consultant might disclose confidential internal information.

- The consultant might have inaccurately analyzed the needs and therefore will give an improper diagnosis.

- The consultant will lack impartiality.

Normally, a consultant will meet a client in the client's office. The client feels comfortable in familiar surroundings and is therefore more relaxed. The advantage to the consultant is having the opportunity to view the client's offices and operations, and to leave diplomatically if the meeting is unproductive or continues too long.

Try not to have a meeting just before lunch, as the client could have a lunch commitment or be distracted by the time or feel hungry.

Attempt to arrange an appointment for the time that you are at your peak of mental clarity so that you will create the most positive impression.

Make sure you arrive on time. Being late automatically creates a negative impression and can destroy the client's desire to deal with you. A small matter such as being late for an important appointment could represent an attitude and management style, which could cause conflict during the consulting project.

c. DURING THE INTERVIEW

The day has now arrived. You made certain you were at the client's office 10 to 15 minutes prior to the appointment to relax and compose yourself. You are feeling self-confident and positive about the meeting because you have thoroughly prepared yourself and worked through in your own mind a role-play of events that are soon to occur.

Arriving early gives you an opportunity to observe the dynamics of the office and personnel, and the general tone of the company. If you are going to have a relationship with a client, these simple factors are important to know beforehand.

When the meeting starts, it is important to shake hands with a firm grasp. A less than firm grasp will betray an insecure personality or lack of confidence in your abilities, and that impression alone could lose a project. It is important to consciously project a confident personality, positive attitude, firm method of speaking, and an attentive and relaxed stance. Exhibit a sense of control and leadership. A client wants to associate with a person who projects himself or herself well.

During the interview, you should spend almost all the time asking questions and little time answering them. After the initial social pleasantries and after you have briefly exchanged backgrounds, control the meeting asking your prepared questions. It is helpful to advise the client that you will be taking notes as this is a fact-finding interview. Having a prepared checklist is evidence of efficient administration and an assurance that no questions will be overlooked and interview consistency will be maintained.

Ask for examples to illustrate general statements. Ask open-ended as well as very specific questions, and let the client do the talking. If a pause occurs, be prepared with the next question or other appropriate reaction. Listen intently to what the client says and how the client perceives the problem. If you want the client to continue elaborating on a situation, use questions starting with how, why, who, what, or where or state, "that's interesting, can you tell me more about that?"

Be aware of non-verbal communication in body posture, mannerisms, voice patterns and behavior. When forming an impression of a client's situation or opinion, restate it back to the client for confirmation.

If a client attempts to ask you a lot of questions, try to deflect the line of questioning back to the client. If the client asks specific questions about how you think the problem can be dealt with, or the various steps or stages that should be considered, don't answer the questions directly. Your first interview is a fact-finding stage and you should not get involved in speculation or offering advice. Tell the client that you will certainly give an opinion later, after you have had an opportunity to review and analyze the facts and determine the options. Say that it would be premature and unprofessional for you to provide an opinion at this early stage. You don't want to give away free consulting, especially based on incomplete information.

At the end of the interview, ask the client if he or she would like to see a proposal and whether it should be a simple or detailed one.

Throughout the interview, be aware of the fears and concerns that might be present. Try to make sure you have dealt with all of them to the client's satisfaction.

d. AFTER THE INTERVIEW

Once the interview is over, you should review the data while it is still fresh in your mind. Identify the problems as you see them, and analyze the needs. Then outline the possible solutions and draft a proposal. The proposal steps are outlined in the next chapter.

The normal steps that follow include writing a thank you letter to the client as soon as possible after the meeting and saying a proposal will follow as soon as it is complete.

e. WHY YOU SHOULD TURN DOWN BUSINESS

After your interview and assessment of the client and project and other factors involved, you may decide that it would be wise not to accept the project. That decision takes insight and foresight, and many consultants find it difficult to make. Consultants may be influenced by factors such as the need for cash flow, seeing a challenge in the project, seeing potential marketing opportunities, desiring some form of activity because of the lack of it, or wanting to help because a client is in need. Some of the reasons you should consider turning down business are as follows:

(a) A client looks as though he or she is on the verge of business failure. (Studies have shown that there are various reasons for business failure, such as management incompetence, imbalanced experience, lack of management experience, or lack of experience in the product or service line. Some of the danger signals may include: lack of a business plan, high overhead costs, low morale, lack of cash flow, lack of understanding of financial information, indecisiveness, backlog of commitments, inefficiency, poor communication, and general chaos. As a consequence, you do not want to be burdened with the stress of a client failure or the risk of not collecting your fee.)

(b) The reputation of a client is to pay late or not pay at all.

(c) The client has a bad reputation for other reasons, and you do not want to be associated with that client.

(d) You do not like the client personally

(e) A proposed project is illegal or unpleasant

(f) You are over-committed with other projects and unable to accept the work and perform satisfactorily and on time

(g) The potential job is too small for your time, priorities or cash flow

(h) The potential job is too large for your ability or desire to administer it

(i) You lack the expertise to perform the job to the standard that would be required

(j) You do not offer consulting services in that client industry area

(k) The client does not want to pay you the fee that you have requested, but wants to pay you less than you feel is fair to complete the project

(l) The project would involve you compromising what you consider to be your professional and ethical standards

(m) The client does not appear to fully appreciate your skills and abilities

(n) The client does not have any money.

f. HOW TO TURN DOWN UNWANTED BUSINESS

Once you have decided that you do not want the business at all, or in the form that is available, there are various tactics and techniques involved in turning down the business in such a way as to maintain goodwill and not hurt the client's feelings.

If the proposed project is simply unsuitable for you, you may wish to turn it down completely. There are different ways of rejecting projects directly:

(a) Tell the client that your present workload is very heavy and unfortunately you are unable to accept the job. This option makes you appear more attractive and desirable to the client for possible future projects.

(b) Tell the client you are unable to technically comply with the job specifications. This typically occurs with government agencies. If you are expected to take a government job because of previous projects, and you want to be considered favorably in the future, you could propose an approach that you feel the client will reject as it may be outside the stated or unstated guidelines.

(c) Tell the client that you do not perform the particular type of service being requested, either because you do not have the capacity, or it isn't your current field. If you normally perform that type of consulting, state that at the present time you are directing your talents and priorities in a slightly different direction.

(d) Bid the job too high. You can quote a fee much higher than you think the job is worth or that other competitors might bid. The risk here, of course, is that your bid might be accepted.

There may be occasions when you would accept a job if it was changed to meet your needs. Some of the techniques you could consider include:

(a) Accept only part of the proposed project. You could encourage other consultants to accept parts of the project you do not wish to handle.

(b) Redefine the project to meet your needs, and offer to conduct the assignment on your own terms. This approach only works if the client's goals, objectives, and expectations can be met without additional costs.

(c) Accept the job but act as project manager and employ other consultants to assist you in completing the job.

17

CONSULTING PROPOSALS

Most initial interviews result in a request for a proposal. The proposal plays a significant role in your ability to obtain consulting assignments. Because of the vital nature of writing and presenting successful proposals, you may wish to refer to the Bibliography for further references. This chapter covers some of the basic concepts and tactics required to succeed in your proposal.

a. WHAT IS A PROPOSAL?

A proposal is a letter or document that you prepare for a client describing your understanding of the client's needs. This is very important as your client, to have confidence in you, must be satisfied that you understand the problem as well as the client does. It states what you intend to do for the client, and indicates in specific terms the anticipated results and potential benefits to the client.

A proposal is a selling document. It is intended to be informative and appealing and convince the client to contract for your services.

b. PRIVATE VERSUS PUBLIC SECTOR PROPOSALS

Public sector proposals tend to be more formal than private sector proposals. When a client requests a proposal, the request is made on the assumption that anyone offering goods or services is properly qualified and equipped to do so. The government requires that you demonstrate your own competence and prove that your facilities, experience, resources and whatever else are adequate to handle the requirements. The client is evaluating not only the merits of the program you propose versus the merits of competitive programs, but also your credentials versus the credentials of your competitors. It is common for government agencies to require that you outline your personal qualifications. One reason government agencies request such information is that they are required by procurement regulation to make an objective evaluation of each proposal. Your qualifications provide one specific comparison.

Goverment agencies have various evaluation factors. An example of the criteria a government agency might use is shown in Appendix 4.

Private sector proposals are far more flexible in their selection requirements as they are not governed by legislation. Therefore, pragmatism and subjective factors have more of an influence on the final decision.

c. SOLICITED VERSUS UNSOLICITED PROPOSALS

Solicited proposals are those requests that are made by a prospective client from the public or private sector. An organization requesting a proposal has already identified some needs. Your proposal will be judged on quality, timeliness, reliability, and effectiveness.

An unsolicited proposal is designed by a consultant who perceives a need and is confident that it can be met through the use of the consultant's services.

Solicited proposals generally involve a competition between large numbers of consultants who bid on the project. In an unsolicited proposal situation, you may be the only person being considered.

d. SIMPLE AND FORMAL PROPOSALS

1. Simple proposal

The simple proposal is simply a written statement, typed on the consultant's stationery, that includes the following items:

(a) A description of the work to be done

(b) The name of the consultant performing the work

(c) The services or personnel to be provided by the client

(d) The date work will begin and the length of time required to complete the assignment

(e) An outline of anticipated categories of costs to be paid by the client

(f) The fees to be paid for services rendered and the terms arranged.

The proposal is signed by the consultant and normally sent by mail or delivered in person to the client. If the proposal is agreed upon, the client should sign a copy of the proposal or letter. The letter of proposal and agreement constitutes a legal contract and is similar to a letter of agreement.

2. Formal proposal

A formal proposal is considerably more detailed in that all aspects of the project are spelled out in full. It is similar to a formal contract and offers protections to both the consultant and the client.

The proposal does not become a legally binding contract until the client reads and signs the proposal document to that effect, or a covering letter referring to the proposal as a binding contract is signed, or a formal contract is made reflecting the contents of the proposal and signed by both parties. A format for a formal proposal is described in the next section.

e. GUIDELINES AND FORMAT FOR A SUCCESSFUL PROPOSAL

The basis for your written contract will be the matters that you discuss at the proposal stage. Make sure you expand on the need, outcome, benefits, and results. Do not and on the process or methods. This protects you from a client rejecting proposal, and performing the project in-house using your proposal as a guide submitting your proposal to other consultants for estimates and then hire someone else who uses the process you detailed.

keep in mind when you are preparing the proposal that your client some of the concerns and fears outlined in the preceeding chapter. minimize any concerns in the content of your proposal.

should consider having a number of standardized proposals if there is y in the type of services you offer. If the standardized documents are on a rocessor, they can easily be adapted to include or exclude paragraphs and ke the document an original. It is also very easy to revise a document on a processor. The standardized proposal contains all the basics of any proal, leaving open those items that are specific to each project. Another advange of a standardized proposal is your ability to deliver the completed proposal to he client within a short time after your initial meeting.

The sample proposal format and guidelines (Sample #16) is rather form and detailed. It may include clauses that are not applicable or appropriate in situations, as each project is unique.

SAMPLE #16
PROPOSAL FORMAT

1. **Table of contents:** Includes headings and page numbers

2. **Introduction:** It is important to persuade the client that you understan and the underlying factors that influence it. Briefly outline and analyze th demonstrate the need. State that the matter is important and warrants outside assistance. Emphasize that you want to help and that you are the riate source of help.

3. **Project purpose:** The purpose and goals of the engagement are out clear and accurate fashion. State the purpose and goals in the client's ow the client can identify with the proposal. During your initial interview y elicit from the client what the client perceived as being the needs or p means to resolve them. Detail the goals in such a way that you car specific and measureable outcomes to have a reference point for mea of the project and satisfying the client.

4. **Project benefits:** Highlight the anticipated benefits the clier promise results you cannot guarantee, but the client has to be giv of success. This is a particularly important section as the client h and recognize the benefits in order to justify the financial and ment. Your client may have to account to other directors assisting your client to assist you, the more detail you provid

e. GUIDELINES AND FORMAT FOR A SUCCESSFUL PROPOSAL

The basis for your written contract will be the matters that you discuss at the proposal stage. Make sure you expand on the need, outcome, benefits, and results. Do not expand on the process or methods. This protects you from a client rejecting the proposal, and performing the project in-house using your proposal as a guide or submitting your proposal to other consultants for estimates and then hiring someone else who uses the process you detailed.

Also keep in mind when you are preparing the proposal that your client might have some of the concerns and fears outlined in the preceeding chapter. Attempt to minimize any concerns in the content of your proposal.

You should consider having a number of standardized proposals if there is similarity in the type of services you offer. If the standardized documents are on a word processor, they can easily be adapted to include or exclude paragraphs and to make the document an original. It is also very easy to revise a document on a word processor. The standardized proposal contains all the basics of any proposal, leaving open those items that are specific to each project. Another advantage of a standardized proposal is your ability to deliver the completed proposal to the client within a short time after your initial meeting.

The sample proposal format and guidelines (Sample #16) is rather formal and detailed. It may include clauses that are not applicable or appropriate in all situations, as each project is unique.

SAMPLE #16
PROPOSAL FORMAT

1. **Table of contents:** Includes headings and page numbers

2. **Introduction:** It is important to persuade the client that you understand the project and the underlying factors that influence it. Briefly outline and analyze the factors that demonstrate the need. State that the matter is important and warrants professional outside assistance. Emphasize that you want to help and that you are the most appropriate source of help.

3. **Project purpose:** The purpose and goals of the engagement are outlined here in a clear and accurate fashion. State the purpose and goals in the client's own words so that the client can identify with the proposal. During your initial interview you attempted to elicit from the client what the client perceived as being the needs or problems and the means to resolve them. Detail the goals in such a way that you can refer to them as specific and measureable outcomes to have a reference point for measuring the progress of the project and satisfying the client.

4. **Project benefits:** Highlight the anticipated benefits the client will receive. Do not promise results you cannot guarantee, but the client has to be given some realistic hope of success. This is a particularly important section as the client has to clearly understand and recognize the benefits in order to justify the financial and administrative commitment. Your client may have to account to other directors or shareholders. You are assisting your client to assist you, the more detail you provide.

c. SOLICITED VERSUS UNSOLICITED PROPOSALS

Solicited proposals are those requests that are made by a prospective client from the public or private sector. An organization requesting a proposal has already identified some needs. Your proposal will be judged on its quality, timeliness, reliability, and effectiveness.

An unsolicited proposal is designed by a consultant who perceives a need and is confident that it can be met through the use of the consultant's services.

Solicited proposals generally involve a competition between large numbers of consultants who bid on the project. In an unsolicited proposal situation, you may be the only person being considered.

d. SIMPLE AND FORMAL PROPOSALS

1. Simple proposal

The simple proposal is simply a written statement, typed on the consultant's stationery, that includes the following items:

(a) A description of the work to be done

(b) The name of the consultant performing the work

(c) The services or personnel to be provided by the client

(d) The date work will begin and the length of time required to complete the assignment

(e) An outline of anticipated categories of costs to be paid by the client

(f) The fees to be paid for services rendered and the terms arranged.

The proposal is signed by the consultant and normally sent by mail or delivered in person to the client. If the proposal is agreed upon, the client should sign a copy of the proposal or letter. The letter of proposal and agreement constitutes a legal contract and is similar to a letter of agreement.

2. Formal proposal

A formal proposal is considerably more detailed in that all aspects of the project are spelled out in full. It is similar to a formal contract and offers protections to both the consultant and the client.

The proposal does not become a legally binding contract until the client agrees and signs the proposal document to that effect, or a covering letter referring to the proposal as a binding contract is signed, or a formal contract is drafted reflecting the contents of the proposal and signed by both parties. A sample format for a formal proposal is described in the next section.

5. Approach, scope, and plan: Compare and contrast several possible approaches to the project, if appropriate. Explain how you will proceed in general terms. Define the scope and limits of the proposed consulting service. Divide the tasks into smaller segments that provide clear stages in the project as reference points for you and your client. As mentioned earlier, provide sufficient information to demonstrate your competence, but not enough about the process and techniques to provide a formula for the client to perform the project without you.

6. Project schedule: Determine the schedule and list the specific tasks required to attain the objectives. State the timing and sequence of tasks according to the various stages. A functional flow diagram might help to graphically assist the client's understanding and provide a reference point for progress.

7. Progress reports: It is important to maintain continual communication with the client. As explained in earlier chapters, the more information you provide your client, the more confidence the client will have in you, and the less risk there is of problems occurring. Progress reports are frequently made at specific stages, when interim bills are sent. A client is more disposed to pay if tangible benefits can be seen and specific problems have been resolved. The frequency and format of periodic progress reports should be specified.

8. Costing summary: Explain your fees, types of fee arrangement, billing procedures, and timing of bills. Detail the expected expenses that will be passed on directly to the client. Your client should understand that your estimate for time and costs is an estimate only. Provide sufficient detail about your fees, so that your client appreciates the correlation between the amount of time expended and the cost of your services. Outline any other terms and conditions or variables that could affect the final cost.

9. Personnel and qualifications: Provide a brief background history of your firm and the personnel who will be consulting on the project. If you have had experience solving problems similar to the client's, make reference to that. Select only those aspects of your background experience that related directly to the client and the proposal.

10. Sub-contracts: If you are sub-contracting or collaborating with other consultants, it is important to specify who they are and what duties they will perform. Specify whether you or the client is responsible for their technical performance to avoid any future problems.

11. Use of client personnel: It is important that the client understand what commitments and obligations will be his or her responsibility. If you are to delegate responsibilities or otherwise receive assistance from the client's staff or executives, you should make it clear that your fee estimate is based on the use of client personnel. Specify personnel duties and time required if possible.

12. Senior management support: Make the executives aware that their support is vital to the success of the project. It is important that support for the project be communicated throughout the organization to gain cooperation and compliance. If regular meetings are going to be held with senior executives, specify the purpose and frequency of such meetings.

13. Steering committee function, if applicable: A steering committee reviews, coordinates, assists, and implements the consultant's work. It provides momentum and organizational credibility and decision-making functions for the project. Detail the purposes, composition, and responsibilities of this committee.

14. Output material included: Describe any reports, surveys, instructional material or other products that are part of the proposal.

15. Management plan: Describe your approach to managing the overall project. Who will be the client contact person, and what will his or her management role and authority be pertaining to the project?

16. Disclaimers: If you have used disclaimers regarding the project, make sure that the reason is outlined. Your role is strictly that of advisor, not a decision-maker, and any benefits achieved is based on both your recommendations and the client's actions and decisions. If your client does not fulfill his or her obligations and support, your responsibility and choices should be outlined. Indicate who has ownership and control over any proprietary information that could develop from your services, for example, instructional material.

17. References: If requested, or if it is your style and wish to provide client references, make sure that you obtain written permission in advance from the references. Update them to make sure they still think highly of you.

18. Summary and closing of proposal: This should be a short restatement of your belief in the importance of the engagement. Mention your availability to answer questions. If you are prepared to begin the project within a short time after the client's acceptance, state that clearly. You want to stimulate the client's need and persuade the client that you can fulfill the need.

f. PRESENTING YOUR PROPOSAL

How you package your proposal is nearly as important as how it is stated. If possible, your proposal should be prepared on a word processor, as that reflects professionalism and quality secretarial resources. Your signature and the date should appear at the end of the proposal.

A covering letter should accompany your proposal thanking your client for the time and cooperation during the meeting and for the opportunity to submit a proposal. Highlight the topics discussed and state that you can help because you have had experience with this type of problem and would like to have the opportunity to be of service. You may want to flatter the client in some way by referring to his or her contribution in the meeting. Offer to answer any questions either by phone or at an arranged meeting. State that you will call within 10 business days to discuss the proposal further. Put that date on your calendar. If you have not heard from the client within that period, make sure that you contact the client on the 10th day.

You may wish to suggest in your covering letter if you didn't mention it in the proposal that references are available on request. You may wish to suggest that the client contact some of your other clients to discuss work you have performed. This should demonstrate your self-confidence and increase the client's trust and confidence in you.

g. PROPOSAL FOLLOW-UP

Your client may be slow in responding to your proposal. You do not want to appear to be pressuring the client, but you may have to take certain steps to clarify the situation or obtain a contract.

You stated in your covering letter that you would contact the client within 10 business days. It is appropriate, then, that you do contact the client on the 10th day to answer any questions. You may receive further questions at that point, or obtain a positive or negative response to your proposal.

If the reason for the delay appears inexplicable, you may wish to wait for a further five business days and then drop in to see the client in person to ask if a decision has been made. This approach may or may not be appropriate in a given situation.

If a client is waiting for a committee decision, determine when the committee will meet to discuss the proposal and follow-up by phone to the client the following day. You may also wish to consider giving an acceptance time limit in your proposal to encourage prompt consideration. In a given situation you might adopt the attitude that you would like to know one way or the other within a certain time. The client could construe the acceptance time limit in a positive fashion, as it could imply that you are in demand and have other projects available to you that require a decision.

h. WHAT TO DO IF YOUR PROPOSAL IS NOT ACCEPTED

It is helpful if you can determine why you received a rejection. It may not be appropriate, practical or possible for you to obtain the answer from the client. Budget restraints, other priorities, or lack of consensus could be reasons. Possibly another consultant was awarded the contract. If possible, find out who obtained the assignment and why that proposal was selected over your own. Rejected proposals can provide a good learning experience.

Regardless of the circumstances, write a thank you letter to the client expressing your appreciation for his or her time, interest, and cooperation, and mention that you would be pleased to submit a proposal for consideration in any future projects.

i. HOW TO AVOID GIVING AWAY FREE CONSULTING

At this stage you should know whether your proposal was rejected or accepted. If it was rejected, you may have provided too much information in your proposal to your client, who in turn used the information for his or her benefit. In other words, you gave away free consulting. If your proposal was accepted, and you now have a contract or a contract is being prepared, you should be aware of the various ways that clients can innocently or intentionally obtain your advice for free.

At times, you may decide to share your knowledge and ideas in an attempt to build goodwill with the client or prospective client. That is a judgment you will have to make at the time. But you are running a business, which requires income and profit. You cannot carelessly give away the only product you have, which is time and skill.

1. Potential client interview or discussion

A potential client may contact you and wish to discuss ideas and problems with you on the telephone, over lunch or at the client's office or your office. The potential client (referred to as "client" for convenience) wants to "pick your brains." You willingly cooperate due to your desire to obtain a consulting assignment.

The strategic solution is to confirm that you do provide service in the area concerned and you are available to the client on a professional basis and would be pleased to establish a relationship. Answer any concerns raised by the client by asking questions aimed at drawing out information. Do not offer solutions but imply that there are solutions to the problems discussed.

If answers are specifically requested, respond that you require far more information before providing an answer. State that it would be unprofessional for you to provide an opinion without sufficient information on which to base that opinion. Again, restate that you would be pleased to discuss the matter further on a professional basis if they so wish.

These deflective techniques are the same ones outlined in the preceeding chapter relating to the initial interview. Ask the client directly if he or she is interested in retaining a consultant to provide assistance in the specific area of concern. Clarify if the client would like you to submit a proposal to resolve the problem. Decide if the client is a serious enough prospect to spend the time on a proposal.

Make it clear throughout the discussion that you are paid for professional services and that you are capable of assisting the client on a fee for service basis.

2. Client need analysis

A client might perceive that a problem exists, but not understand the precise nature of the problem. The client implies to you that if an analysis of the needs is made with recommendations for resolution an attractive contract could immediately result. This teaser can entice unsophisticated or new consultants to provide a thorough diagnosis without fee.

A naive consultant can be easily exploited by this technique. The risk, of course, is that no subsequent contracts materialize or some other consultant is retained. One way of resolving this problem is to recommend that the client enter into a contract with the first stage to be a diagnostic stage. After the diagnosis is made, with recommendations, then the consultant could proceed to the next stage of contract and implement the recommendations. That way the consultant is protected by contract, and the sincerity of the client is assured.

152

An option can be inserted in the contract that if the client elects not to proceed with the recommendation, then the consultant is assured payment of an agreed sum in consideration for the time and energies spent during the diagnostic phase.

3. Free detailed advice in the written proposal

In your proposal you may write a complete, detailed formula with all the necessary instructions together with an outline of the methods and steps required to attain the objective. The client now has the prescription for resolving the problem and can give it to other consultants to submit an estimate or implement the detailed proposal with in-house personnel.

One approach to avoid this problem is to write the proposal highlighting in detail the need that exists, the objectives that must be achieved in order to resolve the client's problem, and the measurable, specific outcomes and benefits that will be attained at specific stages of the assignment. A functional flow diagram graphically illustrating the steps is an effective marketing tool. De-emphasize or omit information on the processes or methods to be used.

4. Potential future benefit

A client may try to convince you that some future benefit, such as goodwill or contacts, could occur if you performed the service. The condition is that you provide the service for free or a reduced amount as the price to pay for future opportunities and contacts.

This technique is normally exercised by larger or more influential clients who take advantage of a consultant's impressionable, desperate or opportunist nature. The client may attempt to blame the lack of financial recompense on budget allocations already spent, internal financial restraints being imposed, or a general hold on all project commitments. From a consultant's viewpoint, the mere association with an influential or prestigious client could be an inducement.

As long as you are aware of the business and psychological dynamics at work, you can make a responsible, pragmatic decision. The decision might be to accede to the client's overtures, resist them, or attempt to negotiate a more realistic package.

5. Additions to the original fixed price contract

You may be asked to perform additional work outside the original contract terms.

It is not uncommon for a client to request additional work, as all needs cannot be foreseen in advance or changing circumstances change the needs. Once you are aware that the request is outside the fixed price contract terms, you should contact the client, draw this fact to the client's attention in a polite fashion and suggest that a modified contract or addendum be negotiated to incorporate the additional work. You would then negotiate the amount and method of payment for the additional work.

This situation reinforces the importance of being specific in a fixed price contract as to the services that are to be performed. Ambiguity in terms could lead to a difference of opinion, an impasse, legal problems, and loss of goodwill as well as loss of a client.

Depending on the circumstances, a formal contract amendment may not be required; a confirmation letter outlining the amendments and signed by both parties may be enough. The method is a matter of style, nature of client, and other circumstances.

6. Free consulting in a follow-up situation

You can run into problems when you have performed your services as outlined in your contract, but the client continues to need your services for operating the project. For example, suppose you recommended a type of computer hardware that was subsequently installed in the client's premises, and the client's personnel had difficulty learning the new equipment. You might feel an obligation to assist the client by explaining the necessary matters to the personnel. You may then be continually phoned by the client requesting you to return to explain various features to the personnel. Unless you are aware of the process occurring, you could be providing considerable free consulting.

The obvious solution is to anticipate the situation in advance, and incorporate provisions for follow-up consultation fees into the original contract. The contract can specify the method of payment and terms. One option is a time retainer contract, which means that you perform a specified service regularly, (e.g., several specified hours or days per month). Another option is an availability retainer contract. This means you are "on call" for a fixed monthly fee as outlined in the terms of the agreement.

7. Relatives, associates, and friends

Relatives and friends may frequently come to you for advice. You must develop ways to maintain the relationship but clarify your role as a professional who provides service for a fee.

You can develop various subtle but effective approaches. One technique is to say that you have a policy of not advising family or friends because of possible conflict of interest or bias. Because you value the relationship and operate by professional standards, you feel it would not be appropriate or responsible or you would prefer not to provide professoinal advice that they might rely on.

Another approach is to say you are unable to provide advice because of incomplete information, and that it would be irresponsible, unprofessional, and unfair on your part to give an opinion based on incomplete facts.

You have choices. You can either decline to provide advice, provide advice for free, or establish your relationship in the context as a business one and negotiate a fee for service. It is also helpful to keep in mind that you can be exposed to professional liability and negligent claims if your advice is followed and problems occur even though you did not charge or get paid for your advice.

18

CONTRACTS

As a consultant, you will quickly become aware of the necessity of written contracts in all your business and client relationships. A contract is the framework within which your obligations, rights, remedies, and remunerations are clarified. There are oral, written, and implied contracts. You want to make sure that your consulting business assumes no commitments or financial outlay without the security of an agreement in writing. Many consultants and other small business people commence their business with the trusting attitude that a verbal agreement is sufficient. It only takes one bad experience to demonstrate the folly of relying on a verbal agreement. This chapter explores some of the important aspects of contracts.

a. ESSENTIALS OF A VALID CONTRACT

A contract is an agreement between two parties to perform mutual obligations. The most common forms of contract are the oral contract and the written contract. The problem with an oral contract is that if the parties disagree, unless there are reliable witnesses or part performance of the agreement, it is difficult to reconstruct what the original bargain was. A written contract simply records in a formal or informal manner the nature of the bargain. For example, if you send a letter to a client confirming your agreement and the five essential elements of a contract are present, you have a simple informal contract.

The five elements of a contract are as follows:

1. Offer

If you are submitting a proposal or a contract to a client, that constitutes your offer to the client to accept your proposal. Your offer, naturally, will be in writing and spell out the particulars in some detail.

2. Acceptance

Acceptance of your proposal must be clearly demonstrated. Normally this takes the form of your prospective client confirming in writing an acceptance of your proposal letter or document or contract, and acknowledging the terms you have outlined.

In certain situations an acceptance can be assumed and the contract made valid by part performance. In other words, it could be argued that your offer was accepted if your client permitted you to perform in part or in full the terms of your written proposal, even though a written acceptance had not been received.

156

Naturally, this is a high risk manner of doing business. Never begin a project without first protecting yourself in writing.

3. Consideration

Consideration is something of value being promised to you or given to you in exchange for your services. Valuable consideration normally refers to money or some other valuable assets, but a promise to pay money or provide some other benefit can be deemed to be consideration.

4. Competency

An agreement will not be considered binding if signed by persons lacking competence to understand the "nature and quality of their actions." This includes minors, the mentally infirm, or a person who is intoxicated at the time the agreement was accepted or signed. The age at which a person ceases to become a minor varies depending upon the jurisdiction. In some circumstances a contract signed by a minor is considered to be binding.

5. Legality

A contract created to perform an illegal act is void. For example, if a number of businesses signed an agreement to price fix in their area of product sales, and one of the parties failed to follow the agreement, the other parties to the agreement would not be able to sue for breach of contract, as the subject matter of the agreement was illegal.

b. WHY A WRITTEN CONTRACT IS NEEDED

There are many reasons why a written contract is essential. Some of the reasons are:

- *Projects professional image:* A written contract enhances your image as a responsible professional and businessperson.

- *Avoid misunderstandings:* It is difficult to remember complex details without having them in writing. Subsequent events and distractions can cloud the recall of earlier conversations. Both parties can have different assumptions and interpretations of what the bargain was on critical points of issue. It only makes sense to prevent this problem by the simple act of writing down the agreement.

- *Untruthful client:* It is not uncommon in verbal agreements for one party to reconstruct the agreement in a self-serving fashion at some later point. This could be to negotiate a more favorable contract or to get out of the contract obligations all together. If it is just one person's word against the other, it is difficult if not impossible for a court to attempt to reconstruct with certainty the original bargain. The time, delay, and expense of attempting to assert your rights eliminates any profit and possibly your business as well.

- *Death of either party:* If either party to the contract dies, the estate of the deceased would have difficulty determining the actual bargain. This could give rise to law suits against the estate of the deceased consultant if the client claimed damages had been suffered because of the death due to breach of contract. The estate of the deceased would be in a difficult position to defend any action, not knowing the exact terms and obligations of both parties.

- *Terms of payment outlined:* If you do not have specific terms of payment in writing, such as monthly or at specific stages in the project, the client could attempt to wait until the end of the job to pay you, claiming there was no other agreement to the contrary. You want to avoid this problem by having written agreement before you expend your time, energy, and resources.

- *Fee for service confirmed:* You want to make clear that you are being paid for your time, and that your efforts are not being supplied free as a marketing device or preliminary assessment.

- *Avoiding and limiting liability:* You want to protect your interests in writing by having provisions in the agreement to protect yourself from liability. For example, you may want to have a contingency clause to the effect that if events occur outside your control you are not to be held responsible. You might also consider a limited liability clause which sets a fixed amount of money that you would be responsible for if you are held liable. For example, you might have a clause stating that your liability is limited to $15,000 or the balance of the contract, whichever is less.

- *Preventing litigation:* If you do not have an agreement in writing, a client could claim that you acted improperly or that the work was not completely done. Unless an agreement in writing spelled out the nature of the services that you were going to provide, it would be difficult for you or your client to show exactly what you agreed upon. Because of this impasse on the terms and obligations of the agreement, litigation might be difficult to avoid.

- *Collateral for financing:* A written contract outlining benefits that you will receive for performing services is as good as money. You can pledge the contract at a bank as security for loan advances. This ability to lever your legal documents for working capital or cash flow purposes is just good business sense. No banker will lend money on the strength of your verbal assurance that you have a consulting agreement with a client.

- *Potential for increase of revenue:* If you have a contract that details the exact services and supplies you are providing, any variation would allow you to negotiate an addendum to the agreement. The problem with an oral agreement could be a dispute over the exact point at which your services and supplies are not included in the bargain.

- *Independent contractor status confirmed:* Without a written agreement specifying your independent status of operating, within the terms of the agreement, without direction or control, you could be considered to be an employee by the tax authorities. Make clear in the written agreement the nature of the roles of the parties. Also, the client might set down his or her own specifications, or question you in detail on an ongoing basis about what you are doing, thereby reducing some of your independence. To prevent this, take the initiative to specify the detail, nature, and form of the services you are going to provide.

- *Encourages contract acceptance:* Many prospective clients feel nervous about agreeing to have you perform a project unless they know the exact detail and terms of the relationship in writing. The person with whom you might be negotiating frequently has to explain the particulars to colleagues or superiors. Without a written contract in writing, you might not win the assignment.

- *Communication:* As mentioned previously, good communication is an essential ingredient for client satisfaction and goodwill. A well-written contract helps build client confidence.

c. STRUCTURE OF A FORMAL CONTRACT

A consulting contract can vary widely in its complexity depending upon the nature and value of the project being performed and the nature of the clients being served. Sample #17 describes the format for a formal contract and discusses clauses that are frequently included. Not all the clauses are necessarily appropriate or applicable in each case. A simple contract or letter of understanding does not need the same detail.

If a proposal letter or document exists, it can be referred to in the contract as part of the agreement and attached as an appendix.

SAMPLE #17
CONTRACT FORMAT

---

1. **Parties involved:** Name all parties involved in the contract and state the date the contract is signed.

2. **Term of contract:** The starting and completion dates of the contract are written here, or a reference is made to an appendix attached in which the dates and hours are described. The contract may state either the beginning and ending dates of an assignment, or both, or a maximum of hours within a fixed time period. The time period can either be closed or open. An open contract simply states that a specific job is to be performed, without giving a deadline for completion. Or, a contract might simply state that an ongoing relationship is commencing, the length of which shall be at the pleasure of both parties.

---

3. Duties of the consultant: Outline your proposed consulting in detail, by specific task and scope. Previous meetings have probably clarified services to be offered during the proposal stage, and the proposal letter or document spells out what you are offering. If this is included in the contract for practical, tactical or legal reasons, or choice of style, the following areas might be be covered:

- Services that you, as consultant, will provide
- The timing of the submission of various documents pertaining to the project
- The nature of reports to be furnished, if any, and the approximate dates when they will be completed
- Any special materials to be prepared, such as brochures, etc.
- The timing and nature of any consultant/client meetings, either on fixed dates or at specific stages in the project or upon mutual request
- Travel that might be required, the nature of compensation, when that is to be paid, and what is required to obtain payment
- Your authority to use client resources, office equipment, computer, files and records, and access to client's customers
- Your right to use third party information; for example, ledgers and journals and other financial information in the possession of the client
- A provision restricting you from performing services for the client's competitors (Be careful of this provision, especially if you intend to develop a clientele base within a certain industry.)

4. Duties of the client: Wherever a consultant requires access to information or to employees, customers, or advisors of the client, it should be specified clearly in the agreement that the client agrees and will have the responsibility of facilitating and performing in those specific areas. For example, if you require information from a third party, you should try to have the client responsible for obtaining the information for you. If the client does not or cannot cooperate and therefore impedes the project, how are you compensated?

5. Payment for services: This is an important section and should state the basis on which your fees will be paid; that is, per diem, fixed rate, fixed price plus expenses, or other form. Various types of fee structures are discussed in chapter 13. When and how the invoices will be rendered should be spelled out clearly, for example, invoices could be rendered at specific identifiable stages throughout the project. If the client is billing on an hourly or daily rate, it should be specified in the contract what that rate is. If a down payment (retainer) is required, that should also be specified.

6. Expenses: Any job-related expenses to be paid by the client are described here. In the case of a fixed price contract, your expenses are incorporated in the fixed price agreed upon. Most other forms of fee structure involve expenses to be paid by the client. Outline what is required for payment.

7. Late payment: The contract should specify when payment should take place — either at specified periods or upon receipt of invoice or 30 days after invoice, or whatever arrangement is agreed upon. A clause can be inserted in the agreement that if the invoice is not paid within the agreed upon billing period, interest on the overdue account will be added. The interest rate is normally slightly higher than the prevailing bank rate to act as an incentive to pay.

8. Stop work clause: This clause allows the consultant to cease providing services on the project until the oustanding fees and interest have been paid. Generally this clause is not applied until a certain period has elapsed and all other attempts at getting payment through goodwill have been unsuccessful. Stopping work is a last resort. It is important that the basis on which you can discontinue your services be stated in the contract.

9.   Independent contractor: State that you are an independent contractor and therefore not eligible to participate in any benefit programs or tax withholding obligations on the part of the client. This clause makes it clear that you are not an employee.

10.   Work delegation: Outline the basis on which you are permitted to hire assistants and delegate work. Depending upon the nature of services you are providing, your personal service and expertise is probably desired by the client. If you plan to sub-contract out to other people, protect yourself by clarifying that in the contract.

11.   Additional work: This clause allows a client to request a modification to the contract and add a provision for additional services. Any modification to the contract should be confirmed in writing with particulars and signed by both parties before any additional service work commences.

12.   Confidentiality: State that any information disclosed to you pertaining to the project or any information that you become aware of during the period of the project will be kept strictly confidential.

13.   Ownership: This clause covers ownership of materials or ideas resulting from your services. Many rejected ideas and plans could be useful for another project. Naturally, it is not in your best interests to have the client own this information. You should require that rejected plans or ideas are to remain your property.

14.   Limited liability of consultant: You may wish to insert a clause saying any liability because of your mistakes or breach of contract is limited to the amount of the contract price, assuming that there is a fixed contract price, or the amount of loss, whichever is lower. If there is no fixed contract price, set a specific maximum to the loss. However, such a clause is difficult if not impossible to enforce. You should also take out professional liability insurance and errors and omissions insurance as a protection. (See chapter 11.)

15.   Contingencies: This clause states that you have complete control of all services rendered, with the exception of events beyond the control of you or the client, such as accidents, delays, strikes or supplier problems. This clause attempts to protect both parties if the contract is not able to be completed.

16.   Advertising: This clause restricts the use of the client's name for media release without the written approval of the client.

17.   Arbitration: Outline the procedures to be followed in the event of disagreement by either party about the terms or interpretation of the terms of the contract. Normally, provision is made for a dispute to be settled by an independent arbitrator, the basis on which the arbitrator will be paid and by whom, and the criteria for selecting the arbitrator.

18.   Governing laws: This clause simply states that the contract shall be governed by the laws of the jurisdiction in which it is written.

19.   Termination: Either party is allowed to terminate services upon written notification a set number of days in advance. Outline the details and the reasons under which termination can take place.

20.   Agreement binding: State that the written agreement is the total agreement between the parties and shall take the place of any previous contracts or verbal or written agreements. This clause normally states that any modification to the agreement must be in writing and agreed between the parties to be enforceable.

21.   Signatures: The parties to the contract sign the agreement. It is very important that a representative of the client who sign has the authority to do so and the position is written on the contract. In some cases, corporate seals are required if corporations are involved.

d. TYPES OF CONTRACTS

There are several types of contracts frequently used in the consulting business. It is important to understand the options that are available to you as they involve various tactical and legal considerations. Following is a brief summary of the most common types of contracts.

1. Letter of agreement

This simple contract is in the form of a letter stating a summary of the agreement between the parties. This includes the nature of services to be performed, the method and time of payment, the starting date and duration of the contract, the resource materials and personnel to be supplied by the client, if applicable, and the consultants who will be involved on the project, if applicable.

The letter of agreement is normally prepared by the consultant and forwarded to the client for signature and approval. An example of a letter of agreement prepared by a consultant is shown in Sample #18.

Sample #19 shows a letter of agreement prepared by the client. Note the differences in tone and format between the two. The one prepared by the client has the appearance of a short formal contract.

2. Letter of agreement with general terms and conditions appended

Another option is to have a letter of agreement accompanied by a statement of standard terms and conditions (see Sample #20). The statement is a standardized form that you can use often for similar type of agreements. It includes such matters as fee structure, reimbursable expenses, sub-contracts, invoices and payments, warranty and limitation of professional liability. Other clauses can be included in this form based on your own needs and precautions. If you prefer this format, the letter of agreement attached to the terms and conditions need not be detailed. It can outline the specific, not general, terms of the agreement.

The letter of agreement and/or general terms and conditions form are frequently used if the client does not want a more formal contract. From a tactical viewpoint, you might feel that a client would be intimidated by a formally structured contract. Another factor might be your personal style of consulting practice. If the contract is not complex and the fee is low, you might favor the simpler contract format

3. Formal contract

A formal contract is preferred if the financial cost of the project is high, if the project is complex, if substantial financial commitment to suppliers or sub-consultants is involved, or if it is the style of the client to require such a detailed contract.

Normally when government contracts are involved, the government prepares the formal contract.

SAMPLE #18
LETTER OF AGREEMENT
(Prepared by consultant)

(Consultant's Letterhead)

_____, 198____

Mary Roberts, President
ABC Corporation
7890 Front Street
Anytown, Anywhere

Dear Ms. Roberts:

Re: Consulting Agreement

This letter will confirm our understanding concerning the terms of retainer and nature of services to be performed for ABC Corporation. These terms are as follows:

1. Term. This agreement will be for a period of _____ commencing on _____. Either of us may terminate this agreement with thirty (30) days' written notice to the other party. In the event of termination, I will be compensated for services rendered through the date of termination.

2. Duties. My duties will include:

   a. Review, analysis, and recommendations for changes in the systems and organizational structure of the research division.

   b. Preparation of weekly reports on the progress of the project.

   c. Preparation of a final report and oral presentation for the management of the company, with recommendations for implementing system and organizational improvements and related costing.

3. Compensation. The compensation for my services shall be at the rate of $450 per day, payable on receipt as billed. Other out-of-pocket costs, such as travel expenses and secretarial services will be billed separately.

Enclosed is a copy of this agreement for your records. Please sign the original and return it to this office in the enclosed envelope. If you have any questions, please contact me.

Sincerely,

David Jones
Consultant

Accepted and agreed to:

_____   _____
Mary Roberts, President   Date
ABC Corporation

SAMPLE #19
LETTER OF AGREEMENT
(Prepared by client)

ABC Corporation
7890 Front Street
Anytown, Anywhere

_____ 198____

Smith Jones & Associates
Consultants
1234 Main Street
Anytown, Anywhere

Dear _____:

Re: Consulting Project

I am pleased to announce that your proposal to ABC Corporation has been accepted. The conditions of our acceptance are as outlined below.

1. **Term.** Your appointment as a consultant to ABC Corporation (hereinafter called "the Corporation") is confirmed for the period _____ to _____.

2. **Services.** You shall perform such work or services as are set forth in Exhibit A, attached hereto and specifically made a part of this Agreement. The work or services to be performed by you may be changed by the Corporation from time to time by letter requests sent to you. You shall keep the Corporation informed on the progress of any work being performed under this Agreement.

3. **Compensation and expenses.**

(a) The Corporation will pay you a total fee of $ _____ for all work performed hereunder on satisfactory completion of the work.

(b) Your compensation will be at the rate of $ _____ per month for all work performed hereunder. You will be paid at the same time you are reimbursed for approved expenses under paragraph 3(c) below.

(c) You will receive reimbursement for the actual cost of reasonable expenses arising out of the work performed under this Agreement (not to exceed $ _____), subject to the approval of the Corporation. You shall deliver an itemized statement to the Corporation on a monthly basis that shows fully the work being performed under this Agreement and all related expenses. The Corporation will pay you the amount of any authorized expenses within thirty (30) days of the receipt of the itemized statement of all expenses, submitted together with receipts for all hotel, car rental, air fare, and other transportation expenses for all other expenses of $25 or more.

4. **Working facilities.** You will be furnished with such facilities and services as shall be suitable for your position and adequate for the performance of your duties under this Agreement.

5. **Reports.** Any and all reports, manuscripts and any other work products, whether completed or not, that are prepared or developed by you as a part of the work under this Agreement shall be the property of the Corporation and shall be turned over to the Corporation promptly at the Corporation's request or at the termination of this Agreement, whichever is earlier.

6. **Independent contractor.** You shall exercise control over the means and manner in which you perform any work requested hereunder, and in all respects your relationship to the Corporation shall be that of an independent contractor serving as a consultant and not as an employee.

7. **Termination.** This Agreement may be terminated upon thirty (30) days' written notice by either party.

8. **Confidential information.** You agree that for the term of your appointment hereunder and for two (2) years thereafter, that you will not disclose to any person, firm or corporation any confidential information regarding the Corporation, its business, directors, officers and employees.

9. **Nonassignable.** This Agreement is personal in nature and is not assignable by you or by the Corporation.

10. **Arbitration.** Any controversy or claim arising out of the interpretation of this Agreement shall allow either party to submit the disputed clause to Arbitration under the Arbitration Act of (name of jurisdiction). The costs of such arbitration to be borne equally by both parties.

11. **Entire agreement.** This letter, including Exhibit A, contains the entire agreement of the parties. It may not be changed orally but only by an agreement signed by the party against whom enforcement of any waiver, change, modification, extension or discharge is sought.

I trust that the terms of this appointment meet with your approval. If so, please indicate this by signing a copy of this letter and returning it to the Corporation. An additional copy of this letter is enclosed for your records.

Very truly yours,

_____
Client signature

Accepted and agreed to this _____ day of _____, 198 _____.

_____
Consultant signature

Other situations where a formal contract might be considered, are if you have a new client, a client who has never used consulting services before, or a client who has a reputation for being difficult in general, or complaining about fees in particular. Naturally, in this latter case, if you have advance notice it would be very wise to reconsider any involvement with that client.

Sample #21 illustrates a formal contract. Table #7 is a checklist of provisions frequently covered in contracts with government or industry.

4. Sub-consulting agreement

This is an agreement between you and any sub-consultants you employ to undertake a part or all of a consulting project you have arranged.

SAMPLE #20
STATEMENT OF GENERAL TERMS AND CONDITIONS

1. FEE STRUCTURE

All time, including travel hours, spent on the project by professional technical and clerical personnel will be billed. The following approximate ranges of hourly rates for various categories of personnel are currently in effect:

Category	Hourly Rate
Principal	$ 70
Consultant	50
Analyst	40
Technician	30
Typist	15

Hourly rates will be adjusted semi-annually to reflect changes in the cost of living index as published by (state name of appropriate government department). If overtime for non-professional personnel is required, the premium differential figured at time and one-half of their regular hourly rate is charged at direct cost to the project. Unless otherwise stated, any cost estimate presented in a proposal is for budgetary purposes only, and is not a fixed price. The client will be notified when 75% of any budget figure is reached, and the budget figure will not be exceeded without prior authorization from the client.

2. REIMBURSABLE EXPENSES

The following expenses will be billed at direct cost plus 15%:

(a) Travel expenses necessary for the execution of the project, including air fares, rental vehicles, and highway mileage in company or personal vehicles, which will, be charged at _____ cents per mile. Air travel will be by tourist class; except when tourist class service is not regularly available.

(b) Telephone charges
(c) Postage
(d) Printing and reproduction
(e) Computer services, including word processing

(f)   Other expenses directly attributable to the project.

Subcontracts will be billable at cost plus 15%.

3. INVOICES AND PAYMENTS

Invoices will be submitted monthly and payment is due on receipt of invoice. A 2% per month service charge will be added to all delinquent accounts. In the event Consultant shall be successful in prosecuting any suit for damages for breach of this agreement, including suits for non-payment of invoices, to enforce this agreement, or to enjoin the other party from violating this agreement, Consultant shall be entitled to recover as part of its damages its reasonable legal costs and expenses for bringing and maintaining any such action.

Rates for foreign contracts are negotiable and the above rates do not apply.

4. WARRANTY

Our professional services will be performed, our findings obtained, and our recommendations prepared, in accordance with generally and currently accepted management consulting principles and practices. The warranty is in lieu of all other warranties either expressed or implied.

5. LIMITATION OF PROFESSIONAL LIABILITY

The Client agrees to limit any and all liability or claim for damage, for cost of defense, or for any expenses to be levied against Consultant to a sum not to exceed $15,000, or the amount of our fee, whichever is less, when such claim arises from any error, omission, or professional negligence on the part of Consultant.

6. OTHER DOCUMENTS

(e.g., Proposal letter dated _____) is hereby made a part of this document.

7. ACCEPTANCE BY CLIENT

Client, by signing below, hereby agrees to these general terms and conditions of Client except as noted below:

CLIENT (typed name of client)

BY: _____

(Signature)

(Name and Designation)

SAMPLE #21
CONSULTING CONTRACT

ABC Trainers Inc. (hereinafter called "the Company") desires to utilize the expert assistance of _____ (hereinafter called "the Consultant") in the field or fields in which the Consultant has professional qualifications.

1. Parties and relationships

The Company is a corporation engaged in the business of consulting and the provision of technical assistance and training to small business through the use of skilled independent contractors. The Consultant is a person who by education, training and experience is skilled in the provision of the service required.

2. Character and extent of services

(a) It is the mutual intent of the parties that the Consultant shall act strictly in a professional consulting capacity as an independent contractor for all purposes and in all situations and shall not be considered an employee of the Company.

(b) The Consultant reserves full control of his activities as to the manner and selection of methods with respect to rendering his professional consulting services to the Company.

(c) The Consultant agrees to perform his activities in accordance with the highest and best state of the art of his profession.

3. Period of service and termination

(a) The period of service by the Consultant under this agreement shall be from _____ through _____ and may be renewed upon the mutual agreement of the parties hereto.

(b) Either the Company or the Consultant may terminate this agreement by giving the other party 30 days' written notice of intention of such action.

(c) The Company reserves the right to halt or terminate the conduct of a seminar-workshop by the Consultant without prior notice or claim for additional compensation should, in the opinion of the Company, such conduct not be in the best interests of the Company.

4. Compensation

(a) Upon the Consultant's acceptance hereof, the Company agrees to pay the Consultant according to the following schedule:

(Insert compenstion rate or fixed fee and any allowance for or schedule of allowable expenses, if any.)

(b) In the event that the Company desires, and it is mutually agreed to by the Consultant, the Consultant's services may be used in the conduct of training/consulting programs not specifically identified in paragraph 4(a). In such cases, the Company agrees to pay the Consultant on the basis of the following schedule:

(Insert compensation rate or fixed fee and any allowance for or schedule of allowable expenses, if any.)

(c) In the event of special circumstances, variations to the fee schedule of paragraphs 4(a) and 4(b) will be allowed as mutually agreed to in writing by the parties hereto.

5. Notification

The Consultant will be notified by the Company in writing to begin his participation in specific training and/or consultation assignments to which the fee schedule of paragraphs 4(a) and 4(b) apply. Such notification will include a statement of the time(s) and place(s) of the intended training/consultation involvement with other necessary information.

6. Expenses

The Consultant, as an independent contractor, shall be responsible for any expenses incurred in the performance of this agreement, except as otherwise agreed to in writing prior to such expenses being incurred. The Company will reimburse the Consultant for reasonable travel expenses incurred with respect hereto.

(A specification of "reasonable" may be inserted here).

7. Method of payment

(a)   The Consultant shall be paid as provided for in paragraphs 4(a) and 4(b) hereof, on the basis of a properly executed "Claim for Consulting Service" form (sample attached).

(b)   The "Claim for Consulting Service" form is to be submitted at the end of the calendar month during which consulting services are performed. Exceptions to this arrangement are allowed with the written approval of the Company.

(c)   Payment to the Consultant will be made by check, delivered by certified mail postmarked no later than _____ days subsequent to receipt of the "Claim for Consulting Service" form as provided for in paragraphs 7(a) and 7(b).

8. Copyrights

(a)   The Consultant agrees that the Company shall determine the disposition of the title to and the rights under any copyright secured by the Consultant or his employee on copyrightable material first produced or composed and delivered to the Company under this agreement. The Consultant hereby grants to the Company a royalty fee, non-exclusive, irrevocable license to reproduce, translate, publish, use and dispose of, and to authorize others to do so, all copyrighted or copyrightable work not first produced or composed by the Consultant in the performance of this agreement but which is incorporated into the material furnished under this agreement, provided that such license shall be only to the extent the Consultant now has or prior to the completion or final settlement of this agreement may acquire the right to grant such license without becoming liable to pay compensation to others solely because of such grant.

(b)   The Consultant agrees that he will not knowingly include any copyrighted material in any written or copyrightable material furnished or delivered under this agreement without a license as provided in paragraph 8(a) hereof or without the consent of the copyright owner, unless specific written approval of the Company to the inclusion of such copyrighted material is secured.

(c)   The Consultant agrees to report in writing to the Company promptly and in reasonable detail any notice or claim of copyright infringement received by the Consultant with respect to any material delivered under this agreement.

9. Drawings, designs, specifications

(a)   All drawings, sketches, designs, design data, specifications, notebooks, technical and scientific data, and all photographs, negatives, reports, findings, recommendations, data and memoranda of every description relating thereto, as well as all copies of the foregoing, relating to the work performed under this agreement or any part thereof, shall be subject to the inspection of the Company at all reasonable times; and the Consultant and his employees shall afford the Company proper facilities for such inspection; and further shall be the property of the Company and may be used by the Company for any purpose whatsoever without any claim on the part of the Consultant and his employees for additional compensation, and subject to the right of the Consultant to retain a copy of said material shall be delivered to the Company or otherwise disposed of by the Consultant, either as the Company may from time to time direct during the progress of the work, or in any event, as the Company shall direct upon the completion or termination of this agreement.

10. Confidentiality

(a)   It is understood that in the performance of his duties, the Consultant will obtain information about both the Company and the Company's client, and that such information may include financial data, client lists, methods of operating, policy statements, and other confidential data.

(b)   The Consultant agrees to restrict his use of such above-mentioned information to the performance of duties described in this agreement. The Consultant further agrees to return to the Company and to the Company's client upon the completion of his duties any and all documents (originals and copies) taken from either organization to facilitate the project described herein.

11. Non-competition

The consultant agrees that he will not perform his professional services for any organization known to the Consultant to be a client of the Company unless the Company has employed the Consultant for the provision of such services to the client. This restriction shall remain in effect for a period of two years after the termination of this agreement. For the purposes of this section, "client" is defined as any organization, which during the said period of restriction, has engaged the Company to promote:

(Provide a list of all the services/products provided by the Company).

12. Applicable law

The parties agree that this agreement is to be construed according to the laws of _____ (state jurisdiction).

13. Assignment

The Company reserves the right to assign all or any part of its interest in and to this agreement. The Consultant may not assign or transfer this agreement, any interest therein or claim thereunder without the written approval of the Company.

14. Integration

This agreement, executed in duplicate, constitutes the entire contract between the parties and may be cancelled, modified, or amended only by a written supplemental document executed by each of the parties hereto.

IN WITNESS WHEREOF, the parties hereto have accepted and executed this agreement this _____ day of _____, 198 ____.

_____   _____

John Smith, Consultant   ABC Trainers Inc.

                                                   by: _____
                                                   (Authorized signatory)

TABLE #4
DETAILED CONTRACT CHECKLIST
(Commonly used for government contracts)

GENERAL

1. Date of agreement

2. Identification of client and consultant, including transfer of responsibility to successors (if the client is a public body, the authority under which it acts and the source of available funds should be specified.)

3. Review of the background and brief definition of the project.

4. Scope of the assignment, including references to any detailed description incorporated in appendices

5. Effective date of commencement of work, when different from 1. and estimated or stipulated time for completion

6. Designation of individuals in client and consultant organizations responsible for policy decisions

7. Work Statement containing a description of the requirements in detail (The description should include the problem to be solved or the objective of the investigation, the approach or method to be used, and the extent or degree of work to be undertaken. The proposed statement of work should be sufficiently descriptive so as to become a usable yardstick).

8. Provision for changes in the work requirements

9. Provision for arbitration of disputes

10. Provision for termination by either party for "cause" or "convenience"

RESPONSIBILITIES OF THE CONSULTANT

1. Specify a project leader, professional help, services, and information to be supplied

2. Work schedule to be maintained

3. Personnel to be supplied (may be detailed in appendix).

4. Availability for conferences with the client

5. Reporting, including the schedule and nature of reports

TABLE #4 — Continued

6. Ownership of designs, blueprints, reports, etc., to be specified in the contract

7. Safeguarding of information supplied by client

8. Guarantee of performance, where required.

9. Limitation of liability of the consultant with regard to loss or damage of reports, third party use of reports, errors or omissions or professional negligence (this provision for the benefit of the consultant)

10. Right to cancel the contract upon written notice of (x) days, provided that nonperformance of the other party can be clearly documented and provided that the defaulting party has been given (x) days to make good nonperformance.

11. Provision for disposal of any or all materials used in the performance of work

RESPONSIBILITIES OF THE CLIENT

1. Information, services, and facilities to be provided

2. Availability for conference with the consultant

3. Number of days of staff support by client agency staff

4. Prompt review and approval of reports and products

5. Changes clause

DURATION OF CONTRACT

1. Stipulation of termination, either by stating a specific date, or by indicating the duration of the operation from the execution of the contract

2. Provision and mechanism for the modification of the specified date by mutual agreement

3. Provision for extension or renewal

4. Provision and mechanism for early termination by either party

5. Termination by reason of events beyond control of either party

6. Provision against delays

FINANCIAL PROVISIONS

1. Total financial commitment by the client

2. Method and schedule of billing by the consultant

3. Method of payment

4. Currency or currencies of payment and conversation rates

5. Guarantee of payment by the client

6. Payment of interest on delayed payments

7. What are patent requirements? Who has copyright in reports and other products? Who has publication rights and under what circumstances?

8. Payment shall be made within (x) days of billing, billing to be by arrangement

TABLE #4 — Continued

> 9. Allowable costs or expenses to be billed separately from labor costs shall include but not be limited to:
>
> Telephone
> Postage and courier
> Travel
> Accommodation & miscellaneous
> Photocopying and printing
> Graphics
> Special typing support
> Translation
> Miscellaneous special materials
> Computer costs
> Subcontractual services

It is quite common for consultants to sub-contract work out to other consultants. You may use sub-consultants to keep overhead low, or if you are unable to perform the task yourself because you lack expertise in the area, or because a large project requires a large number of support resource personnel.

Generally you need not explain to your client that you are using sub-contracting services, unless your client specifically asks. Sometimes a client would like to have the qualifications of a sub-contractor clarified. You are ultimately responsible for the quality of the work performed by your sub-consultants and therefore must be very selective. You should monitor and approve all work performed by the sub-consultant. All services performed by the sub-consultant are performed under your consulting company's name. All correspondence pertaining to the project is printed only on your stationery. In all outward respects, the sub-consultant is your employee under your direction.

Your sub-contracting agreement should clearly spell out that the relationship of the sub-consultant to you is one of an independent contractor. You should also seriously consider a non-competition clause in the contract restricting the sub-contractor from taking advantage of access to your clients to sell consulting services directly. A non-competition clause or restrictive covenant can vary depending upon the circumstances and the laws of your jurisdiction. Legal advice should be obtained before you complete any contract to be certain that the non-competition clause would be reasonably upheld as fair and appropriate if it were contested. The clause normally states that the sub-consultant shall not perform professional services independently of your firm to any of your clients past or present. The exception would be under your direct employ as an independent contractor. A two-year time period for the restriction is fairly common. The restriction covers a wide or narrow geographic base depending on the nature of your services.

A summary of the standard clauses that should be considered include:

(a) The parties to the contract

(b) Independent contractor status of sub-consultant

(c) The responsibilities of the sub-consultant fully specified

(d) Term of the contract

(e) Amount and method of payment for fees and expenses

(f) A cancellation provision in case the contract is cancelled

(g) The method and amount of remuneration to be paid to the sub-consultant up to the point of cancellation

(h) A confidentiality provision stating that all the client information accessible to the sub-consultant is to be held in strict confidence

(i) All documents obtained by the sub-consultant are to be returned to the consultant or client

(j) Provision that the contract cannot be assigned or duties delegated without the written consent of both parties

(k) Other "standard" or "unique" provisions

Sample #21 which shows a consultant contract can also be used as a format for a sub-consulting contract.

5. Agency agreement

An agency agreement is a contract that would be prepared if you were acting for a client as an external agent: for example, if you were selling a product on behalf of a client, or negotiating on behalf of the client with the government for funding purposes. The clauses in this type of contract vary considerably. Generally the client prepares the agreement for you to sign.

6. Letter of retainer agreement

This is an agreement that you outline in a letter. One form of retainer relationship is when you are available "on call" at the request of a client based on need of your services. The consultant charges the client for being "on call" and available, even though the consultant may not be used.

Another form of retainer relationship is if you provide a service on a periodic basis, for example, monthly or quarterly.

e. PREPARING YOUR OWN CONTRACT

You should consider having several standardized contracts with variations depending on the different types of consulting services you perform. Space can be left in the contract for inserting the unique features of a specific consulting project. If your contracts are stored on a word processor or a personal computer with word processing capabilities, each contract can easily be personalized in an original format for each consulting job.

The process of preparing your own contract is not difficult. Try to obtain as many sample forms of contracts as possible from your competitors and from contract books that are available from your local library or law school. Then refer to the various headings outlined in this chapter or shown in the sample contracts or checklists. Outline the areas that you feel are important for your particular type of consulting services or problems. As soon as you have completed this exercise, expand on the points in a descriptive paragraph and then sub-divide into clauses in a format appropriate to your needs and in a style you prefer.

Take your draft contracts to your lawyer to evaluate. It is to your benefit to save your lawyer's time and your money by preparing the documents yourself. You are most familiar with your work and the important factors of your projects. Your lawyer can review your draft contracts and rewrite them or add additional clauses if required.

Major companies or government frequently have their own standardized contracts and send them to you for signature. In some cases there is room for negotiation; in other cases no negotiation is possible. If you are presented with the contract, you should review it thoroughly yourself and mark the areas that cause you concern. Also, note the areas that are not in the contract that you would prefer to have covered. Then discuss the contract with your lawyer. If you have any doubts about the required provisions of the contract, it is best to either negotiate those provisions out if possible, or not accept the project. If a contract is not completely to your liking, the degree of risk or dissatisfaction on your part or your client's part is high.

If a client wants to make changes to your contract, it is better to make the changes rather than have them make up their own contract. A client-prepared contract could have clauses or conditions you do not want.

In summary, attempt to prepare all your own contracts. The client relationship will therefore be established on *your* terms. Your initiative and leadership in preparing the contract should have a positive effect on the dynamics of the relationship with your client.

19

EXPANDING YOUR PRACTICE

There are many ways of acquiring clients. The simplest way is to keep your existing clients happy and nurture the present and past clients well. Studies show that over 70% of a consultant's business is based on repeat business or referral business from existing clients. A marketing formula shows that the average person has over 200 contacts including friends, relatives, and associates. By carefully developing this client potential you can expand your practice rapidly.

For example, from one satisfied client you could obtain numerous projects sufficient to keep you busy on an ongoing basis. If your client gives you repeat work on a regular basis and also recommends you to 10 other business associates in the same industry and 5 of them become clients, your business will grow. Former employees of the first client or referral clients may go to work for other firms in the private or public sector. If they enjoyed working with you, they will request your services again or refer work to you. The possibilities are limitless.

An effective way of keeping your clients satisfied is to create client dependency. The more the client relies on you because of your specialty, the more repeat business you will generate. The more your client respects you for your knowledge and leadership, the more the client will look to you for guidance.

It is important that the client feel in control at all times. You must maintain your image as a unique commodity. Your role is to complement staff. You do not want to be perceived as just another person on staff.

If there are particular tasks that the client does not enjoy, and you can fill the void and have the skills and ability to perform the task, and the situation seems appropriate, this could create further dependency. If the outcome of a project is particularly successful and considerable positive feedback occurs, make a point of having your client share the glory with you. A satisfied client will appreciate your value, and provide you with more consulting contracts.

There are other ways of developing your practice. Expanding your line by adding additional services that are natural extensions of your first service is effective. If you have clients that retain you for one service, you are creating a potential two or three-fold growth pattern with all your clientele. Because you already have the credibility with the client for one project, it will be much easier for you to market your skills for the other services.

Sub-contracting is another way of expanding your practice. You can locate sub-contractors from your contract contact network and through referral. They can be effectively used to increase your earnings by providing depth and greater capacity for your business. You would be in a position to make proposals for larger or more complex projects using past, present or future clients as your base. If a client has been satisfied with your service on a smaller project or a particular service line, and you have additional service lines and a greater depth and capacity, the prospects are endless. Naturally, sub-contracting will involve more administration for you, but the independent contractor status of sub-consultants will allow you flexibility to hire them on a need basis.

Other ways of expanding your practice are to review all aspects of your operation on an ongoing basis, note the weak areas and develop a specific plan for dealing with them. Areas such as self-promotion and more efficient follow-up on leads can also enhance your clientele base.

A free brochure about seminars, mail order books, and tapes concerned with consulting practices is available upon request.

Please send your comments about this book, or your request for further information to:

Professional Development International
#310 - 1070 West Broadway
Vancouver, British Columbia
V6H 1E7

or

#200 - 15 Veteran Way
Oakland, California 94602

BIBLIOGRAPHY

a. GENERAL CONSULTING

Altman, Mary Ann & Weil, Robert I. *Managing Your Accounting and Consulting Business.* Matthew Bender, 1978.

Bailey, Geoffrey. *Maverick: Succeeding as a Freelance Entrepreneur.* Lester & Orpen Dennys, 1983.

Blake, Robert R. & Mauton, Jane S. *Consultation.* Addison Wesley, 1970.

Gore, George J. & Wright, Robert G. *The Academic Consultant's Connection.* Kendall-Hunt Publishing Co., 1979.

Guttman, H.P. *The International Consultant.* McGraw-Hill, 1976.

Holtz, Herman. *How to Succeed as an Independent Consultant.* John Wiley & Sons, 1983.

Johnson, Barbara L. *Private Consulting.* Prentice-Hall, 1982.

Kelley, Robert E. *Consulting: the Complete Guide to a Profitable Career.* Charles Scribner's Sons, 1981.

Lant, Jeffrey L. *The Consultant's Kit.* JLA Publications, 1981.

Lippitt, Gordon & Lippitt, Ronald. *The Consulting Process in Action.* University Associates Inc., 1978.

McGonagle, John J. *Managing the Consultant: a Corporate Guide.* Chilton Books, 1981.

Pickens, Judy E. *The Freelancer's Handbook.* N.J.: Prentice-Hall, 1981.

Pilon, Daniel H. & Bergguist, William H. *Consultation in Higher Education.* Council for Advancement of Small Colleges, 1979.

Shenson, Howard L. *Consulting Handbook.* Howard L. Shenson Inc., 1982.

———————— *The Successful Consultant's Guide to Fee Setting.* Howard L. Shenson Inc., 1980.

_____ _____ *How to Strategically Negotiate the Consulting Contract.* Bermont Books, 1980.

Spiro, Herbert T. *Financial Planning for the Independent Professional.* John Wiley & Sons, 1978.

Stanley, C.M. *The Consulting Engineer.* John Wiley & Sons, 1961.

Steele, Fritz. *Consulting for Organizational Change.* University of Massachusetts Press, 1975.

Smith, Brian R. *The Country Consultant.* Consultant News, a Division of Kennedy & Kennedy, Inc., 1982.

b. CONSULTING NEWSLETTERS

Consultant's News (monthly). Kennedy & Kennedy Inc., Templeton Road, Fitzwilliam, NH 03447.

Consulting Opportunities Journal (bimonthly), 1629 K Street, N.W., Suite 520, Washington, DC 20006.

Granstmanship Center News (8 times a year). The Grantsmanship Center News, 1015 West Olympia Blvd., Los Angeles, CA 90015.

International Consulting News (semi-annually). International Consultants Foundation, 5605 Lamar Road, Washington, DC 20016.

The Professional Consultant (monthly). Howard L. Shenson Inc., 20121 Ventura Blvd., Woodland Hills, CA 91364.

c. GOVERNMENT CONSULTING

Bermont, Hubert. *The Successful Consultant's Guide to Winning Government Contracts.* Bermont Books, 1981.

Bermont, Hubert & Garnin, Andrew. *How to Win with Information or Lose Without It.* Bermont Books, 1981.

Cohen, W.A. *How to Sell to the Government.* John Wiley & Sons, 1981.

Gowan, Vincent Q. *Consulting to Government.* Ottawa: Infoscan Ltd., 1979.

Holtz, Herman. *The $100 Billion Market: How to do Business with the U.S. Government.* AMACOM, 1980.

_____ *Directory of Federal Purchasing Offices: Where, What, How to Sell to the U.S. Government,* John Wiley & Sons, 1981.

_____ *Government Contracts: Proposalmanship and Winning Strategies.* Plenum Publishing Corp., 1979.

Murphy, Harry. *Grantsmanship Consulting.* Howard L. Shenson Inc., 1981.

d. MANAGEMENT CONSULTING

Albert, Kenneth J. *How to be Your Own Management Consultant.* McGraw Hill Book Company, 1978.

Fuchs, Jerome H. *Making the Most of Management Consulting Services.* American Management Association, 1975.

_____ *Management Consultants in Action.* Hawthorne Books Inc., 1975.

Greiner, Larry E. & Metzger, Robert O. *Consulting to Management.* Prentice Hall, 1983.

How to Control the Quality of a Management Consulting Engagement. Association of Consulting Management Engineers, 1972.

Klein, Howard J. *Other People's Business: A Primer on Management Consultants.* Mason-Charter Publishing, 1977.

Kubr, M. *Management Consulting: A Guide to the Profession.* International Labor Office, 1982.

Kuttner, M. *Managing the Paperwork Pipeline.* John Wiley & Sons, 1978.

Schein, E. *Organizational Psychology.* Prentice-Hall, 1965.

Thompson, A.A. and Strickland, A.J. *Strategy Formulation and Implementation.* Business Publications, 1980.

e. MARKETING

Gray, Douglas A. and Cyr, Donald G. *Marketing Your Product.* Self-Counsel Press, 1987.

Hammeroff, Eugene & Nichols, Sandra. *How to Guarantee Professional Success: 765 Tested, Proven Techniques for Promoting Your Practice.* Bermont Books, 1982.

Holtz, Herman. *Winning Clients.* John Wiley & Sons, 1988.

Johnston, Karen and Withers, Jean. *Selling Strategies for Service Businesses.* Self-Counsel Press, 1988.

Kennedy, James H. *Public Relations for Management Consultants.* Consultants News.

Kotler, Philip and Bloom, Paul N. *Marketing Professional Services.* Prentice-Hall, 1984.

Lant, Jeffrey. *The Unabashed Self-Promoter's Guide.* Jeffrey Lant Associates Inc., 1983.

Mahon, J.J. *The Marketing of Professional Accounting Services.* John Wiley & Sons, 1978.

Marcus, Bruce W. *Competing for Clients.* Probus Publishing, 1986.

Shenson, Howard L. & Schacter, J. *Marketing Your Professional Services.* Howard L. Shenson Inc., 1981.

Todd, Alden, *Finding Facts Fast: How to Find Out What You Want to Know Immediately.* William Morrow & Company, 1972.

Watson, Dr. Ken, *The Consultant's Guide to Business Development.* Evaluation & Strategic Management Associates Ltd., 1984.

Webb, Stan. G. *Marketing and Strategic Planning for Professional Service Firms.* Amacom, 1982.

Weiner, Richard D. *Professional's Guide to Public Relations.* Richard Weiner Inc.

Wilson, Aubrey. *The Marketing of Professional Services.* McGraw Hill, 1972.

Withers, Jean and Vipperman, Carol. *Marketing Your Service.* Self-Counsel Press, 1987.

f.   NEGOTIATING

Coffin, R.A. *The Negotiator.* American Management Association, 1973.

Cohen, Herb. *You Can Negotiate Anything.* Bantam Books, 1980.

Fisher, Roger & Ury, William. *Getting to Yes: Negotiating Agreement Without Giving In.* Houghton-Mifflin, 1981.

Karrass, Chester L. *Give and Take: The Complete Guide to Negotiating Strategies and Tactics.* Thomas Y. Crawell Publishers, 1974.

Levin, Edward. *Negotiating Tactics: Bargain Your Way to Winning.* Fawcett Columbine Books, 1982.

Niremberg, Gerard I. *The Art of Negotiating.* Cornerstone Library, 1968.

_____ *The Art of Creative Thinking.* Simon & Shuster, 1982.

_____ *Fundamentals of Negotiating.* Hawthorn/Dutton, 1968.

_____ *How to Give and Receive Advice.* Editorial Correspondents Inc., 1975.

Niremberg, Gerard I. & Calero, H. *How to Read a Person Like a Book.* Simon & Shuster, 1971.

_____ *Meta-talk: How to Uncover the Hidden Meanings in What People Say.* Simon & Shuster, 1973.

Schatzki, Michael. *Negotiation: The Art of Getting What You Want.* New American Library, 1981.

Warschaw, Tessa Alberta. *Winning by Negotiation.* McGraw-Hill, 1980.

g. NEWSLETTERS

Beach, Mark. *Editing Your Newsletter.* International Self-Counsel Press, 1983.

Holtz, Herman. *Successful Newsletter Publishing for the Consultant.* Bermont Publishing, 1983.

Hudson, H.P. *Publishing Newsletters.* Charles Scribners Sons, 1980.

The Newsletter on Newsletters. Newsletter Clearinghouse.

Shenson, Howard L. *How to Develop and Promote Your Own Newsletter for Profit and/or Personal Image Building.* Howard L. Shenson, Inc., 1980.

h. PRESENTATIONS AND PUBLIC SPEAKING

Boettinger, Henry M. *Moving Mountains: The Art of Letting Others See Things Your Way.* MacMillan.

Carnegie, Dale. *How to Develop Self-Confidence and Influence People by Public Speaking.* Simon and Shuster, 1936.

Dunckel, Jacqueline & Parnham, Elizabeth. *The Business Guide to Effective Speaking.* International Self-Counsel Press, 1984.

Leech, Thomas. *How to Prepare, Stage and Deliver Winning Proposals.* Amacom, 1982.

Lewis, David V. *Secrets of Successful Writing, Speaking and Listening.* Amacom, 1982.

Shenson, Howard L. *How Consultants Can Build a Lucrative Paid Speaking Business.* Howard L. Shenson Inc., 1982.

Spicer, Keith. *The Winging It Logic System.* Doubleday, 1982.

i. PROPOSAL WRITING AND REPORTS (see also Writing and Publishing)

Ammon-Wexsler, J. & Carmel, C. *How to Create a Winning Proposal.* Mercury Publications, 1978.

Bermont, Hubert. *The Successful Consultant's Guide to Writing Proposals and Reports.* Bermont Books, 1979.

Dunnigan, J.A. & Shenson, Howard L. *The Consultant's Guide to Proposal Writing.* Howard L. Shenson, 1981.

Ewing, D.W. *Writing for Results in Business, Government, Science and the Professions.* John Wiley & Sons, 1979.

Gallagher, William J. *Report Writing for Management.* Addison-Wesley, 1969.

Holtz, Herman and Schmidt, Terry. *The Winning Proposal: How to Write It.* McGraw Hill, 1981.

Kapp, R.P. *The Presentation of Technical Information.* Constable & Company Ltd., 1973.

Mandel, S. & Caldwell. *Proposal and Inquiry Writing.* MacMillan, 1962.

Program Planning and Proposal Writing. The Grantsmanship Center News.

Strunk, W. & White, E.B. *The Elements of Style.* MacMillan Publishing, 1972.

Watson, Dr. Ken. *Preparing Winning Proposals.* Evaluation & Strategic Management Associates Ltd., 1982.

j. SELF-EVALUATION AND DEVELOPMENT

Bolles, Richard N. *The Three Boxes of Life and How to Get Out of Them.* Ten Speed Press.

_____ *What Color is Your Parachute: A Practical Manual for Job-hunters and Career Changes.* Ten Speed Press, 1984.

Crystal, John C. and Bolles, Richard N. *Where Do I Go From Here With My Life.* **Ten Speed Press, 1981.**

Gray, Douglas A. *The Entrepreneur's Complete Self-Assessment Guide: How to accurately determine your potential for success.* **International Self-Counsel Press, 1986.**

Lakein, Alan. *How to Get Control of Your Time and Your Life.* **The New American Library, 1973.**

Molloy, John. *Dress for Success.* **Warner Books, 1975.**

Traxel, K. *Manager's Guide to Successful Job Hunting.* **McGraw-Hill, 1978.**

k. SMALL BUSINESS MANAGEMENT

Albert, Kenneth J. *How to Pick the Right Small Business Opportunity.* **McGraw-Hill, 1977.**

Armstrong, Michael. *Be a Better Manager.* **International Self-Counsel Press Ltd., 1984.**

Baumbeck, Clifford M. & Lawyer, Kenneth. *How to Organize and Manage a Small Business.* **Prentice-Hall, 1979.**

Brown, Beaner. *The Entrepreneur's Guide.* **Ballantine Books, 1982.**

Curtin, Richard T. *Running Your Own Show: Mastering the Basics of Small Business.* **New American Library, 1982.**

Dible, D. *Up Your Own Organization: A Handbook to Start and Finance a New Business.* **The Entrepreneur Press, 1978.**

Gray, Douglas A. and Gray, Diana L. *The Complete Canadian Small Business Guide.* **McGraw-Hill Ryerson, 1988.**

Greene, Gardiner G. *How to Start and Manage Your Own Business.* **New American Library, 1983.**

James, Jack. *Starting a Successful Business in Canada.* **International Self-Counsel Press, 1986.**

Mancuso, Joesph R. *How to Start, Finance and Manage Your Own Small Business.* **Prentice-Hall, 1978.**

_____ *Small Business Survival Guide.* **Prentice-Hall, 1980.**

Maumes, William. *The Entrepreneurial Manager in the Small Business.* **Addison-Wesley, 1978.**

Timmons, J., Smollen, L. and Dingee, A. *New Venture Creation: A Guide to Small Business Development.* Richard D. Irwin Inc., 1977.

l. TIME/STRESS MANAGEMENT

Anderson, R. *Stress Power.* Human Science Press, 1978.

Benson, H. *The Relaxation Response.* Avon Books, 1975.

Bliss, E. *Getting Things Done.* Charles Scribners Sons, 1976.

Friedman, M. & Rosenman, R. *Type A Behavior and Your Heart.* Fawcett Crest, 1974.

Lahaye, Tim. *How to Manage Pressure Before Pressure Manages You.* Zonderervan Publishing House, 1983.

Lakein, A. *How to Get Control of Your Time and Life.* The New American Library, 1974.

Mackenzie, R. Alec. *The Time Trap: How to Get More Done in Less Time.* McGraw-Hill, 1972.

McCay, James T. *The Management of Time.* Prentice-Hall, 1950.

McRae, Brad. *Practical Time Management.* Self-Counsel Press, 1988.

Neidhardt, E. J.; Weinstein, M. S.; and Conry, R. F. *Managing Stress.* Self-Counsel Press, 1985.

Rosen, G. *The Relaxation Book.* Prentice-Hall, 1977.

Selye, Hans. *Stress Without Distress.* New American Library, 1974.

Taylor, Harold L. *Making Time Work For You: A Guidebook to Effective and Productive Time Management.* General Publishing Co. Ltd., 1981.

_____ *Managing Your Memory.* General Publishing Ltd., 1982.

_____ *Personal Organization: The Key to Managing Your Time and Your Life.* Time Management Consultants Inc., 1983.

Warshaw, Leon J. *Managing Stress.* Addison-Wesley Publishing Co., 1979.

m. WRITING AND PUBLISHING (see also Proposal Writing and Reports)

Applebaum, Judith and Evans, Nancy. *How to Get Happily Published.* Harper & Row.

Bermont, Hubert. *The Successful Consultant's Guide to Authoring, Publishing and Lecturing.* Bermont Books, 1979.

Davidson, Marion and Blue, Martha. *Making It Legal: A Law Primer for the Craftmaker, Visual Artist and Writer.* McGraw Hill, 1979.

Ewing, David W. *Writing for Results in Business, Government and the Professions.* John Wiley & Sons, 1974.

Goodman, Joseph. *How to Publish, Promote and Sell Your Book.* Adams Press, 1980.

Mathiew, Aron. *The Book Market: How To Write, Publish and Market Your Book.* Andover Press, 1981.

The Writers Handbook. The Writer Inc.

Provost, Gary. *The Freelance Writer's Handbook.* New American Library, 1982.

Wilbur, Perry L. *How to Write Articles That Sell.* John Wiley & Sons, 1981.

_____ *How to Write Books That Sell.* Contemporary Books, 1979.

n. SEMINARS AND WORKSHOPS

Murray, Sheila L. *How to Organize and Manage a Seminar.* Prentice-Hall, 1983.

Shenson, Howard L. *How to Create and Market a Successful Seminar or Workshop.* Howard L. Shenson Inc., 1981.

Watson, Walter; Pardo, Luis & Tomouic, Vladislav. *How to Give an Effective Seminar.* General Publishing, 1978.

SOURCES OF PROCUREMENT AND CONTRACTS INFORMATION

a. SCIENCE PROCUREMENT INFORMATION NETWORK (CANADA)

This is a computerized "source information system" maintained by the Department of Supply and Services as a service to client departments. All consultants should ask for their capabilities to be entered on the system. This can take four to six months from the time of application.

Consultants' names are retrieved from the system by a "keyword" coding. The department has a book of keywords that covers location, industry groups, science fields, and specialization: *The Index of Science Procurement Key Words.*

Searches are normally done sequentially. First with a full list of desirable keywords, then, depending on the response, with less specific or demanding lists.

Write to:

Data Administrator
Science Procurement Information
    Network & Main Sourcing List
Supply and Services Canada
Place du Portage, Phase 3
Floor 10C1
11 Laurier Street
Hull, Quebec
K1A 0S5

Professional Services Branch
    Sourcing List (Canada)
Science and Professional Services Directorate
Place du Portage, Phase 3
11 Laurier Street
Hull, Quebec
K1A 0S5

b. THE R & D BULLETIN (CANADA)

The R & D Bulletin is published by the Canadian federal government in the second week of each month and contains three main sections:

(a) Projects for which proposals are expected to be invited

(b) Statistical summary

(c) Contracts awarded during the previous month

The first section describes selected research and development requirements for which the Science Centre of the Department of Supply and Services expects to solicit proposals. Organizations interested in submitting proposals may get further information from the science contract manager, listed against each requirement, at the following address:

Science Centre
Supply and Services Canada
Place du Portage, Phase 3
11 Laurier Street
Hull, Quebec
K1A 0S5

c. BULLETIN OF BUSINESS OPPORTUNITIES (CANADA)

This is a weekly listing of contracts awarded. Its only interest is perhaps the general one of seeing what other firms and departments are doing. Occasionally useful for identifying a subcontracting opportunity.

Information Services
Supply and Services Canada
Place du Portage, Phase 3
11 Laurier Street
Hull, Quebec
K1A 0S5

Program Export Market Development (Canada)
Department of External Affairs
125 Sussex Drive
Ottawa, Ontario
K1A 0G2

d. MULTILATERAL PROJECT INFORMATION SYSTEM (CANADA)

Each month Industry, Trade and Commerce (Canada) distributes project updates on multilateral projects worldwide. Distributed only to Canadian companies and organizations.

Office of Overseas Projects
Department of Industry, Trade and Commerce
Ottawa, Ontario
K1P 3X4

e. COMMERCE BUSINESS DAILY (U.S.)

The *Commerce Business Daily* (CBD) is published each weekday by the U.S. Department of Commerce. It identifies proposed defense procurements valued in excess of $10,000, and civilian agency procurements in excess of $5,000. It also lists contract awards over $25,000 for civilian agencies and $50,000 for military agencies. It is an essential source of information for the consultant.

The announcements are in a form similar to newspaper classified ads. A complete list of the classification headings is currently given on the back of the subscription form.

The principal sections of the CBD include:

(a) Business news: Announcements of procurement conferences, trade fairs, seminars, and small business assistance conferences.

(b) Procurement of services:

- Experimental development, test and research work
- Expert and consultant services
- Maintenance and repair of equipment
- Modification, alteration and rebuilding of equipment
- Technical representative services
- Operation and maintenance of government-owned facility
- Installation of equipment
- Medical services
- Architect — engineer services
- Housekeeping services
- Photographic, mapping, printing and publication services
- Training services
- Transportation services
- Lease or rental, except transportation equipment
- Miscellaneous
- New construction and major additions to existing buildings
- Maintenance repair and operation of real property

(c) Procurement of supplies, equipment and material

(d) Research and development sources sought

In order that potential sources may learn of research and development programs, advance notice of the government's interest in a specific research field is published here. Firms having the research and development capabilities described are invited to submit complete information to the purchasing office listed. Information requested generally includes: the total number of employees and professional qualification of scientists, engineers, and personnel specially qualified in the R & D area outlined, and description of general and special facilities, an outline of previous projects including specific work previously performed or being performed in the listed R & D area; statement regarding industrial security clearance previously granted; and other available descriptive literature. Note that these are not requests for proposals. Respondents are not notified of the results of the evaluation of the information submitted, but the sources deemed fully qualified are considered when requests for proposals are solicited. Closing date for submission of responses is 14 days from publication of the notice, unless otherwise specified.

(e) Contract awards

(Same subdivisions as earlier "procurements" section.)

(f) Trade leads

(Foreign construction and direct sales opportunities.)

CBD notices inform the reader whether response may be in the form of a request to be included among a list of possible contractors who will each be sent a formal request for proposal, or whether potential contractors should respond with a resume of experience, qualifications and capabilities to provide the advertised service, material or research. In the latter case, the RFP will be sent only if the qualifications are considered suitable for the proposed project.

(g) Numbered notes

As a space-saver the first issue of each week contains a definition for each of a series of numbered notes that are used in subsequent issues.

By the time a Request for Proposal appears in the CBD, the project will have been under active development within the government department for several months.

(h) Exemptions from publication in the CBD

Contracts of less than $10,000, classified contracts for reason of national security, and contracts resulting from an unsolicited proposal containing proprietary information.

A sole source procurement is published as an announcement for information only. This usually is a procurement where the government has been conducting research under contract with a certain firm and desires to extend the work for an additional period of time.

(i) Sources sought

A Sources Sought publication normally describes an area of research and development, rather than a specific program. It is used to cut down on the volume of synopses and to restrict those firms receiving copies of the Request for Proposal to only those actually qualified.

The information asked for will be equipment and facilities available, previous experience, resumes of key personnel, management ability, etc. It does not call for specific answers to specific problems but only for information to establish your capability to do research in the area of interest. It usually will have a response cutoff date and a prompt reply is

192

to your advantage. Sources Sought are published throughout the year, but usually during the summer to cover the coming fiscal year's program which begins October 1. After the responses to Sources Sought are evaluated, the respondents are not officially informed of their evaluation, but those found qualified are placed on a source list as a potential contractor in that area of interest. It is generally possible to confer with the evaluation team members concerning their assessment of your capabilities.

Government buyers are not allowed to give out either the size of the source list or the names of the sources. In all cases, the engineer and the buyer have the option, if they feel the firm is qualified, of adding firms to the source list even though those firms did not respond to the publication in the *Commerce Business Daily*.

(j) CBD subscription information

To order send remittance with full mailing address to:

Superintendent of Documents
Government Printing Office
Washington, DC 20402
(202) 783-3238.

Purchase order must be accompanied by payment. Make checks payable to Superintendent of Documents. Allow approximately six weeks for delivery of first issue.

f. COMMERCE CLEARING HOUSE REPORTS

Government Contracts Reports (U.S.) and numerous other U.S. and Canadian reports are available from:

Commerce Clearing House Inc. (U.S.)
425 13th Street, N.W.
Washington DC 20004

CCH Canada
6 Garamond Court
Don Mills, Ontario M3C 1Z5

g. FOUNDATION RESEARCH SERVICE (U.S.)

Foundation Research Service (F.R.S.), a subsidiary of Lawson & Williams Associates Inc., a management consultant firm, has dealt with the 1,000 largest foundations that account for 90% of all grants to all types of programs. They have introduced a new fundraising aid, called *The Foundation 500*. This publication is a cross-referenced system that matches foundations with 70 detailed subject categories such as arts, education, health, religion, international, science, welfare, etc. It also provides recipient-by-state categories showing what foundations have given in which of the 70 categories and in which of the 50 states and the District of Columbia.

Contact:

Foundation Research Service
c/o Lawson & Williams Associates, Inc.
39 East 51st Street
New York, NY 10022

h. THE CATALOGUE OF FEDERAL DOMESTIC ASSISTANCE

CFDA is the basic research tool for government grant seekers. Entries include complete information on numerous grant programs, and are cross-indexed.

Of special interest are Information Contacts and Related Programs. The former tells you where to find additional information on the program; the latter tells you where in CFDA you can find similar projects.

It gives information on grants, loans, loan guarantees, scholarships, mortgage loans, and insurance or other types of financial assistance. It also lists sources of assistance in the form of provision of federal property, facilities, equipment, goods, or services — including the donation of surplus, real, or personal property.

The CFDA is organized into three indexes: a functional index, a subject index, and an agency program index. Detailed program descriptions in the center portion of the catalogue are listed in the same order as the agency program index, alphabetically by name of the agency.

Continuous updating keeps the catalogue as current as possible, but the rapidity with which federal programs are wiped out and new ones established is such that it cannot be assumed that any listing is completely accurate at any given time.

The CFDA, a publication of the Executive Office of the President, Office of Management and Budget, may be ordered from:

Superintendent of Documents, U.S.
Government Printing Office
Washington, DC 20402

i. THE GRANTS REGISTER

The Grants Register is a broad research tool containing information on international granting programs as well as those conducted in the United States.

The Grants Register (current edition), Roland W. Turner (ed.), St. Martin's Press, Inc., New York, NY.

j. FUNDRAISING MANAGEMENT

This magazine has information about fundraising, such as computerized mailing lists, capital campaigns and whether you should use a window envelope for your direct mail piece. As one of the few commercial publications in the fundraising field, *Fundraising Management* is loaded with ads about direct mail lists, volunteer and donor recognition items, and conferences.

Write to:

Hoke Communications
224 Seventh Street
Garden City, Long Island, NY 11530

k. THE GUIDE TO FEDERAL ASSISTANCE (U.S.)

This is an information service on federal assistance programs, updated monthly. It includes consultation by "hot line" with staff. Write to:

The Guide to Federal Assistance
5791 Beaumont Avenue
La Jolla, CA 92037

l. THE FEDERAL REGISTER (U.S.)

The Federal Register, which is published every weekday by the U.S. Government, is a vital source of information about new programs and program changes. When legislation authorizing a program is signed into law, regulations implementing the legislation are supposed to be developed before funds are obligated. Those regulations must be published in the *Register*.

The Federal Register often contains valuable information on government contracts and/or grant programs described in *The Catalog of Federal Domestic Assistance*. Announcements related to programs usually deal with changes, expansions, or clarifications of programs already in existence. The *Register* is indexed monthly.

The Federal Register
Superintendent of Documents
U.S. Government Printing Office
Washington, DC 20402

m. LOCAL GOVERNMENT FUNDING REQUEST

Although oriented toward the concerns of local government, this newsletter may be of interest to consultants in that it offers fairly extensive coverage of developments in a number of policy and program areas. Write:

Government Information Services
752 National Press Building, N.W.
Washington, DC 20004

n. WASHINGTON RESEARCHERS (U.S.)

This information service provides clients with background reports, sources of information, expert opinions, documents from federal departments and agencies, facts and statistics, and Washington representation. The emphasis is on locating sources of information in the federal government. It includes:

- *The Information Report.* Quarterly. Free to clients
- Sources of information on corporations
- List of country experts in the federal government
- List of industry analysts in the federal government
- List of foreign firms with U.S. affiliates
- Sources of information for selling to the federal government

Write to:

Washington Researchers
2612 P Street N.W.
Washington, DC 20007

o. PROFESSIONAL SERVICES MANAGEMENT JOURNAL

Contains a variety of information useful to consultants in the design, architectural, and engineering fields, including current developments in contracting, marketing, time management, quality control, and consulting.

Practice Management Associates Ltd.
Ten Midland Avenue
Newton, MA 02158

p. CONSULTING DIRECTORIES

(a) *Consultants & Consulting Organizations Directory (Gale Research Company)*

Edited by Paul Wasserman and Janice McLean. 1,034 pages; 5,314 entries. Cross index of subjects; subject index of U.S. and Canadian firms by location; index of foreign firms; index of individuals.

Entries cover 10 major points of information:
- Name of organization
- Address
- Telephone number
- Date founded
- Branch offices
- Principals: officials and titles
- Type of clients
- Non-profit or profit-making

- Description of services: type of consulting performed
- Code numbers for subjects in which firm is active

Entries cover 146 fields of activity (cross-referenced).

(b) *Who's Who in Consulting (Gale Research Company)*

Edited by Paul Wasserman and Janice McLean. Cross index of subjects; subject index of consultants by location. Contains 7,500 entries; each entry covers 9 points:

- Individual's name
- Addresses, business and home
- Date and place of birth
- Education: institutions attended, degrees and dates
- Career data
- Current position(s)
- Memberships in professional associations
- Consulting specialties
- Published works

Cross-referenced by subject area and geographic location

(c) *A Periodic Supplement to Consultants and Consulting Organizations Directory (Gale Research Company)*

Edited by Paul Wasserman and Janice McLean. Each issue contains approximately 250 new entries and two cumulative indexes:
- Subject index of firms by location
- Alphabetical index of individuals

(d) *Management Consultant's Bibliography (Institute of Management Consultants, N.Y.)*

q. NATIONAL TECHNICAL INFORMATION SERVICES

This division of the U.S. Department of Commerce offers a wide variety of reports and information services based on federally funded research. Subjects include technical information, business, industry, economics, government and health planning. NTIS, 5285 Port Royal Road, Springfield, VA 22161.

r. THE WORLD BANK: OPERATIONAL SUMMARY OF PROPOSED PROJECTS

The World Bank has launched a quarterly publication listing projects up for tender around the world. Besides giving details of the projects, worth in total billions of dollars each year, it states their current status: either identification, feasibility, appraisal, negotiation, approval or procurement.

197

The Johns Hopkins University Press
Journals Division
Baltimore, MD 21218

s. OTHER RESOURCE INFORMATION MATERIAL

1. Canada

Corpus Almanac and Canadian Sourcebook, Vol. 1 & 2, Gage Publishing, 1989.

Directory of Associations of Canada (4th edition), Micromedia, 1989.

Canadian Government Programs & Services CCH Canada, 1989.

Handbook of Grants & Subsidies of the Federal and Provincial Governments (Canada) STM Research & Publication, Montreal, 1989.

Canada: Trade and Commerce, *Selling to the Canadian Government*, Ottawa

Canada: Treasury Board, *Contracts for the Services of Individuals*, Ottawa

Canada: Treasury Board, *Fee Guidelines for Personal Service Contracts with Industries*, Ottawa

Canada: Supply and Services, *Selling Goods and Services to the Federal Government.*

2. United States

National Trade and Professional Associations and Labor Unions of the U.S. and Canada (23rd edition), Columbian Books, 1988.

Directory of Management Consultants, second edition, 1980. Available from publisher, Kennedy & Kennedy, Templeton Road, Fitzwilliam, N H   03447.

Encyclopedia of Professional Management, second edition, 1980. Kennedy & Kennedy, Fitzwilliam, NH.

Findex: Directory of Market Research Reports, Studies and Surveys. Offers a place to check for proposal-writing information. Information Clearing House, NY.

A Guide to Management Services, Dun and Bradstreet, New York, 1968. Describes numerous services that are marketed by consultants. Includes references for additional information.

How to Find Information about Companies. Identifies sources, such as public records, credit reporting and trade associations. Washington Researchers, Washington, DC

APPENDIX 2

CONSULTING ASSOCIATIONS
(U.S. AND CANADA)

AAHC American Association of Hospital Consultants
Suite 830 - 2341 Jefferson Davis Highway
Arlington, VA 22202

AAMLC American Association of Medico Legal Consultants
2200 Benjamin Franklin Parkway
Philadelphia, PA 19130

AAPBC American Association of Professional Bridal Consultants
42 Woodridge Circle
West Hartford, CT 06107

AAPC American Association of Political Consultants
Suite 1406 - 1101 North Calvert Street
Baltimore, MD 21202

ACCCE Association of Consulting Chemists &
  Chemical Engineers, Inc.
50 East 41st Street
New York, NY 10017

ACEC American Consulting Engineers Council
Suite 802 - 1015 15th Street, N.W.
Washington, DC 20005

ACF Association of Consulting Foresters
Box 369
Yorktown, VA 23690

ACME Association of Consulting Management Engineers
230 Park Avenue
New York, NY 10017

AERC Association of Executive Recruiting Consultants, Inc.
30 Rockefeller Plaza
New York, NY 10020

AFCCE   Association of Federal Communications Consulting Engineers
         525 Woodward Avenue
         Bloomfield Hills, MI 48013

AHCC   Academy of Health Care Consultants
         Suite 3342 - 875 North Michigan Avenue
         Chicago, IL 60611

AICPA-MAS   American Institute of Certified Public Accountants,
             Management Advisory Services Division
         1211 Avenue of the Americas
         New York, NY 10036

APA   American Psychological Association — Division of Consulting
             Psychologists
         1200 17th Street, NW
         Washington, DC 20036

APEC   Automated Procedures for Engineering Consultants, Inc.
         Miami Valley Tower, Suite M-15
         Dayton, OH 45402

APMHC   Association of Professional Material Handling Consultants
         1548 Tower Road
         Winnetka, IL 60093

APS   Association of Productivity Specialists
         One Illinois Center
         Chicago, IL 60601

ASAC   American Society of Agricultural Consultants
         Suite 470, Enterprise Center
         8301 Greensboro Drive
         McLean, VA 22102

ASCA   American Society of Consulting Arborists
         12 Lakeview Avenue
         Milltown, NJ 08850

ASEC   Association of Consulting Engineers of Canada
         Suite 616 - 130 Albert Street
         Ottawa, Ontario
         K1P 5G4

ASCP   American Society of Consultant Pharmacists
                2300 9th Street, South
                Arlington, VA   22264

ASCP   American Society of Consulting Planners
                1717 North Street, NW
                Washington, DC   20036

CABC   Canadian Association of Broadcast Consultants
                2639 Portage Avenue
                Winnipeg, Manitoba
                R3J 9P7

CAMC   Canadian Association of Management Consultants
                Suite 805
                121 Bloor Street E.
                Toronto, Ontario
                M4W 3M5

FFCS   Food Facilities Consultants Society
                135 Glenlawn Avenue
                Sea Cliff, NY   11579

FCSI   Foodservice Consultants Society International
                1400 Pickwick Avenue
                Glenview, IL   60025

IABPC   International Association of Book Publishing Consultants
                52 Vanderbilt Avenue
                New York, NY   10017

ICCA   Independent Computer Consultants Association
                Box 27412
                St. Louis, MO   63141

IMC   Institute of Management Consultants
                Room 810 - 19 West 44th Street
                New York, NY   10036

NAFC   National Association of Financial Consultants
                Suite 114 - 11059 East Bethany Drive
                Aurora, CO   80014

NAMAC   National Association of Merger and Acquisitions Consultants
              Suite 282 - 4255 LBJ Freeway
              Dallas TX   75234

NAPCA   National Association of Pension Consultants & Administration
              Suite 300 - Three Piedmont Center
              Atlanta, GA   30305

NAPENA   National Association of Public Employer Negotiators and
                  Administrators
              1400 N. State Parkway
              Chicago, IL   60610

NCAC   National Council of Acoustical Consultants, Inc.
              66 Morris Avenue
              Springfield, NJ   07081

NICMC   National Institute of Certified Moving Consultants
              222 West Adams Street
              Chicago, IL   60606

NPC   National Personnel Consultants
              Suite 1702 - Pennsylvania Building
              Philadelphia, PA   19102

MCDAM   Managerial Consultation Division of the Academy of
                  Management
              College of Business
              University of Southern Florida
              Tampa, FL   33620

PMI   Project Management Institute
              Box 43
              Drexel Hill, PA   19026

PRSA   Public Relations Society of America, Inc.
              845 Third Avenue
              New York, NY   10022

RAAA   Relocation Assistance Association of America
              950 17th Street
              Denver, CO   80202

SMCAF   Society of Medical Consultants to the Armed Forces
           Box 4033
           Harrisburg, PA   17111

SPBC   Society of Professional Business Consultants
           221 North LaSalle Street
           Chicago, IL   60601

FREE OR NOMINAL COST BUSINESS PUBLICATIONS

a. UNITED STATES

1. Small Business Administration (SBA) Publications

A number of business publications are available from SBA. For copies call 800-433-7217 (in Texas call 800-729-8901) or write to:

Small Business Administration
P.O. Box 15434
Fort Worth, Texas 76119

There are publications available under these headings:

(a) Management Aids

(b) Small Marketers Aids

(c) Small Business Bibliographies

(d) Small Business Management Series

2. Internal Revenue Service

The IRS publishes many free pamphlets and guides to help the small business person. Request a complete list from your local IRS office.

3. Bank of America

Following is the list of business pamphlets from the *Small Business Reporter Series* available at nominal charge from the Bank of America. For copies, contact your local branch.

Beating the Cash Crisis

Avoiding Management Pitfalls

Business Management; Advice from Consultants

Cash Flow/Cash Management

Financing Small Business

Understanding Financial Statements

Equipment Leasing

Personnel for the Small Business

Steps to Starting a Business

Advertising Small Business

Marketing New Product Ideas

b. CANADA

1. Royal Bank of Canada

Following is the list of business pamphlets from the *Guide to Independent Business Series: Your Business Matters* available at no charge from the Royal Bank of Canada. For copies, contact your local branch.

Starting a Business

Market Planning

How to Finance Your Business

Planning and Budgeting

Control Over Direct Costs and Pricing

Good Management — Your Key to Survival

Advertising and Sales Promotion

Control Over Inventory Investments

Financial Reporting and Analysis

Credit Management and Collection

Evaluation and Management of Fixed Assets

Management of Liabilities and Equities

Pointers to Profit

Taxation

Management Audit

Managing Time for Profit and Growth

Exporting — Importing

Managing the Future

2. Federal Business Development Bank (FBDB)

Numerous publications, kits and other materials are available at no charge from the FBDB. Contact a local office for further information.

PROPOSAL EVALUATION CHECKLIST

a. GENERAL FACTORS

(a) Has the bidder responded with an appropriate technique or is he or she trying to fit the problem to a favorite technique?

(b) What priority will this project receive from the consultant? How important will it be to his or her firm?

(c) Does the proposal meet the Terms of Reference and the intended scope of the study?

(d) How useful or capable of implementation will the end product be?

(e) What degree of originality is present in the proposal?

(f) Are the submission of progress reports and presentation of interim briefings required? What progress reports and interim briefings are planned?

(g) What degree of direct consultant-client liaison is proposed? Does the consultant-client relationship include a training component for the client's personnel? What type of training is proposed?

(h) Is the proposed content of progress reports in accordance with the requirements of the client? Will progress reports contain a monthly statement of costs incurred, commitments, and, if necessary, a revised estimate of total costs?

(i) When the project is completed, how does the consultant intend to hand over the project?

(j) What degree of follow-up and/or debriefing is proposed? To whom do the relevant data belong and what happens to them when the project is completed?

b. PAST PERFORMANCE

(a) Is the usual business of the offeror closely related to the proposed work?

(b) Do the references to past experience include activities specifically related to the requirements of the proposed study?

(c) Has the proposer been honored by professional societies because of the performance in a specific professional area?

(d) What reputation does the firm hold in the area of the proposed study?

(e) Has the firm worked for this client before, and if so with what success?

(f)   Are the statements of past performance worded in a meaningful way so you can identify what work was actually performed?

(g)   Are there aspects of past performance that indicate particular weaknesses or strengths?

c. SCOPE OF WORK

(a)   Has the proposal demonstrated an understanding of the problems to be solved?

(b)   Is this research area new to the company?

(c)   Has the offeror made an accurate assessment of the problem based on an interpretation of the requirements set forth in the work statement?

(d)   Has the offeror presented an approach that will achieve the stated objectives?

(e)   Is the proposed approach supported with justification of why it should achieve the evaluation objectives?

(f)   Do you think the suggested approach will work?

(g)   Has the offeror introduced unanticipated events which may result in a project overrun or an expanded scope of work?

(h)   Does the proposal distinguish between the simpler and the more difficult performance requirements?

(i)   Does the proposal convincingly show a depth of understanding of the problem?

(j)   Are the technical problems clearly delineated or are they merely "parroted" from the proposal request?

(k)   Have the limits of the problem been specified to show that the proposed study will be restricted to an appropriate scope?

(l)   Is there a concise but adequate review of literature? Is the literature review merely an annotated bibliography or is it a scholarly critique?

(m)   Are the specific objectives of the proposal clearly stated? Are these goals realistic in view of time, equipment, budget, and professional experience of the principal investigator?

(n)   Does the plan, in fact, permit an unequivocal test of the stated hypotheses of research questions?

(o)   Does the proposal represent a unique, imaginative approach?

(p)   Is the technical program fully responsive to all written requirements and specifications?

(q)   Are there any apparent discrepancies or omissions?

(r)   Are "products" clearly defined and presented?

d. PERSONNEL

(a) Is it clear which tasks in the study specific personnel will be assigned to and for what amount of time?

(b) Are the personnel assigned to specific tasks qualified by training and experience to successfully perform the tasks?

(c) Is there a clear organization chart depicting project management? Is the apportionment of personnel level and time to specific tasks realistic?

(d) What assurances are made concerning the availability of personnel proposed? Was a contingency plan requested if certain personnel become unavailable?

(e) Have enough time and personnel been included to provide adequate administrative management of the study?

(f) Is the author of the proposal one of the key personnel?

(g) Does the success of the project depend, to a large degree, upon personnel not directly associated with the prospective firm?

(h) Do biographies relate specific experience of personnel to the specific needs of this project?

(j) Does the proposal show the capabilities of the management to handle a project of the size contemplated?

(k) Is the position of the program manager in the overall organization and the limits of his or her authority and responsibility shown?

(l) Are the type, frequency, and effectiveness of management controls and method for corrective action shown?

(m) Does the task organization integrate the overall organization in terms of effective lines of authority and communication, and in terms of effective integration of research, development, design, drafting, technical writing, and where appropriate test functions?

(n) Is it clearly demonstrated that top-level management will continue a high level of interest and assume responsibility for successful accomplishment of the program?

(o) Is the proposal dependent upon recruitment of key personnel?

e. PLANNING AND MANAGEMENT

(a) Has the work schedule been specified clearly, and is it realistic in terms of time and money? Does it fit with available personnel?

(b) If time of performance is important and is a competitive evaluation factor, is the proposed schedule supported by the technical proposal?

(c) Is the planning realistic? Does it follow recognized and accepted procedure?

(d) Does the proposal show that the delivery schedule will be met and how it will be met?

(e) Is sufficient detail regarding master scheduling, programming, follow-up, and other like functions given to reinforce the foregoing assurance?

(f) Are the various technical phases of the project detailed and realistically scheduled?

(g) Are effective review, evaluation, and control provided at specific checkpoints?

(h) Has the offeror allowed for all necessary clearances; e.g., OMB (U.S.), Statscan (Canada)?

f. FACILITIES

(a) Are the facilities and equipment needed for successful completion of the study specified in the proposal?

(b) How does the offeror intend to access facilities not at the contractor's site?

(c) Does the use of facilities outside of the contractor's firm require a subcontract? If so, is the proposed subcontractor specifically mentioned, along with an explanation of its required qualifications?

(d) Is the planned use of facilities, such as printing, data processing, etc., realistic?

(e) If computer services are required, are there controls built into the processing so corrective action can be taken at intermittent points if necessary?

(f) Is any government-furnished equipment required?

(g) Are the proposed laboratory and test facilities adequate for the requirements of the technical scope of work?

(h) Are resources overly committed?

g. COST

(a) Is the overall cost within range of your (the contracting agency's) budget?

(b) What is the relationship between the cost figures and equivalent items in the technical proposal?

(c) Are the personnel costs reasonable according to the tasks to be performed?

(d) Are the appropriate personnel assigned to perform the appropriate tasks?

(e) Have expenditures been set aside for subcontracting requirements, such as data processing?

(f) If a large-scale questionnaire must be mailed, has an adequate sum been set aside for postage?

(g) Have costs for development of instruments, purchase of materials, such as scoring sheets, etc., been included?

(h) Does the travel seem reasonable when compared to the tasks to be accomplished?

(i) If consultants or experts are included, is their daily rate reasonable and within the proper financial range? Is the proposed time reasonable?

(j) Is an appropriate type of contract requested?

(k) Is the schedule of payment acceptable?

(l) Have appropriate procedures been used to estimate costs?

OTHER TITLES IN THE
SELF-COUNSEL BUSINESS SERIES

PREPARING A SUCCESSFUL BUSINESS PLAN
A practical guide for small business

This book will guide you through the creation of an exciting and authoritative business plan that will also lay the foundation for a dynamic process of planning and reviewing your business agenda over the long term. $14.95

THE BUSINESS GUIDE TO PROFITABLE CUSTOMER RELATIONS
Today's techniques for success

You need good service to attract customers and keep them coming back, and this book provides plans and programs that have been proven successful by other businesses and that you can use to increase your profits. $7.95

ASSERTIVENESS FOR MANAGERS
Learning effective skills for managing people

This book explains the uses of assertive skills and provides a step-by-step approach for learning the techniques that are most useful in the business world. Worksheets are included. $9.95

THE BUSINESS WRITING WORKBOOK
A guide to defensive writing skills

This writing guide provides exercises and worksheets to practice skills that are directly applicable to anyone in a supervisory or management setting. $9.95

EVERY RETAILER'S GUIDE TO LOSS PREVENTION
Keep your profits! Stop theft!

This book covers planning and implementing a loss prevention program, training employees to spot and foil shoplifters, dealing with internal theft, identifying counterfeit currency, how to act during a robbery, and much more. The authors' proven techniques will help you make your retail business more secure and let you stop paying thieves out of your profits. $12.95

MARKETING YOUR PRODUCT
A planning guide for small business

This practical book explains what a comprehensive marketing plan can do to ensure that your product succeeds in a competitive marketplace. The in-depth checklists included in this book will take you, step by step, toward a successful, profitable marketing strategy. $12.95

MARKETING YOUR SERVICE
A planning guide for small business

There are 32 worksheets for you to develop your own specific marketing plan based on the procedures the authors describe. $12.95

SELLING STRATEGIES FOR SERVICE BUSINESSES
How to sell what you can't see, taste, or touch
The key to success in the service business is selling—and selling yourself. This book provides a step-by-step system for selling your service in a way that you can feel comfortable with. Worksheets are provided for planning and maintenance. $12.95

CHAIRING A MEETING WITH CONFIDENCE
An easy guide to rules and procedure
The author uses everyday language to demystify the art of conducting a meeting in a fair, orderly, and efficient manner. This is not a rules book, but a simple guide on how to run a meeting according to the rules of order. Your meetings can become an effective tool in dealing with the business of the day and the venue for discussion that is productive and to the point. $7.95

THE BUSINESS GUIDE TO EFFECTIVE SPEAKING
Making presentations, using audio-visuals, and dealing with the media
Effective communication has always been the key to business success and this book provides a straightforward businesslike approach to developing and improving on-the-job speaking skills. $7.95

BASIC ACCOUNTING FOR THE SMALL BUSINESS
Simple foolproof techniques for keeping your books straight and staying out of trouble
The book enables a business person to do preliminary bookkeeping and organize financial matters in a manner that makes accounting easier and more accurate, as well as less expensive. The day-to-day accounting problems encountered in the running of a business are discussed and the solutions given. U.S. edition $6.95, Canadian edition $7.95

A PRACTICAL GUIDE TO FINANCIAL MANAGEMENT
Tips and techniques for the non-financial manager
This book goes beyond basic financial control advice to a thorough discussion on how to define information needs to communicate more clearly with your accounting department and make decisions more effectively based on financial information. $7.95

FINANCIAL CONTROL FOR THE SMALL BUSINESS
A practical primer for keeping a tighter rein on your profits and cash flow
Many small business people are frightened by the prospect of balancing ledgers, drawing up income statements and balance sheets, and comparing their current assets to their liabilities. However, this book takes the mystery out of accounting. In easy-to-understand language, this book takes you through the "after the basics" accounting procedure for the small business. $6.95

A SMALL BUSINESS GUIDE TO EMPLOYEE SELECTION
Finding, interviewing, and hiring the right people

This book offers employers practical information on how to successfully select productive employees. It includes sample advertisements, application forms, suggested interview questions, and role-play exercises for the interviewer/applicant exchange. $6.95

READY-TO-USE BUSINESS FORMS
A complete package for the small business

Running a small business and keeping it in order can be made much simpler if efficient systems are in place and the paperwork is up to date. This handy guide of tear-out forms is just what your small business needs to help you take the worry out of daily record-keeping and routine tasks and put more time into keeping on top of your competitors. $10.95

BUSINESS ETIQUETTE TODAY
A guide to corporate success

In this guide you will learn about table and party conversation, telephone talk, company protocol, keeping clients and colleagues waiting, and the new rules of behavior emerging as women and men find themselves at the same conference table. $7.95

START AND RUN SERIES
A step-by-step buisness plan

Our *Start and Run Series* shows you how to set up and run a business in the following areas. These specific guides tell you how to set up shop, sell your product or service, hire employees, plan and arrange financing, design marketing strategies for individual business types, find sources of funding, budget, and identify legal considerations.

START AND RUN A PROFITABLE CRAFT BUSINESS $10.95

START AND RUN A PROFITABLE RESTAURANT $10.95

START AND RUN A PROFITABLE RETAIL BUSINESS $12.95

DESIGN YOUR OWN LOGO
A step-by-step guide for business, organizations, and individuals

A well-designed logo can be an organization's most valuable asset. However, the cost of a commercial artist's work is prohibitive for most small businesses, clubs, and individuals. This handy guide provides an option; it gives background information to the psychology of effective logos and includes a step-by-step guide to designing one for any purpose. $9.95

ORDER FORM

All prices are subject to change without notice. Books are available in book, department and stationery stores, or use this order form. (Please print)

Name_____

Address_____

_____

Charge to:

☐ Visa   ☐ MasterCard

Account Number_____

Validation Date _____

Expiry Date _____

Signature_____

☐ **Check here for a free catalogue which outlines all of our publications.**

Please add $2.50 for postage & handling.

IN CANADA
Please send your order to the nearest location:

Self-Counsel Press
1481 Charlotte Road
North Vancouver, B. C. V7J 1H1

Self-Counsel Press
2399 Cawthra Road, Unit 25
Mississauga, Ontario L5A 2W9

IN THE U.S.A.
Please send your order to:

Self-Counsel Press Inc.
1704 N. State St.
Bellingham, WA 98225

YES, please send me:

_____ copies of **Preparing a Successful Business Plan**, $14.95

_____ copies of **The Business Guide to Profitable Customer Relations** $7.95

_____ copies of **Assertiveness for Managers** $9.95

_____ copies of **Every Retailer's Guide to Loss Prevention** $12.95

_____ copies of **Marketing Your Product**, $12.95

_____ copies of **Marketing Your Service**, $12.95

_____ copies of **Selling Strategies for Service Businesses**, $12.95

_____ copies of **Chairing a Meeting With Confidence**, $7.95

_____ copies of **The Business Guide to Effective Speaking**, $7.95

_____ copies of **Basic Accounting for the Small Business**, U.S. $6.95; Cdn. $7.95

_____ copies of **A Practical Guide to Financial Management**, $7.95

_____ copies of **Financial Control for the Small Business**, $6.95

_____ copies of **A Small Business Guide to Employee Selection**, $6.95

_____ copies of **Ready-To-Use Business Forms**, $10.95

_____ copies of **The Business Writing Workbook**, $9.95

_____ copies of **Business Etiquette Today**, $7.95

_____ copies of **Start & Run a Profitable Craft Business**, $10.95

_____ copies of **Start & Run a Profitable Restaurant**, $10.95

_____ copies of **Start & Run a Profitable Retail Business**, $12.95

_____ copies of **Design Your Own Logo**, $9.95